Discourse Analysis beyond the Speech Event

Discourse Analysis beyond the Speech Event introduces a new approach to discourse analysis. In this innovative work, Wortham and Reyes argue that discourse analysts should look beyond fixed speech events and consider the development of discourses over time. Drawing on theories and methods from linguistic anthropology and related fields, this book is the first to present a systematic methodological approach to conducting discourse analysis of linked events, allowing researchers to understand not only individual events but also the patterns that emerge across them.

Discourse Analysis beyond the Speech Event

- provides a method for detailed examination of speech, writing and other communication
- introduces students and researchers to the discourse analytic tools and techniques required to analyze the relationships between discourse events
- offers explicit guidelines that direct the reader through different stages of discourse analytic research, including worked examples from conversation, magazines and social media
- incorporates sample analyses from ethnographic, archival and new media data.

This book is essential reading for advanced students and researchers working in the area of discourse analysis.

Stanton Wortham is Judy and Howard Berkowitz Professor at the University of Pennsylvania. He has written on classroom discourse and the linguistic anthropology of education, interactional positioning in media discourse and autobiographical narrative, and Mexican immigrant communities in the New Latino Diaspora.

Angela Reyes is Associate Professor of English (Linguistics) at Hunter College and Doctoral Faculty in Anthropology at The Graduate Center, CUNY. She has written on language and racialization, Asian American youth, and ideologies of mixed race/language in the Philippines.

Discourse Analysis beyond the Speech Event

Stanton Wortham and Angela Reyes

Routledge
Taylor & Francis Group

LONDON AND NEW YORK

First published 2015
by Routledge
2 Park Square, Milton Park, Abingdon, Oxon OX14 4RN

and by Routledge
711 Third Avenue, New York, NY 10017

Routledge is an imprint of the Taylor & Francis Group, an informa business

British Library Cataloguing-in-Publication Data
A catalogue record for this book is available from the British Library

Library of Congress Cataloging-in-Publication Data
A catalog record for this title has been requested

ISBN: 978-0-415-83949-5 (hbk)
ISBN: 978-0-415-83950-1 (pbk)
ISBN: 978-1-315-73520-7 (ebk)

Typeset in Baskerville
by Graphicraft Limited, Hong Kong
Printed and bound by CPI Group (UK) Ltd, Croydon, CR0 4YY

For Ben and Rachel—*S.W.*
For Anna—*A.R.*

Contents

List of figures   viii
List of tables   x
Acknowledgments   xii

1   Discourse analysis across events   1

2   Central tools and techniques   40

3   Discourse analysis of ethnographic data   72

4   Discourse analysis of archival data   110

5   Discourse analysis of new media data   143

6   Conclusions   171

Appendix A: Transcription conventions   183
Appendix B: Abbreviations of names in Wortham transcripts   184
References   185
Index   189

Figures

1.1   The example of Tyisha and her cat   4
1.2   The outcome of the example   9
1.3   The example of "Tyisha the courageous liar"   26
1.4   The outcome of the example   29
1.5   Parallelism across speech events   32
1.6   The pathway across three events   34
1.7   The final examples   35
2.1   Narrated events in the central example   46
2.2   Narrated events in the Columbine example   68
3.1   The example of "Maurice the beast"   75
3.2   The example of the Sirens   84
3.3   Maurice caught in the middle   88
3.4   Parallelism across narrated and narrating events   92
3.5   "Samsung" as potential nickname for Samuel Jung   100
3.6   Potential nicknames for Samuel Jung and Sam Park   102
4.1   Geisha speech   112
4.2   Strange speech   116
4.3   Advertisement for Pāru Nerikōyu (Pearl Paste Perfumed Hair Oil), by Hirao Sanpei Shōten (Hirao Sanpei Company), *Jogaku sekai*, 1912, 12(15), unpaginated. © Hakubunkan Shinsha Publishers, Ltd.   120
4.4   Advertisement   122
4.5   Untitled image of a *moga*, *Fujin sekai*, 1931, 26(5), unpaginated. © Jitsugyō no Nihon Sha, Ltd.   123
4.6   Advertisement for Bikutoria Gekkeitai (Victoria Menstrual Garment), by Yamato Gomu Seisakusho (Yamato Rubber Manufacturing Company), *Fujin sekai*, 1925, 20(1): 333. © Jitsugyō no Nihon Sha, Ltd.   124
4.7   Haymaker   127
4.8   Paddy Blake   131
4.9   Young gentleman   133
4.10   Skanger youngwan   138
5.1   Super-competitive   148

5.2　"Acting black"　154
5.3　*Lazy Sunday* and *Friday!*　159
5.4　Storylines in *Lazy Sunday* and *Friday!*　162
5.5　*Lazy Sunday* storyline　163
5.6　*Friday!* storyline　163
5.7　Story enhancements in *Lazy Sunday* and *Friday!*　165

Tables

1.1	Components of a within-event discourse analysis for the "Tyisha the beast" example	14
1.2	Components of discourse analysis within and across speech events	22
1.3	Components of a cross-event discourse analysis for Tyisha	24
1.4	Analysis of the discrete event "Tyisha the courageous liar"	30
1.5	Cross-event discourse analysis of Tyisha across the pathway	37
2.1	The phases and components of discourse analysis	42
2.2	The components of our approach to within-event discourse analysis	63
2.3	The phases and components of discourse analysis beyond the speech event	67
3.1	Analysis of "Maurice the beast" early in the example	77
3.2	Initial elaboration of the "Maurice the beast" example	79
3.3	Initial cross-event analysis of Maurice's pathway	83
3.4	Emerging pathway for Maurice	86
3.5	Maurice's pathway, including preliminary analysis of May 10	89
3.6	The full cross-event analysis of Maurice's predicament	93
3.7	Initial analysis of the nicknames across events	103
3.8	Cross-event establishment of "Samsung" as an unremarkable nickname	105
3.9	The cross-event analysis of "Samsung"	107
4.1	Initial analysis of Takeuchi's text	113
4.2	Cross-event analysis of commentaries on "schoolgirl speech"	118
4.3	Initial analysis of the 1912 advertisement	122
4.4	Cross-event analysis of the three advertisements	125
4.5	Initial analysis of the Irish bull	128
4.6	Cross-event analysis of representations of Irish speech	136
4.7	The final cross-event analysis of Irish accent	140
5.1	Initial analysis of the "not in my house" event	149
5.2	First 11 comments that directly quote "not in my house" (adapted from Chun, 2013)	150
5.3	Cross-event analysis of "not in my house"	151

5.4	Comments with marked and unmarked orthographic representations of "my"	152
5.5	Standard and nonstandard spelling by country	153
5.6	Initial analysis of the "acting black" event	155
5.7	Five comments from the 15 that criticized Wu's racial essentialism (adapted from Chun, 2013)	155
5.8	Analysis of the initial pathway of events about "acting black"	156
5.9	Selected comments from the 60 that aligned with Wu's experience of "acting black" (adapted from Chun, 2013)	157
5.10	Four of the seven comments by black authors who align with Wu (adapted from Chun, 2013)	157
5.11	The cross-event analysis of "acting black"	158
5.12	Within-event analysis of *Lazy Sunday*	166
5.13	Analysis of *Friday!* as juxtaposed with *Lazy Sunday*	166
5.14	Analysis of "ironic blackness" across events	168

Acknowledgments

This book is about discourse analysis across pathways of linked events. Just as we emphasize the importance of cross-event discourse in the understanding of social processes, we acknowledge its significance in the writing of this book. The ideas we present here are a result of our own participation in pathways of events involving many scholars, over many years. We owe enormous gratitude to Elaine Chun, Miyako Inoue, Rob Moore, and Betsy Rymes for their generosity and trust in allowing us to use their exemplary scholarship as the centerpieces of Chapters 4 and 5. Special thanks to Rob Moore for reading drafts and providing generous feedback in the early stages of writing. We also acknowledge many others who have participated along pathways of linked events throughout the writing process, with Asif Agha, Adrienne Lo, Michael Silverstein, and Reed Stevens playing crucial roles. We thank Betty Deane and Lauren Hallden-Abberton for their help with preparing the final manuscript. We also thank our patient and skilled editors at Routledge: Rachel Daw, Nadia Seemungal, and Helen Tredget. Finally, we are grateful to our families who provided support and encouragement throughout the long process of writing.

Stanton Wortham
Philadelphia, June 2014

Angela Reyes
New York City, June 2014

1 Discourse analysis across events

Discourse analysis is a research method that provides systematic evidence about social processes through the detailed examination of speech, writing and other signs. This book describes an approach to discourse analysis drawn primarily from the field of linguistic anthropology (Agha, 2007; Duranti, 1997; Silverstein, 1976, 2003)—a discipline that studies language use in social and cultural contexts— although we also borrow concepts from related fields. Our approach makes two significant contributions. First, we clearly delineate a linguistic anthropological method for doing discourse analysis, offering transparent procedures and illustrations. Second, we extend discourse analysis beyond the speech event, showing how to study the pathways that linguistic forms, utterances, cultural models, individuals and groups travel across events.

Recent theoretical and empirical work has made clear that many important social processes can only be understood if we move beyond single speech events to analyze pathways across linked events (Agha, 2007; Agha and Wortham, 2005; Wortham, 2012). Learning, for example, involves systematic changes in behavior from one event to the next. A learner has experiences in one or more events and then behaves differently in subsequent events. In socialization, to take another example, a novice experiences events characteristic of a group and then participates more competently in subsequent events. No matter how sophisticated our analyses of discrete events, we cannot offer empirically adequate analyses of processes like learning and socialization unless we study pathways across linked events, because such processes inherently take place across events. In order for discourse analysis to be a useful method for studying processes like learning and socialization, it must uncover how people, signs, knowledge, dispositions and tools travel from one event to another and facilitate behavior in subsequent events. This book presents the first systematic methodological approach to doing discourse analysis of linked events.

An example

Consider the following example, taken from a ninth grade combined English and history classroom in an urban American school. The two teachers are discussing Aristotle's *Politics* with 18 students—six boys and 12 girls, mostly African

American. See Wortham (2006) for more information on this classroom. The class is exploring Aristotle's account of human nature, specifically the question of what distinguishes humans from animals. In the passage they read, Aristotle says: "he who is unable to live in society, or who has no need because he is sufficient for himself, must be beast or god" (Aristotle, *Politics*, 1253a, line 29). This implies that an individual who lives outside society is more like an animal than a human. Teachers and students discuss what criterion Aristotle would have used to distinguish humans from "beasts."

Right before segment 1, one teacher has tentatively proposed a criterion: humans have goals and animals do not. A student, Tyisha, objects. (Transcription conventions are in Appendix A and B; "TYI" is Tyisha; "T/B" is Mrs. Bailey, one of the two teachers running this classroom discussion.)

Segment 1: Tyisha's cat as a beast

525 *TYI:*   Mrs. Bailey? I- I have to <u>disagree</u>
                  ((class laughter))
      T/B: can I- can I finish this before you disagree, okay. the idea that he's putting out here is that they- they <u>have</u> goals, and that they can in discussion decide the best way to accomplish their goal. now, Tyisha what's your
530   disagreement?
      TYI: becau(hh)- because if a- like- if my- o<u>kay</u>, if my cat want to- um you know to get to the top of something, you know, he might sit there and be ((3 unintelligible syllables)) and he'll sit there and try <u>every</u>day. and then finally he will do it, that was the <u>goal</u> to try and get up there. he had a <u>goal</u>.
535 *T/B:*   okay (1.0) he's got a [<u>goal</u> but
      ST: [was his goal really <u>ne</u>cessary? ((laughter from class))
      T/B: let's- let's- let's take what- (3.0) <u>let's</u> take what your <u>cat's</u> doing that every day he sees that- <u>coun</u>ter that he wants to get on, and every day when he passes that <u>coun</u>ter he tries to get up there. that's a goal. okay[=
540 *ST:*   [yeah.
      T/B: =how is that different than your <u>goal</u>, the <u>goal</u> that you might have had last night when you had this reading, or-
                  ((some chattering))
      TYI: °I don't know°

In the first line (525), Tyisha states explicitly what type of action she is performing: disagreement. Such an explicit statement can be useful, as it offers discourse analysts guidance in interpreting the event. Discourse analysis would be easy if analysts could rely on people's explicit descriptions of what they are doing. This cannot suffice as a methodological approach, however, for two reasons. First, speakers sometimes lie, speak ironically or make mistakes. Maybe this event is a disagreement, but perhaps not. Second, speakers cannot be depended upon to provide explicit interpretations of their discourse. Most of the time, both participants and analysts must interpret implicit messages and infer what type of action is occurring.

Our approach to discourse analysis depends centrally on a distinction between what Jakobson (1957/1971) called a **narrated event** and an "event of speaking" or **narrating event** (we place important technical terms in bold when introducing and defining them). The narrated event is what is being talked about, while the narrating event is the activity of talking about it. Narrated content includes more than just narratives. Jakobson uses "narrated event" to refer to any denoted content, and we use "narrating event" to refer to any discursive interaction among participants, whether or not the speakers tell stories. From lines 527–529, for example, the teacher describes Aristotle's theory. This narrated event has consistently been the topic of conversation for several minutes. From lines 525–527 and 529–530 the speech event itself is the narrated event, as the teacher and Tyisha mention her impending "disagreement." Even in cases where the speech event is not explicitly described, any discursive interaction always involves an event of speaking, the interaction between speaker and audience within which narrated events are described. In this passage the narrating event involves teachers and students having a classroom conversation about Aristotle.

Teachers and students could be doing various other things in this narrating event as well. They could be teasing each other, excluding and mistreating some participants, flirting, taking political stands, or various other possible social actions. In our approach to discourse analysis, the central goal is to uncover systematic evidence of the types of social action that are occurring in the event of speaking. An initial step is mapping out the relationship between narrated and narrating events, because content communicated in the narrated events provides crucial resources for accomplishing action in the narrating event.

In the passage above, speakers create two additional narrated events in addition to Aristotle's theory and the "disagreement" in the classroom interaction itself. At line 531 Tyisha gives an example. There are now three narrated events: (1) the teacher's claims about Aristotle's theory of humans and animals; (2) Tyisha's explicit characterization of the next phase of their conversation as a "disagreement"; and (3) Tyisha's cat as an example of a "beast" which appears, contrary to the teacher's claim, to have goals. Then at line 541 the teacher introduces Tyisha herself as a contrasting example, a human who—she will go on to argue—has different kinds of goals than a beast. We could treat this as a fourth narrated event, but we will instead treat it as the introduction of a second character (Tyisha) into the third narrating event, the example about Tyisha's cat.

Figure 1.1 represents the narrated and narrating events. We will use figures in this format throughout the book to present narrated and narrating events visually. The external rectangle represents the narrating event, the interaction between teachers and students in the classroom. We represent the main characters as ovals, and we separate teachers from students because of their different institutional statuses—differential roles that can be seen in the teachers' right to direct conversation and evaluate students, for example. At this point in the conversation we represent Tyisha as part of the class, in the same group as the other students, because she is participating in the conversation as many of her peers do. The embedded box on the right represents the narrated event about Aristotle's theory

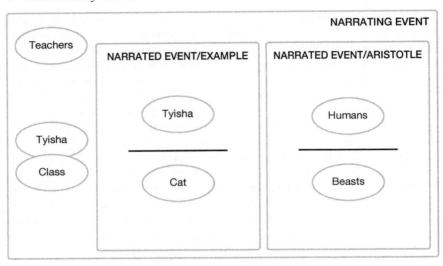

Figure 1.1 The example of Tyisha and her cat

of humans and beasts. Aristotle distinguishes between the two and the class discusses what separates one from the other, exploring whether humans have goals and beasts do not, for example. The embedded box on the left represents the example of Tyisha and her cat. Tyisha offers this example in order to argue that animals have goals just like humans, and Mrs. Bailey elaborates it by discussing whether Tyisha herself has goals similar to her cat's. The example borrows the distinction between humans and beasts from Aristotle, and it presents Tyisha and her cat as exemplars of these two categories. We do not represent the third narrated event, the explicit characterization of their interaction as a disagreement, partly to save space and partly because this topic does not recur until later.

In order to identify the social action occurring in the narrating event, discourse analysts must analyze narrated events, because the characterization of narrated characters and events is one of the most important resources that speakers use to accomplish social acts in discursive interaction. In this example, the distinction between humans and beasts—established in their discussion of Aristotle—and the characterizations of Tyisha and her cat—established through the example— become crucial tools for teachers and students as they position Tyisha herself in the classroom conversation.

The first step in discourse analysis, then, involves mapping out the narrated and narrating events, as illustrated in Figure 1.1. Early in an analysis we often do not know what types of social action are occurring in the narrating event, so we just make a provisional sketch of positioning in the narrating event and revise it later in the analysis. The next step is to figure out how signs that speakers use to describe the narrated event also communicate information about social action occurring in the narrating event. As described more extensively in Chapter 2, we recommend that discourse analysts first attend to certain types of signs that often carry information about the narrating event. **Deictics**, for example, inevitably link narrated and narrating events (Silverstein, 1976). We give a more precise definition of these forms in Chapter 2, but for now we can define them as linguistic signs whose referential value (what they communicate about the narrated event) depends on information about the (narrating) speech event itself. In line 532, for example, Tyisha refers to her cat as "he." Participants and analysts only know the referent of "he" because they heard her use the term "my cat" in prior discourse, at line 531. If we entered the conversation at line 532, the referent of "he" would not be clear. At line 541, the teacher uses "you" to refer to Tyisha. We only know the meaning of this term if we have information about the speech event itself, specifically about the identity of the addressee. The systematic use of "he" and "you" in this and subsequent passages distinguishes two focal characters in the events described, and this ends up having implications for the narrating event.

Deictics often provide important information about the social action accomplished through discourse, because they presuppose things about the narrating event at the same time as they describe the narrated event. Distinguishing between "we" and "they," for example, does more than refer to two groups. It also presupposes a boundary between one group that includes the speaker and another group that excludes him or her. This boundary sometimes becomes salient in social action, as when a speaker systematically places some people beyond the boundary, in an out-group. In the classroom example of Tyisha and her cat, teachers and students use "you," "he" and other signs to distinguish between and characterize Tyisha and her cat. As the conversation continues, this distinction between Tyisha the human and her cat the beast becomes central to the social action.

Segment 2: Similarities between Tyisha and her cat

550 *ST:*   humans can do more things than cats can do, like they can <u>build</u>
     TYI: no that's not- just a goal. my <u>goal</u> is to <u>win</u> in Nintendo and
               ((laughter by a few girls in the class))
     ST: that's your <u>goal</u>?
     TYI: it's a <u>go:al</u>, so
555 *T/B:*   okay maybe winning at Nin<u>ten</u>do is like your <u>cat's</u> goal of getting on top of
               the-
     TYI: right
     T/B: the- the counter. but aren't- don't we have more [=
     ST: [better
560 *T/B:*   =long ranged goals than your <u>cat</u> getting on top of the <u>coun</u>ter, or you
               winning Nintendo?
     TYI: but I'm just saying they're goals. you said animals can't have <u>goals</u> or
               something, so I just told ya I disagree.
     T/B: okay, but can we- can we <u>qualify</u> that then.
565 *TYI:*   yeah.
     T/B: can we <u>qualify</u> that and say that <u>man</u> (2.0) doesn't just have im<u>me</u>diate
               goals, but also has- long range goals.

In the narrated events from lines 550–558, teachers and students continue to discuss the example of Tyisha and her cat. From lines 558–567, they return to their discussion of Aristotle's and their own theories about the distinction between humans and beasts. Note the use of **reported speech** in lines 562–563. We will define the term more precisely in Chapter 2, but for now we mean direct and indirect reports of what someone said. Reported speech connects narrated and narrating events, reproducing and characterizing something from the narrated event to accomplish action in the narrating event. Tyisha uses indirect discourse to describe what the teacher said ("you said animals can't have goals") and herself ("I just told ya I disagree"), as she reviews what their debate is about. The teacher had claimed that animals do not have goals, but Tyisha offered a convincing counterargument with the example of her cat—who clearly seems to have goals when he jumps on the counter. At lines 555–558, the teacher accepts her argument, although at lines 558–561 the teacher goes on to propose a different kind of distinction between human and animal goals.

Here Tyisha uses reported speech to summarize the earlier phase of the argument, in which she successfully disagreed with the teacher's claim. Thus she explicitly marks her successful use of a counterargument. In Chapter 2 we describe how reported speech is often important to establishing social action in the narrating event. Reported speech links characters in the narrated event and participants in the narrating event, as participants put words into characters' mouths and in so doing inevitably characterize and evaluate them. Such identification of characters is one important device through which participants act. Tyisha, for example, summarizes her earlier speech in a way that characterizes her past self—the person who disagreed with the teacher a couple of minutes earlier—as confident and matter-of-fact in her demeanor ("I just told ya I disagree"). This positioning helps make Tyisha herself, the student participating in the narrating classroom interaction, seem an intelligent, balanced, successful contributor to substantive classroom conversation. As we describe more fully in Chapter 2, discourse analysts should examine deictics and instances of reported speech early in their analysis because these types of linguistic signs often do important work in evaluating characters and positioning participants.

In this passage Tyisha characterizes her narrated self in other ways as well. By exploring these characterizations, we can analyze more fully how the narrated events become resources for teachers and students as they perform social action in the narrating event. For example, when Tyisha says that her goal is to win Nintendo video games, she might be characterizing her narrated self as pursuing rudimentary, unintellectual goals. In Chapter 2 we will describe this as **voicing**, the characterization of a narrated person as occupying a recognizable social position (Bakhtin, 1935/1981; Wortham, 2001). In this case Tyisha might be voicing her narrated self as intellectually unengaged, as an unmotivated teenager wasting time on video games. Note that we have used evaluative language in making this characterization. It would be possible to evaluate video game playing more positively. Among a group of video game enthusiasts, for example, Tyisha's description of her narrated self could be grounds for praise or envy. But in the passage above other participants evaluate it negatively. At line 553 a student says "that's your goal?" in a disbelieving tone. At lines 555–558 the teacher compares this goal to an animal's goal. And at line 559 another student presupposes that human goals are "better," with animal-like goals including Nintendo thus being worse.

Tyisha herself probably intended her Nintendo-playing self as an example of lower, animal-like goals, because she is arguing that humans and animals have similar goals. The teacher had claimed that humans have goals while animals do not, and Tyisha made a plausible counterargument. Now the teacher has acknowledged that animals do have goals (at line 539), but she continues to pursue the idea that humans are different than animals by introducing the idea that humans and animals have different kinds of goals (at line 558). By characterizing herself as having lower, animal-like goals—like playing video games—Tyisha presents her (human) self as having goals similar to her cat's. She is trying to win the argument by denying the teacher's claim that human goals make us different from animals.

Tyisha apparently does not anticipate the teachers' response, however. At line 558, the teacher used an inclusive "we" to refer to humans—she herself, Tyisha and the other students are humans, and the teacher claims that all humans have goals that are different from animals'. As the conversation continues in the following segment, however, the teachers and other students exclude Tyisha from their group. As noted above, deictics like "we" often make important contributions to social action in the narrating event. In the next segment teachers and students make clear that Tyisha is no longer included with the other humans in the category of beings that have higher-level goals. By voicing or characterizing herself as having lower-level goals, Tyisha has made herself vulnerable to this exclusion. "T/S" in this segment refers to Mr. Smith, the second teacher running this class discussion along with Mrs. Bailey.

Segment 3: Tyisha the beast

	T/S:	what <u>goal</u> did you have in mind this morning, <u>e</u>ven when you went to sleep.
	TYI:	((laughing)) I didn't h(h)ave o(h)ne.
580	*T/S:*	sure you did. didn't you- didn't you have the goal you had to wake up at a certain <u>time</u>, get <u>dressed</u> in a- by a certain <u>time</u>, <u>get</u> to a place
	TYI:	yeah that's true.
	T/S:	so <u>you</u> had goals even before you s[tarted
	TYI:	[but not in the summertime. I
585		just got up, see, just like
	T/S:	<u>ah</u>, and in summertime when you got up because you <u>had</u> to come to school what was your goal or was it to sleep until three in the after<u>noon</u>? or to get up and play with your friends?
	TYI:	the same goal my cat had, to go to <u>sleep</u>, and get up and <u>eat</u>.
590	*T/B:*	ahhh, isn't that i:nteres[ting? ((rise-fall intonation contour; "mocking" effect))
	T/S:	[a:hhhh
	T/B:	same goals as her (1.0)[=
	ST:	[cat had

595   *T/B:*   =cat had. wow.
     ST: so you are like an animal.
     T/B: so you <u>are</u> like an <u>a</u>nimal.
     TYI: I'm not saying, I just don't have somewheres to be at.
     T/B: okay, but that's not- <u>don't</u> con<u>fuse</u> the issue. <u>one</u> point at a <u>time</u>,
600   Tyisha. you throw out seventeen things and then- nobody can even be<u>gin</u>
           to address any of these things.
    MST: tss ((hissing laughter))

Tyisha keeps trying to win the argument, refusing the distinction between her own (human) goals and her cat's goals at lines 584–585 and 589. Up until this point, the teachers have acknowledged her reasonable claim that animals and humans share some similar goals, but they have argued that people also have uniquely human types of goals. At line 590, however, they shift the interactional positioning in the narrating event. They mark this with distinctive intonation at line 590 and line 592, indicating that something important has been said or implied. At lines 593–597 one teacher states this new information explicitly: Tyisha and her cat have similar goals, and thus perhaps Tyisha is different from the rest of us humans. Tyisha has been arguing for the similarity between human and animal goals all along. But now, instead of trying to establish that all humans have some goals different from animals', the teachers and students argue at lines 596–597 that Tyisha in particular—unlike other humans—has goals like an animal. They accomplish this, in part, through the two instances of "you" in lines 596–597. "You are like an animal" sets Tyisha apart from humans by positioning her with other animals instead. Thus they imply that she is different from the other students in the classroom, and perhaps not fully human. At line 598 Tyisha sees the danger and tries to backtrack, but she fails.

Note how the description of a narrated event—the example of Tyisha and her cat, together with the voicing or social identification of characters in that event— has facilitated social action in the narrating event. The teachers and other students eventually position Tyisha in the narrating event as different from the rest of them, as more like an animal because of the instrumental, lower-level, short-term goals that she allegedly pursues. Figure 1.2 represents the relationship between the narrated and narrating events at this point in the discursive interaction. In the narrated example of Tyisha and her cat, the characterization has shifted such that Tyisha is now positioned along with her cat as having beast-like goals. Aristotle's distinction between humans and beasts helps organize both narrated and narrating events, and in both realms Tyisha has switched from being positioned as human to being positioned as a beast. The dashed lines represent the parallelism established between narrated and narrating events. The teachers and other students distinguish Tyisha from themselves and position her as less than fully human, in the narrating event, by using a model of society and evaluative characterizations drawn from the narrated events. They are not talking simply about Tyisha the hypothetical video game enthusiast, nor are they merely discussing the narrated event involving Tyisha and her cat. They are also using

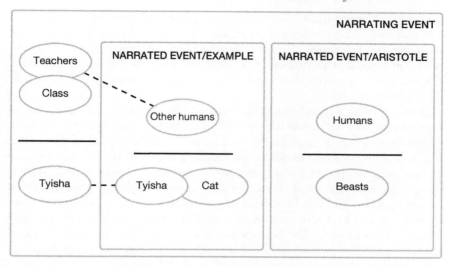

Figure 1.2 The outcome of the example

these narrated events to position Tyisha herself in the narrating event. Just as a beast cannot cooperate sufficiently with others to live in human society, Tyisha cannot follow the rules of classroom engagement and participate productively in group discussion.

The last lines of segment 3 provide another illustration of how reported speech contributes to narrated events in ways that can accomplish social action in the narrating event. At line 600 the teacher says to Tyisha: "you throw out seventeen things and then nobody can even begin to address any of these things." The verb "throw out" here describes a type of speech event, portraying Tyisha as making lots of points, in scattershot fashion, without offering others an opportunity to engage them productively. In Chapter 2 we will show how descriptions of others' speech are potent ways of characterizing others and accomplishing social action. Reporting others' speech—directly, indirectly or generically—is one crucial way speakers establish narrated events that have implications for social action. At lines 599–601, the teacher characterizes Tyisha as a disruptive student who refuses to engage productively in classroom conversation, explicitly describing her undesirable behavior. In subsequent chapters we will see how reported speech can also more subtly contribute to social action in the narrating event by positioning narrated characters and actual participants.

The example of Tyisha and her cat begins to illustrate how discourse analysts systematically explore patterns of sign use. In our approach, discourse analysts first trace how speakers use linguistic and paralinguistic signs as they create narrated events, then make inferences about how these patterns of sign usage contribute to social action in the narrating event. In the example about Tyisha, we have illustrated the first two steps in how such analysis proceeds: first mapping out the narrated events, and then looking for types of signs that often communicate information about how narrated events and characters have implications for the narrating event. Chapter 2 gives a more detailed account of how to identify particular signs that accomplish this work. For now, we have illustrated how deictics, reported speech and voicing can provide important signals about the social action occurring.

Before offering a more detailed account of how discourse analysis proceeds, however, we must distinguish between discourse analysis of discrete speech events and discourse analysis across pathways of events. Traditionally discourse analysis has been done on single events or on recurring types of events. Our linguistic anthropological approach to discourse analysis was largely developed for analyzing discrete events, and most of the methodological tools we present come from this earlier work. In this book we extend the approach to analyze pathways of connected events over time, because many crucial human processes take place across chains of linked events. The next section describes traditional work on discrete speech events. Then we sketch how a linguistic anthropological approach can be extended to do discourse analysis beyond the speech event.

Speech events and their contexts

The analysis of discrete speech events over the past several decades has been enormously fruitful (e.g., Goffman, 1981; Gumperz, 1982; Hymes, 1964; Sacks, Schegloff & Jefferson, 1974; Silverstein, 1992), and our approach uses many tools that have been developed to analyze individual events. Founding figures of discourse analysis such as Goffman (1981), Hymes (1974), Jakobson (1960) and others have described the central components of any given speech event. Every speech event includes **participants**—a speaker, an addressee and often an audience or overhearers. It includes a **message**, communicated over some channel that connects speaker and addressee, "encoding" the message in some denotational **code**. The speech and nonverbal signs that constitute the event have an **organization**—at least a beginning, middle and end, and often more complex kinds of poetic patterning. The communication takes place in some context, both a physical **setting** and a social world with **norms** about social identities and social events. The event has social **consequences** and accomplishes social action.

Different approaches to discourse analysis offer different accounts of how these elements interrelate. Our approach is not the only useful one. Different research questions will require different approaches. On our account, a discourse analyst must uncover the social functions of a speech event, and this centrally includes the social identities or positions that participants assign themselves and others in narrated and narrating events. For example, exclusion is a type of social action, and teachers and students end up excluding Tyisha in part by characterizing her as a "beast" in the narrated event. Participants accomplish social action in the narrating event by organizing their messages, using signs systematically to position themselves and other participants. For example, the narrated events—the discussion of Aristotle's definition of human nature and the example of Tyisha and her cat—established the distinction between humans and beasts, and speakers systematically applied this distinction to Tyisha herself so as to exclude her from the classroom conversation.

Put briefly, then, on our account *discourse analysis uncovers the social actions performed in discursive interaction, by showing how narrated characters are voiced and actual participants are positioned, as this positioning is accomplished through the systematic organization of signs that communicate explicit and implicit messages, and as this organization is accomplished by making aspects of context relevant.* Chapter 2 presents a more detailed procedure for doing discourse analysis. In the rest of this chapter we provide conceptual background for our approach, defining central terms in the italicized sentence and describing key aspects of discursive interaction both within and across speech events. First we want to clarify that, by presenting social action in the narrating event as the target of our approach to discourse analysis, we emphatically do not mean to imply that participants necessarily *intend* the social action they perform. Sometimes participants accomplish action that they do not intend, and sometimes they are unaware of social actions that they demonstrably orient to but do not consciously understand. In many cases, discourse analysis reveals mechanisms of social action that participants use but do not consciously recognize. The parallel between Aristotle's description of humans and beasts and the teachers' distinction between Tyisha and other students with "higher" goals was a central part of the discursive mechanism through which Tyisha was excluded from classroom conversation, for example, but in interviews Wortham (2006) found that the teachers and students were not consciously aware of this mechanism. They were aware of the broader social function, realizing that Tyisha had been excluded, but they were not aware of the mechanisms through which this action had been accomplished.

Silverstein (1992, 1993) shows that the central problem in discourse analysis is determining **relevant context**. As described in Chapter 2, deictics, reported speech and evaluative indexical signs, among other cues, signal relevant context. When Tyisha describes herself as playing Nintendo video games at line 551, for example, she could be identifying herself as intellectually unsophisticated. But this utterance could signal something else if different aspects of the context were salient. If everyone knew that Tyisha was a diligent student who always read more than the teachers required and conducted scientific experiments in her spare time, her comment about Nintendo would more likely be a joke or a counterfactual. If everyone knew that the boys in the classroom were obsessed with video games and played them constantly instead of doing schoolwork, while Tyisha and the other girls were all diligent students, then Tyisha's comment could be read as an insult to the boys with no implications for herself. In order to interpret the implications this utterance has for the positioning of participants and social action occurring in the narrating event, we must know what aspects of context are relevant.

Relevant context gets established as speakers organize their messages systematically so as to foreground certain aspects, and as other speakers subsequently presuppose the same aspects of context. As we describe in Chapter 2, participants do this largely through the systematic deployment and uptake of **indexical signs** that presuppose or create aspects of context. An indexical sign signals its object by pointing to it (Peirce, 1932; Silverstein, 1976). For example, "throw out" in line 600 can describe undisciplined, careless speech—the kind of speech that disruptive, unpromising students might engage in. Participants and analysts know that this expression has these implications because it points to or presupposes many other contexts in which they have heard the term used to describe disruptive, unintelligent or careless people. To take another example, "dude" presupposes a certain kind of (young male) speaker, the type of person who would normally use the word. Deictics are also indexical, pointing to their referents in the context—with "you" pointing to the addressee, a verb in the past tense pointing to a time prior to the event of speaking, etc.

As a speech event unfolds, indexical signs normally accumulate and point to similar contexts, presupposing certain aspects of context as more and more likely to be relevant. After Tyisha talks about playing Nintendo, the teachers return to the distinction between humans and animals without presupposing that Tyisha herself is beast-like. At line 558 the teacher's "we" seems to include Tyisha as a human like others in the class, and at line 580 Mr. Smith describes some of Tyisha's activities as involving human-like goals. But at line 584 Tyisha points out that during the summer she has no complex goals and just lies around like her cat, and at line 589 she concludes by saying that she has "the same goal my cat had, to go to sleep, and get up and eat." These utterances at lines 551, 584 and 589 all point to similar context as relevant—to a culturally familiar model of intellectually unengaged people who lie around and do mindless activities like playing video games.

Silverstein (1992, 1993) calls this accumulation of signs that point to similar aspects of context **contextualization**, the process through which the context relevant to interpreting a speech event is established. Over the course of a discursive interaction a series of indexical signs comes to presuppose some aspects of the context as relevant. One sign alone cannot establish relevant context. If teachers and students had followed Tyisha's comment about Nintendo with discussion of how she is in fact a diligent student, and if she had not subsequently characterized herself as lazy in the summer, then the comment about Nintendo would not have positioned her as lazy and beast-like. But several utterances did in fact presuppose this, and thus that model of a beast-like, lazy person became relevant context for interpreting both the characterization of Tyisha in the narrated event and her position in the narrating event.

Even after these utterances, of course, Tyisha might not ultimately have been positioned as beast-like. Teachers and students could have switched to emphasizing Tyisha's character as a good student, or they could have talked about how inappropriate it would be to compare humans to animals. Any social action accomplished through discursive interaction can be refigured or undone, if subsequent discourse provides robust enough signals to that effect. In the next class, or even years later at a class reunion, these teachers and students could have recalled this conversation and tried to establish that they were just teasing and knew all along that Tyisha was a promising student. In practice, however, relevant context usually solidifies such that participants and analysts can treat a given action as accomplished and routinely presupposable.

In Silverstein's (1992, 1993) terms, this is to say that speech events become **entextualized**. They become stable and identifiable as some kind of social action, after a series of indexical signs has established relevant context and speakers routinely infer that a given social action has occurred. In Tyisha's case entextualization is established in lines 590–601, as teachers and students explicitly state that Tyisha is like an animal and the teacher disciplines Tyisha for her manner of class participation. At this point the social action being accomplished in the narrating event—the exclusion and disciplining of Tyisha—becomes firmly established, and Tyisha is robustly positioned as disruptive and failing to collaborate in class discussion, as like a "beast" who cannot participate productively in collective human activities. This social action is established as a pattern of indexical signs comes to presuppose relevant context.

Any entextualization is a contingent interactional accomplishment. The positions of participants and the nature of the social action can be changed later in the discursive interaction, or in future events. This means that the boundaries of a speech event are sometimes fluid and contested. After line 600, teachers and students go on to discuss another topic and Tyisha stays silent. But they could have taken up the issue of Tyisha's identity, tacitly or explicitly, and then the segment of discursive interaction after line 600 would have been part of the segment we have been analyzing. One central task for discourse analysis is **segmentation** of discursive interaction, the determination of where speech events begin and end (Jefferson, 1978). There are no unambiguous rules for determining the boundaries of a speech event, because these boundaries depend on the relevant context and social actions that are accomplished. In practice, participants normally establish robust entextualization in recognizable ways, making it clear that some sort of speech event or discursive activity has run its course and is now completed.

The goal of discourse analysis, in our approach, is to uncover the type of social action participants perform. Discourse analysts start by identifying signs that do the work of contextualization, signs that make aspects of context relevant. In the classroom conversation above, for example, Tyisha's utterances at lines 551, 584 and 589 collectively make the model of a lazy, intellectually uninvolved teenager relevant. Discourse analysts then look for signs organized systematically into what we will call in Chapter 2 a **configuration of signs** or a poetic structure (Jakobson, 1960; Silverstein, 1992, 1993), signs that collectively establish relevant context. In Tyisha's case, the distinction between humans and beasts is established in the narrated event as teachers and students use Aristotle's account to explore the narrated example of Tyisha and her cat, and then the label "beast" is drawn from these narrated events and used to position Tyisha herself in the narrating event. Many signs presuppose the human/beast distinction and then apply this distinction to Tyisha herself, and the configuration of these signs, accumulating over the course of the interaction, comes collectively

Table 1.1 Components of a within-event discourse analysis for the "Tyisha the beast" example

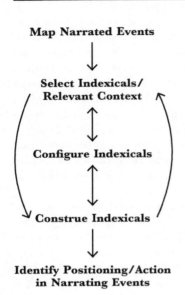

Map Narrated Events	As represented in Figures 1.1 and 1.2, map out the roles of the teachers, Tyisha and other students in the narrating event and the various characters in the narrated events
Select Indexicals/ Relevant Context	Identify deictics, reported speech and other indexical signs that presuppose relevant context; for example, "playing Nintendo" presupposes intellectually unengaged youth
Configure Indexicals	Look for patterns of mutually presupposing indexical signs that collectively come to presuppose a particular account of relevant context, like the various signs identifying Tyisha as beast-like
Construe Indexicals	Interpret salient indexical signs and relevant context, inferring the identification of narrated characters and the positioning of participants, like "Tyisha the beast"
Identify Positioning/Action in Narrating Events	Once a pattern of signs has solidified and an interpretation of the social action has gelled, determine the positioning and action that has occurred, like the exclusion of Tyisha

to presuppose the voicing of Tyisha as a beast and her exclusion from classroom conversation.

The column on the left in Table 1.1 represents the five main pieces in our approach to discourse analysis of discrete events. As the circular arrows indicate, these pieces are not strictly sequential. There are three phases in any analysis. First, as represented on the first line, we map out the narrated and narrating events, anticipating that aspects of the narrated events (like the distinction between humans and beasts) will be relevant to accomplishing social action in the narrating event. Second, as represented on the middle three lines, we engage in the dialectic of contextualization and entextualization, identifying relevant signs and interpreting the voicing, evaluation and interactional positioning that they signal. Third, as represented on the last line, we infer the type of social action occurring among participants in the narrating event.

As described more fully in Chapter 2, it is crucial to see that the three components of the second phase—the middle three lines—represent an iterative, dialectic process, as represented by the circular arrows. Discourse analysts start this phase by identifying indexical signs that point to relevant aspects of the context (for example, "Nintendo" might signal a type of young person who is seen as wasting time in intellectually dulling activities). Then, as represented on the fourth line, analysts construe those signs and the relevant context, inferring what type of interactional positioning and social action is likely occurring (for example, inferring that Tyisha is different from the other students because she pursues lower-level, more animal-like goals). The two components of contextualization and entextualization depend upon each other, such that one process is not prior to the other. Through contextualization relevant context emerges and supports one account of the voicing, evaluation and interactional positioning that is occurring. But at the same time, an account of the emerging voicing, evaluation and interactional positioning constrains inferences about what context might be relevant. Any segment always contains more potentially salient indexical signs than will in fact play an important role in the analysis. Only by making provisional inferences about the entextualization occurring can both participants and analysts narrow down the potentially relevant indexical signs and potentially relevant context.

This cycle of interpretation, from relevant signs to inferred construals of those signs and back—represented by the circular arrows in the table—is provisionally stopped when a configuration of mutually presupposing signs solidifies (Silverstein, 1992, 1993). This is represented on the third line, with the arrows above and below indicating that a solidified configuration of signs constrains both the indexical signs and relevant context that become salient and the plausible construals of those indexicals. In the example of Tyisha, we have pointed out indexical signs in lines 551, 584 and 589 that together presuppose the model or stereotype of a lazy, intellectually unengaged young person. Cultural models or stereotypes like this become potentially relevant context that participants and analysts use to interpret signs and make inferences about voicing, positioning and social action. When combined with the utterances at lines 593–597, the signs in Tyisha's utterances contribute to a configuration that provisionally stops the dialectic of contextualization and entextualization. Collectively, these signs strongly presuppose that the stereotype of a lazy, intellectually unengaged young person is being applied to Tyisha and that she is being contrasted with other students in the classroom. Once this has been established, participants and analysts can go on to the third phase of discourse analysis and infer the social action occurring, in this case the exclusion of Tyisha, as represented on the fifth line of the table. We will use tables with this format to represent the central aspects of our approach to discourse analysis throughout the book, applying it to the sample analyses provided in Chapters 2–5. At this point the meaning of some key terms may not be fully clear, but Chapter 2 will provide more extensive definitions and examples.

Discourse analysts aim to uncover participants' own tacit or explicit accounts of what has happened in an interaction. Analysts argue that an interpretation is plausible by pointing to participants' actions, which make certain signs and contexts salient and indicate that participants themselves are orienting to those signs and to the accounts of social action that can be inferred from them. In other words, discourse analysts must identify patterns in discursive interaction, showing what participants themselves respond to as they contextualize and entextualize their utterances. Discourse analysis is thus empirical, because an interpretation can only be supported by pointing to signs that participants themselves use. This does not mean that participants are necessarily aware of their actions or the mechanisms they use to accomplish them, but it does mean that participants must at least tacitly orient to the signs that accomplish these actions.

It should be clear from our account so far that any adequate discourse analysis must include context beyond the speech event itself. Part of discourse analysis focuses on **co-text**, that component of context composed by the other signs in the speech event. In order to interpret the importance of Tyisha's comment about Nintendo, we took into account comments elsewhere in the text—about what became understood as her lower-level, animal-like goals during summer vacation at lines 584–589, for example. But co-text never suffices, because relevant context always extends beyond the speech event. In this case, the model or stereotype of lazy, intellectually unengaged youth is crucial to interpreting the exclusion of Tyisha. Participants and analysts must be familiar enough with the social context to recognize this stereotype and signs that index it. Potentially relevant context is indefinitely large—extending from signs in the same utterance to locally established stereotypes to widely circulating, institutionalized models. So any discourse analysis focuses on contexts beyond the speech event, pre-supposing models of identity and social life that are necessary to interpret the significance of indexical signs and determine the type of social action occurring. In this book we go beyond this claim to make a stronger argument about context beyond the speech event. We argue that pathways across linked events are central to many social processes and represent an important new focus for discourse analysis.

Speech chains and enregisterment

Sometimes discourse analysts have to know what happened in some other event to interpret a discursive interaction, and adequate discourse analyses always presuppose something about models that have been created and learned in other events. Wortham and Rhodes (in press) make this argument more extensively, describing for narrative discourse in particular two different types of context beyond the speech event: context beyond the event that is inevitably presupposed even when the analysis focuses on a discrete individual event, and context that involves pathways of linked events. In the example of Tyisha and her cat, so far, we have shown how a discourse analyst must presuppose models or stereo-types that have been created in other events and learned through prior experi-ence, in order to interpret the social action that teachers and students accomplish in this discrete event. We will see later in the chapter that this example also participates in a pathway of linked events that socially identify Tyisha across several months.

When we ask certain kinds of research questions, discourse analysis can require a unit of analysis that extends beyond the individual speech event to several events linked in a pathway. Many central human processes take place across and not within events. Socialization requires an individual to develop repertoires of cultural models, skills and habits across events and apply those repertoires more appropriately across time. Fashions and trends involve the dissemination of objects or behaviors, along with their associated evaluations, across events to broader audiences. Learning involves increasingly competent participation in social activities across events, with exposure and practice in one event facilitating participation in subsequent events. Few human processes take place exclusively within single events—although some interesting research questions do focus on pivotal patterns that emerge within one event—and most social scientific research explicitly or tacitly studies processes that involve linked events of one kind or another (Agha, 2007).

Our emphasis on pathways of linked events does not compete with the claim that all discourse analysis inevitably draws on contexts beyond the speech event. It is true *both* that any discrete event of speaking can only be understood by presupposing information, models and evaluations from beyond that event *and* that many functions of discourse are best understood in terms of cross-event pathways. Our focus on linked pathways of events does not imply that event-focused analyses have no value. For some research questions, a focus on discrete events—together with their presuppositions about information, models and evaluations from beyond the speech event—is adequate and productive. Furthermore, many insights developed through analyses of discrete speech events are essential to our own and others' work analyzing pathways across events. With our account of cross-event discourse analysis, we draw attention to another productive unit of analysis for understanding discourse and the social processes that it facilitates. We are foregrounding a new object of investigation that builds on and can complement the important work on discrete events.

Our focus on cross-event pathways raises an important question for discourse analysis. If the research method excels at revealing the structure and function of discrete events, how can it provide systematic evidence relevant to processes like learning and socialization that occur only across events? One response would be to study pivotal events, cases where a process that occurs across a series of events is strongly influenced by one event that becomes an inflection point. Another response would be to study typical events, where the same type of event recurs and has similar functions across time and space. Both of these strategies make sense, in cases where pivotal events do in fact occur or where one event is typical of others in relevant ways. But most human processes do not involve just these two types of cases. Occasionally an individual's socialization depends centrally on one or two pivotal events, for example, and we can provide an adequate account by doing discourse analysis on these. But most of the time socialization involves more complicated pathways across various events, with smaller changes and cross-contextual links accumulating. Sometimes a social type is stable and repeated in some place and time, such that discourse analysis of one typical event can illuminate important patterns. But even in such cases social typifications emerge historically and change as they are disseminated, such that analysis of discrete or typical events will miss important changes and influences.

The alternative response is to do discourse analysis across pathways of events, studying the linkages that allow individuals, signs, stereotypes and objects to travel across events and participate in a social process like socialization or learning. Instead of assuming that an event is pivotal or typical, discourse analysts must develop methods for systematically tracing linkages across events and showing how relevant social processes are accomplished across pathways. This book shows how to do such analyses, extending techniques developed for analyzing discrete events to the analysis of pathways across linked events. Significant empirical analyses have been done that illuminate cross-event processes (Agha, 2007; Agha and Wortham, 2005; Silverstein and Urban, 1996; Wortham and Rhodes, 2013). This book codifies the discourse analytic procedures used in this body of work and presents a systematic linguistic anthropological approach to discourse analysis across speech events. Before giving a more detailed introduction to our methodological approach, in Chapter 2, we must first develop a conceptualization of how pathways of linked events emerge and function.

Linguistic anthropologists have studied the **recontextualization** of speech events for several decades (Bauman and Briggs, 1990; Silverstein and Urban, 1996). Bauman and Briggs describe work on narratives and other discursive genres, tracing how a telling in one context can be recreated in a new context, with participants retaining some features while recontextualizing others to fit the new event. Silverstein and Urban present research on the movement of texts from one event to another and the work of recontextualizing texts in new events. Mehan (1996), for example, describes how a student becomes "learning disabled" as ways of speaking about him move from less formal discussions among educators and parents into more formal documents and diagnostic settings, then into official institutionalized accounts. No one event is pivotal, and the characterizations change in some respects from event to event, but across the pathway of events the student's identity emerges and becomes durable.

Agha (2007) provides a powerful general theory of cross-event pathways. He starts with **register**, a model of discursive behavior that links signs—ways of speaking or behaving—with evaluative typifications about people. Only certain kinds of speakers typically say "dude," for example, and anyone who utters this form seems either like a younger male associated with certain subcultures or like someone quoting or making fun of such a person. Registers are collections of such links, with a set of signs that presuppose some recognizable social type of speaker, hearer and/or event. Agha argues that any association between a sign and a typification (or stereotype) has a **domain**, the group of speakers who will recognize this linkage. He then explains how these three elements of a register (sign, typification and domain) change over time as speakers use and re-use signs across events. The domain expands or contracts, and the signs that index a typification, plus the nature of the stereotype itself, change as the register is used across events.

Folk sociology posits large-scale, enduring groups and stereotypes as fundamental units of analysis. Agha shows how social groups, and the semiotic forms that seem naturally to index them, are created and presupposed through semiotic processes and inevitably change over time. In doing so he points out another kind of indeterminacy that discourse analysis must confront. In the first half of this chapter we showed how signs do not univocally signal their social functions within a speech event, but that participants and analysts must instead infer from relevant context what a given sign means about the social action occurring in the event of speaking. Sometimes that meaning changes as subsequent context leads participants to reinterpret focal signs (Garfinkel, 1967). Similarly, Agha argues that large-scale stereotypes do not persist such that we can take for granted the groups and stereotypes that they presuppose. Analysts must study the emergence and maintenance of registers (and the social groups that they index and evaluate) over historical time.

Instead of assuming that a speaker who uses "dude" comes from a defined group, for example, we must investigate how the term has been and is being used, across contexts, investigating empirically how the sign, the stereotype and the domain emerge, solidify and change. Kiesling (2004) does this analysis, tracing the various meanings of "dude" across a range of social contexts over the past few decades. In Tyisha's case, we cannot assume that she is simply identified as a member of some stable social type. She started the academic year being identified by teachers and other students as a good student who made productive contributions to classroom discussion. Many other girls in the class were identified similarly, throughout the year. But as shown in Wortham (2006), by December Tyisha was being identified as more of a problem. For several months she was positioned as someone who refuses to cooperate with others in productive class-room discussion and she was often excluded, as in the discussion of Tyisha and her cat above. Toward the end of the year, however, she was again identified as making more positive contributions to class discussions. From Agha's perspective, we must study the changing stereotypes that were used to identify Tyisha, and the signs that indexed these, across the months-long pathway from good student to disruptive outcast and back.

Agha presents two central concepts for describing the emergence and trans-formation of registers: **speech chains** and **enregisterment**. Empirically, associations between signs and the social typifications they index emerge across chains of linked events. In the simplest case, someone hears a certain association ("dude" being used by a certain type of young male) and then in a subsequent event uses that term to index a similar social type (while telling a story about such people, for example, perhaps using reported speech to voice a narrated character). A register emerges across such linked events, as sign–stereotype links are established and re-used by members of a growing social domain. In this book we use the term **pathway** to describe a linked series of events that compose what Agha calls a speech chain. "Trajectory" is another possible term (used in Wortham, 2006, for example), but it presupposes a path predetermined from the start, whereas linked speech events in practice change and branch unexpectedly— more like pathways than trajectories or chains.

"Enregisterment" is the term Agha uses to describe how recurring signs become linked to social typifications across speech events over time. Enregisterment describes how an identity for an individual or a stereotype about a group can become widely recognized. Cultural patterns like registers do not stay stable for a bounded group, as presupposed in many simple theories of society and culture. Instead, links between signs and stereotypes emerge and shift. Participants in interaction must coordinate their heterogeneous repertoires in practice, not draw on a stable set of shared categories (Bourdieu, 1972/1977; Rymes, 2014). A register emerges and changes as speakers repeat the use of certain signs across events, indexing presupposed stereotypes. Often a register has evaluative content, construing speakers positively or negatively. Sometimes registers are institutionalized, when schools, governments or other institutions codify guidelines for usage or disseminate sign–stereotype linkages. These evaluations and institutionalizations can provide stability to a register, but signs, typifications and domains continue to change, and individuals who come to the register at different points in the pathway often use it in heterogeneous ways. Analysis of any register thus requires attention to historically emerging changes.

Enregisterment happened across the pathway of events in which Tyisha was socially identified in Mrs. Bailey's class. In several events from December through February, teachers and students made analogies between events in the curriculum that described iconoclasts, individualists or outcasts and Tyisha herself. A typification or model emerged, both in descriptions of the curriculum and in presupposed accounts of Tyisha's social identity, in which an individual insists on his or her own positions or desires and refuses to cooperate in the ways required to form a cohesive nonauthoritarian society. Various signs—like the term "beast" as used by Aristotle, referring to a person who refuses to live in human society—came to index this model, across a pathway of events. The domain of this model included the teachers and students in the class, who over time came to associate these signs and the model. Below we will analyze other events from this pathway, illustrating how events became linked and socially identified Tyisha over time.

Following Agha (2007), we argue that cross-event chains or pathways constitute a different unit of analysis, larger than individual speech events but smaller and more dynamic than macro-level sociological essentializations. In order to analyze pathways of linked events, a discourse analyst must study the individual events that make up the pathway, using the tools introduced above and elaborated in Chapter 2. But discourse analyses of processes like learning, socialization and social identification must also study how cross-event linkages emerge and solidify. In this book we provide a systematic method for doing such analyses.

We argue that cross-event discourse analysis borrows crucial principles from within-event discourse analysis, but that it also has some distinctive characteristics. As Silverstein (2005) argues, the principles for **interdiscursive** enregisterment are in many ways similar to those for **intradiscursive** entextualization. Many of the same principles we use to explain the solidification of social action within an event can be extended to explain the emergence of registers across events. Configurations of mutually presupposing signs emerge within a discrete event, as the characterizations of Tyisha as a "beast" did in the discussion of Tyisha and her cat. Similarly, sign–typification linkages across events come to presuppose each other and establish a more robust pathway that has a clear shape and direction. That is, across a set of linked events participants signal particular typifications and position others in ways that become familiar and robustly established. As participants across events presuppose the sign–typification linkage, it becomes more durably presupposed. Tyisha, for example, did not become an outcast in the classroom only during the discussion of humans, beasts and her cat. Her status as an outcast, as a student who disrupts collective activity and should be excluded from the community, emerged across many events over several months as indexical signs came durably to presuppose this model of her identity. The emergence of sign–typification links across events can be analyzed using the same tools introduced above and elaborated in Chapter 2, identifying configurations of indexical signs across events that presuppose each other and establish more robust pathways that accomplish cross-event processes like socialization and learning.

As we have described above, the social action accomplished in an event emerges as relevant context is established, as configurations of signs become organized such that they position narrated and actual participants as accomplishing social actions. When we do discourse analysis on pathways of linked events, something similar but more complicated happens. Table 1.2 compares discourse analysis within and across events. Discourse analysis across events includes the same general components as discourse analysis within events, but several additional components are required to analyze a pathway of linked events.

Discourse analysis across speech events is similar to discourse analysis of discrete events, focusing on how narrated events and indexical signs create relevant context as signs are configured poetically, thereby establishing participants' positions and social actions. But discourse analysis across events has three additional features. First, when discourse analysis extends across events, we must select the events to focus on, identifying which events are linked in a pathway. Linked events become relevant context for each other, often through devices like reported speech, recurring narrated events or other sorts of parallelism. These linked events form a special kind of context, **cross-event context**, that is important to establishing social action both within and across events. Second, indexical signs across linked events provide a more extensive set that can be configured into mutually presupposing structures and thus establish relevant context. In order to explain how social action and social processes are accomplished across pathways of events, analysts must describe a cross-event configuration of indexical signs. Third, pathways across linked events can accomplish more complex social processes and more durable results than are typically achieved in single events. Analysts must describe how actions and processes are accomplished as a pathway of linked events takes on a definite shape. Discourse analysis across events shows how participants use signs to accomplish a more rigid pathway—establishing robust positioning, social action and social processes—as configurations of signs across events link together and come to presuppose relevant context.

Table 1.2 Components of discourse analysis within and across speech events

	Within Events: Contextualization and Entextualization	Across Events: Recontextualization and Enregisterment
Narrated events serve as resources	**MAP NARRATED EVENTS** Discursive interactions describe narrated events, which communicate content (this communication itself being a type of action) and provide resources for other social action in the narrating event. Mapping narrated events identifies potential resources that may be important to the discourse analysis.	**SELECT LINKED EVENTS AND MAP NARRATED EVENTS** Narrated events have been established in prior discursive interactions, and these are often presupposed such that they become resources in subsequent events. Analysis must identify linked events that might make up a pathway and map the narrated events within each of these.
Indexical signs presuppose and create relevant context	**SELECT INDEXICALS AND IDENTIFY RELEVANT CONTEXT** Indexical signs point to potentially relevant aspects of the context. Participants and analysts attend to these signs and make inferences about what context is relevant. This is the process of contextualization, in which relevant context emerges for understanding what is happening in the speech event.	**SELECT INDEXICALS AND IDENTIFY RELEVANT CROSS-EVENT AND OTHER CONTEXT** Indexical signs point to past and future events along the pathway, tying events together. Other events along the pathway are established as a central part of relevant context, through indexical links like reported speech, shared narrated events and recurring evaluations. Focal indexical signs from across linked events point to cross-event context (context from other events linked in a pathway) and to other aspects of context that become relevant to understanding social actions and processes accomplished across the pathway.
Poetic configuration of signs establishes relevant context and supports an account of social action	**CONFIGURE INDEXICALS** Not all potentially salient indexical signs point to aspects of context that become relevant, and not all possible interpretations of social action become plausible. Signs are configured such that they presuppose clusters of other signs, making some indexicals more salient. Ultimately, a poetically organized configuration of mutually presupposing indexical signs ends the back-and-forth construal of relevant context and possible interpretations, such that one account of social action becomes the most plausible.	**DELINEATE CROSS-EVENT CONFIGURATIONS OF INDEXICALS** A set of signs and relevant context is established as indexicals across events are poetically configured, as signs from several events come to presuppose each other. As this cross-event configuration of signs solidifies, it provisionally ends the back-and-forth construal of relevant context and establishes the social actions and processes that are being accomplished across events, thus establishing a more rigid pathway.

Relevant context grounds inferences about voices, evaluations, positions and actions	**CONSTRUE INDEXICALS** Narrated events and indexical signs make certain aspects of the context relevant to interpreting the discursive interaction. Through entextualization, participants construe these signs and contexts, providing possible interpretations of the voicing, evaluation, positioning and social action occurring in the narrated and narrating events. Rows 2, 3 and 4 in this Table are iterative, with the selection of relevant context and the construal of that context shaping each other, until a configuration of signs solidifies and makes one interpretation of the positioning and social action most plausible.	**CONSTRUE INDEXICALS AND TRACE THE SHAPE OF PATHWAYS** As linked events collectively come to presuppose overlapping relevant context (e.g., relevant stereotypes that recur in the larger society), a pathway becomes more rigid and particular interpretations of social action become more highly presupposable. Instead of entextualization, we have the broader process of enregisterment, with a pathway of events collectively accomplishing social actions and processes. This is a dialectic process, with newly relevant context in a current event providing opportunities for reinterpreting the pathway, while a firmer account of the pathway constrains the context that might be relevant. When cross-event configurations of signs become stable, they make one construal of the actions and broader social processes most plausible.
Participants' positions in and across narrating events can be inferred from relevant context, and social action is accomplished as participants come to presuppose one version of what happened	**IDENTIFY POSITIONING AND SOCIAL ACTION IN NARRATING EVENTS** Relevant context allows participants and analysts to infer the interactional and evaluative positions being occupied by narrated characters and participants in the narrating event. These positions, together with other relevant context, allow inferences about the types of social action occurring in the narrating event. Inferences are always provisional, but in practice stable interpretations of an event usually come to be presupposed.	**IDENTIFY EMERGING CROSS-EVENT ACTIONS AND PROCESSES** Participants and analysts attend to relevant context across events and make inferences about positioning and social action both within and across events. Pathways across events can accomplish more complex, durable social actions and processes, like socialization, learning and social identification. Over time pathways across events become rigid and presuppose certain outcomes, but these can change with future recontextualizations.

Table 1.3 Components of a cross-event discourse analysis for Tyisha

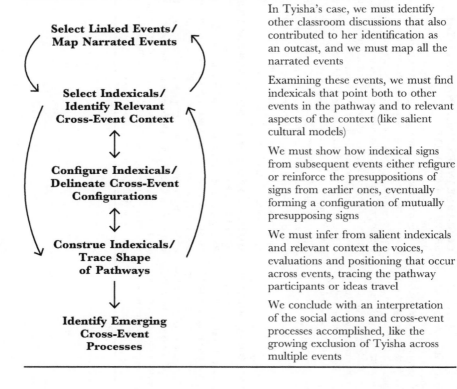

Select Linked Events/ Map Narrated Events	In Tyisha's case, we must identify other classroom discussions that also contributed to her identification as an outcast, and we must map all the narrated events
Select Indexicals/ Identify Relevant Cross-Event Context	Examining these events, we must find indexicals that point both to other events in the pathway and to relevant aspects of the context (like salient cultural models)
Configure Indexicals/ Delineate Cross-Event Configurations	We must show how indexical signs from subsequent events either refigure or reinforce the presuppositions of signs from earlier ones, eventually forming a configuration of mutually presupposing signs
Construe Indexicals/ Trace Shape of Pathways	We must infer from salient indexicals and relevant context the voices, evaluations and positioning that occur across events, tracing the pathway participants or ideas travel
Identify Emerging Cross-Event Processes	We conclude with an interpretation of the social actions and cross-event processes accomplished, like the growing exclusion of Tyisha across multiple events

Table 1.3 represents discourse analysis beyond the speech event, using a slightly modified version of the five-line table introduced above. We will use this format throughout the book when presenting cross-event analyses. In the first stage, represented on the first line, the analyst infers which events are potentially linked in a pathway. There is a set of (smaller) circular arrows in the margins, connecting the first line to the second, because the process of determining relevant linked events requires inference, and this inference depends on which indexical signs and aspects of context become relevant. Many events might potentially be part of a pathway, and the analyst must examine signs in these events in order to decide which ones are in fact linked. After identifying linked events, the analyst describes the narrated events for each. In the next stage, represented on the second and fourth lines, the discourse analyst engages in the iterative process of identifying relevant indexicals that occur across linked events, then inferring from the relevant context signaled by these indexicals the types of voices, evaluations and positioning that might be occurring across events. Construals of voices, evaluations and positioning make certain indexicals salient, but then newly considered indexicals make new construals plausible, in a back-and-forth interpretive process. This dialectic ends provisionally when a configuration of mutually presupposing indexical signs from across events solidifies and establishes some interpretation

as most plausible. This cross-event configuration of signs is represented on the third line of the table. In the last stage, represented on the last line, analysts infer the social actions and processes accomplished across the pathway.

We will briefly illustrate discourse analysis beyond the speech event by examining classroom discussions that involved Tyisha both before and after the discussion of her cat on January 24. In this section we will discuss three other speech events. Any event participates in multiple pathways, and an analyst must select a pathway of linked events relevant to the research question being addressed. For example, an analyst might be interested in the development of a teacher's pedagogical skills over time. Such an analyst could productively trace a pathway across events that included Mrs. Bailey or Mr. Smith using a particular pedagogical tool in more skillful ways. The study presented in Wortham (2006) asks research questions about social identification in Tyisha's classroom, and it follows the emerging identities of Tyisha and some other students across the academic year. Because the research question focuses on Tyisha's identity, we used two criteria for select-ing events to include in our pathway for the current analysis: events in which Tyisha's social identity is explicitly characterized by teachers and other students; and events in which Tyisha becomes a character in an example—as she did in the discussion of Tyisha and her cat—in ways that have implications for her social identity. Wortham (2006) provides a more extensive analysis that justifies the selection of events and describes other relevant events in the pathway.

On January 18, several days before the conversation analyzed above, the class was also discussing Aristotle's *Politics*. They had not yet reached the section on "beasts," but were instead discussing Aristotle's account of courage. Before the segment excerpted below, the teachers had asked whether a person can "obey courageously." Students readily understood that one can resist authority in ways that require courage, but they were not sure whether one could obey authority in a courageous way. At this point Tyisha introduced herself as an example.

Segment 4: Tyisha the courageous liar

280   *TYI:*   okay, I(hhh)- I had a <u>friend</u>. and she was like,
                sneaking out with a <u>boy</u>, and she lied and said that she was
                going with her <u>friends</u>. (hh) a(h)nd she told <u>me</u>, if my
                mother call, to tell her she was at the <u>zoo</u> with her friend
                <u>Stacey</u>. now that took her <u>courage</u> to te(h)<u>ll</u> me.
285   *FST:*   (hh[h)
      TYI: [and it took c(hh)oura(h)ge for <u>me</u> to tell her
                <u>mo</u>ther that.
      FST: °mhm°
      T/B: did it take courage for [her to tell her mother tha[t?
290   *FST:*   [no   [I
                don't think so
      T/B: why would th[at
      TYI: [<u>yeah</u> it took <u>cou</u>rage to tell my
                <u>Mo</u>ther

295   *FST:*   ((3 unintelligible syllables))
      MRC: I don't think it took courage.

In lines 280–284, Tyisha creates a new narrated event. Before this, the primary narrated event in this discursive interaction focused on Aristotle's view of courage, together with teachers' and students' views on this topic. Tyisha gives an example about her friend and the lie that Tyisha told to keep her friend's mother from discovering her friend's activity. As in the example of Tyisha and her cat, this example of Tyisha the courageous liar might characterize Tyisha as morally questionable. Tyisha describes her narrated self as courageously doing something that comes to be understood as immoral. This example does not illustrate the idea of courageous obedience that the teachers were exploring, but the class proceeds to discuss whether it can be courageous to perform an immoral act.

When analyzing events in a pathway, a discourse analyst must also analyze individual events. We will not do a full analysis of the January 18 classroom conversation here. See Wortham (2006) for more detail on this and the other events described below. Figure 1.3 maps the narrated and narrating events after Tyisha introduces her example. The curricular topic involves Aristotle's definition of courage and the question of whether different kinds of acts can be courageous, as represented in the narrated event on the right. The solid lines indicate the curricular question of whether the various actions—like resisting authority or acting immorally—can in fact be courageous. The example presents Tyisha's act of lying to her friend's mother and asks whether this was courageous. No complex action is occurring in the narrating event yet, besides an academic discussion among teachers and students. The laughter embedded in Tyisha and another student's speech at lines 280–286 might indicate that she is making a joke, and so the narrating event might involve humor, but this is not yet clear.

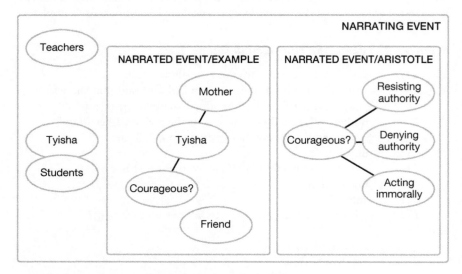

Figure 1.3 The example of "Tyisha the courageous liar"

As the discussion continues, one of the teachers argues that it would have been courageous to tell her friend's mother the truth, instead of lying.

Segment 5: *Lying in a mother's face*

	T/S:	then, which is <u>courage</u>?
	T/B:	Shhh
310	FST:	[so you gonna sit there and <u>lie</u> to [her face
	T/S:	[lying [to <u>lie</u>: or to tell the
		truth be[cause you=
	FST:	[°to tell the truth°
	T/S:	=knew that she was wrong.
315	CAN:	°cause it's wrong°
	FST:	tell the <u>truth</u>. tell the <u>truth</u>
	TYI:	<u>both</u> of them=
	JAS:	both of them take courage [to me
	TYI:	[=both of them take
320		cou[rage, you all wrong
	T/S:	[explai:n how both.
	TYI:	because (hhhh[h)
	FST:	[because
	T/S:	let her
325	TYI:	if I lyin'- If I'm sittin' here lying in another person
		<u>mo</u>ther <u>face</u>, that took courag(h)e. [and if I'm=
	T/S:	[why?
	TYI:	=telling her be<u>cause</u> you don't-
	FST:	lies.
330	T/S:	have you never <u>lied</u> to your mother?
	FST:	°hnuh°
	TYI:	no- not- not to no one <u>else</u>'s momma, <u>no</u>.
	T/S:	have you ever <u>lied</u> to a <u>tea</u>cher who is a mother?
	FST:	uh(hhh)
335	TYI:	that's <u>dif</u>ferent.
	FST:	aw <u>man</u>.
	STS:	((2 seconds of laughter))
	TYI:	that's <u>very</u> different um- I mean that's <u>dif</u>ferent. I'm
		always over there visiting this <u>friend</u> and her mother, might
340		have had trus- trust in me and I come over and tell her this
		big, <u>bo:ld</u> faced lie.

Substantively, the disagreement about "courage" is relatively simple. The teacher and several other students argue that an immoral act like lying cannot be courageous because, as they articulate later, courage is a virtue and cannot be manifested in an immoral act. Tyisha (joined by Jasmine at lines 317–320) argues that lying to her friend's mother took courage, although she acknowledges that telling the truth would also have been courageous. Tyisha's argument seems plausible, but the other implications of her example take over the discussion and push substantive issues to the background.

The narrated events involving Aristotle's account of courage and Tyisha's lie provide resources that teachers and students use to position each other in the narrating event. For instance, they draw on Aristotle's evaluative distinction between courageous and not courageous. Tyisha tries to position herself as courageous and thus good or admirable. But she does so using an example of herself doing something immoral. Her laughter at lines 280–286 and 322–326 might indicate that she is enjoying the tension between claiming virtue while describing an immoral act, and perhaps also enjoying the opportunity to describe immoral acts as part of a substantive classroom discussion. At the same time, the teachers and some students use the content of the example to position Tyisha as different from the other students, as immoral and something of an outcast.

Tyisha's example includes various indexical signs that signal relevant context and allow inferences about voicing, evaluation and positioning, like the evaluative characterizations of her narrated self as doing something wrong. Consider the **verbs of speaking** used to describe Tyisha's statement to her friend's mother. As mentioned above and as discussed extensively in Chapter 2, reported speech and the verbs of speaking used to characterize speech are powerful resources for socially identifying others. When introducing the narrated example Tyisha initially used "tell" to describe the act of speaking to her friend's mother, at line 283. The teacher reframed this as a "lie" at line 301, in a segment not reproduced here (cf. Wortham, 2006, for the transcript), and he contrasted lying with "telling the truth" at lines 311–312. Another student made this more highly presupposing, saying "so you gonna sit there and lie to her face" at line 310. Tyisha herself embraced this characterization of her act at lines 325–326: "I'm sitting here lying in another person mother face." At the end she produces another colorful formulation: "Her mother might have had trust in me and I come over and tell her this big bold-faced lie" (lines 339–341). These more and more highly presupposing terms for describing Tyisha's lie communicate an increasingly robust characterization of her narrated self. The terms describing her utterance more and more highly presuppose flagrantly immoral behavior. The indexical presuppositions of these verbs of speaking form a configuration, such that this characterization of Tyisha as immoral becomes more firmly established, at least in the narrated event.

At line 333 one of the teachers makes clear that this characterization has implications for Tyisha's own position in the narrating event. He asks: "have you ever lied to a teacher who is a mother?" Everyone in the class knows that the other teacher, Mrs. Bailey, has a teenage daughter. Everyone knows that many mothers of teenage daughters worry about their daughters lying and sneaking off with boys. The first teacher's question at line 333 does not contribute to the substance of his argument, because for the purposes of defining courage it is irrelevant whether a person lies to a teacher or to someone else. But his question establishes a parallelism between the narrated character Tyisha lied to in the

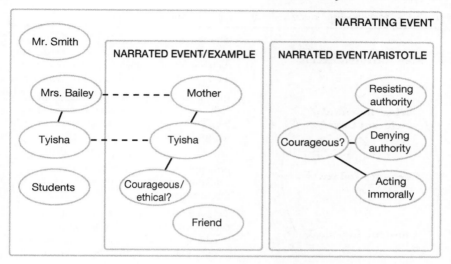

Figure 1.4 The outcome of the example

example and Mrs. Bailey herself, and thus it makes Tyisha's immoral narrated behavior relevant to her position in the narrating event. It opposes her to the second teacher, on an issue of substantial emotional import, because Mrs. Bailey may worry about being lied to by people like Tyisha.

Figure 1.4 represents this parallelism between narrated and narrating events. The discussion about Tyisha in the narrated event has raised the issue not only of whether she was courageous but also of whether she was ethical. By the time they get to the "big bold-faced lie" at line 341, Tyisha is clearly voiced as unethical in the narrated event. By talking about "a teacher who is a mother," Mr. Smith has established the parallelism indicated with the dashed lines: the relationship between the narrated characters Tyisha and her friend's mother may be similar to the relationship between the narrating Tyisha and Mrs. Bailey—at least insofar as Mrs. Bailey might identify with the friend's mother and condemn Tyisha. Mr. Smith has put into play the question of whether Tyisha herself might engage in unethical behavior that would affect people like Mrs. Bailey.

So far we have focused on the indexicals/relevant context/contextualization and voices/evaluations/positioning/entextualization that occurred within the speech event on January 18. This is not a complete analysis of the event, as we give only enough detail to make our forthcoming points about discourse analysis across events. Table 1.4 represents our brief analysis. At the end of the conversation, as we will see in the next segment below, Tyisha is positioned as disrupting classroom conversation and as an outcast from the classroom community. This social action is similar to the exclusion described above from the January 24 discussion of Tyisha and her cat.

Table 1.4 Analysis of the discrete event "Tyisha the courageous liar"

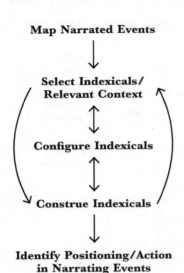

Map Narrated Events	The example of Tyisha the courageous liar provides an opportunity to voice Tyisha, and the concept of courage from Aristotle raises the issue of ethical and unethical behavior
Select Indexicals/ Relevant Context	Indexicals like the verbs of speaking, from "tell" to "lie" to "bold faced lie" and "lie in her face" presuppose a model of increasingly serious unethical behavior
Configure Indexicals	The accumulating and increasingly highly presupposing verbs of speaking form a configuration that solidifies the relevance of this model
Construe Indexicals	Tyisha embraces and others adopt a characterization of her as flagrantly unethical; Mrs. Bailey's status as a mother positions her as opposed to Tyisha the liar
Identify Positioning/Action in Narrating Events	Tyisha is separated out from the teachers and other students, as a less moral person, and she is excluded from class because she is positioned as disruptive

This similar social action provides a link between Tyisha's positioning in the courageous liar discussion on January 18 and in the January 24 discussion of "beasts." On both days Tyisha disagrees with the teachers about the academic topic under discussion, giving relatively convincing arguments. On both days Tyisha presents an example that ends up characterizing her narrated self as morally questionable and as different from and lesser than most humans, including the teachers and other students. On both days the teachers and other students try to engage with her argument substantively but end up foregrounding her morally questionable characteristics and positioning her in the event of speaking as an outcast who disrupts the classroom community. On both days the interaction ends with teachers explicitly disciplining her, as we can see in the following excerpt from January 18.

Segment 6: Tyisha disrupting the class

LIN: I don't think that's <u>cou</u>rage to go and steal a <u>can</u>dy bar
       [because <u>cou</u>rage- right=
MST: [it's stupid
395 LIN: =cause courage, the virtue of courage, what we read
       of courage was to <u>do</u> something- something <u>goo:d</u>, not to
       do <u>some</u>thing and go and do <u>some</u>thing [<u>e</u>vil.
TYI: [that's <u>not</u>
       true

```
400  FST:                                      [yeah that's
                    right
     TYI:           courage is not just doing something goo:d.
                    ((students talking at once))
     TYI:           if I go [shoot you in the head
405  T/B:                  [shhhhh
                    ((students arguing))
     T/B:           ahh, if we can- if we can talk about courage as being
                    something good, the virtue of courage, and go back to that
                    definition, and I know you never bought into it, but the rest
410                 of us seem to be, using this as a definition, so therefore,
                    we'd ask you to kind of go along with it.
     FST:           okay.
     T/B:           the idea of courage, was not just doing things you're
                    afraid to do, but doing things that- overcoming your fear
415                 for a good reason. Linda?
     LIN:           I was saying what Tyisha said, if you go shoot
                    somebody in the head, you gonna call that courage? or you
                    is gonna call that stupid?
```

At lines 409–411 the teacher speaks explicitly to Tyisha about her behavior and the rules of engagement in classroom discussion. She makes clear that Tyisha is prone to make up her own definitions and disrupt productive classroom conversation, and she effectively excludes Tyisha from the discussion for the next several minutes. Linda follows up at line 418 by calling Tyisha's argument stupid (echoing comments made at lines 394 and 397), but the teacher's preceding statement has made clear that Tyisha should not defend her alternative position any further.

When the discussion of Tyisha and her cat occurred on January 24, students and teachers could presuppose that Tyisha is morally questionable and prone to disrupt class more easily than if the January 18 discussion had not occurred. At lines 599–601 in the segment presented above from that January 24 conversation, Mrs. Bailey characterizes Tyisha as a disruptive outcast, in a way that echoes lines 409–411 from the January 18 conversation. Mrs. Bailey and others were able to use fewer indexical signs in order to presuppose these characterizations on January 24, because these signs now index not only a general stereotype of immoral and disruptive adolescent behavior but also the specific conversation on January 18 in which a similar stereotype was also presupposed and attached to Tyisha. In other words, the configuration of signs indexing this stereotype includes mutually presupposing signs from both speech events, and each event becomes relevant cross-event context for the other.

Entextualization within the discussion of Tyisha and her cat—the identification of Tyisha as (metaphorically) less human than other students and as disruptive, and the act of disciplining and excluding her from classroom conversation—is facilitated not only by relevant context that includes circulating social stereotypes

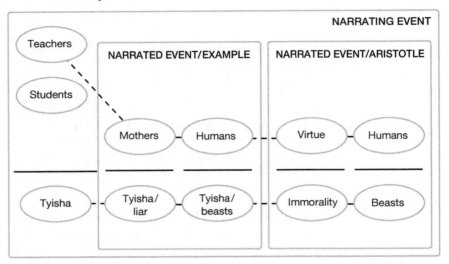

Figure 1.5 Parallelism across speech events

but also by cross-event context, by indexical links with preceding classroom conversations like the one on January 18. In fact, Wortham (2006) describes other events beyond these two that participate in the pathway that established Tyisha's social identity over several months. But these two examples illustrate how cross-event configurations of indexical signs can contribute to social action in the subsequent event of speaking. Figure 1.5 represents the parallelism between and the characterizations across these two events of speaking. Each of the narrated events in the figure represents voices and evaluations from the January 18 discussion on the left and the January 24 discussion on the right. Both narrating events end up separating Tyisha from the rest of the class, positioning her as less human or morally questionable and as a disruptive outcast to be excluded from classroom conversation.

By examining these two conversations together we can also begin to see enregisterment occurring, the emergence of Tyisha's social identity across events. In this case an individual is being socially identified in a classroom over an academic year. The social domain is small—two teachers and 18 students recognize the model of identity being established for Tyisha. But even within this small spatiotemporal envelope, social identification can have significant consequences for Tyisha's personal development and institutional credentials, as well as significant consequences for students' socialization into norms about "good" students who are "likely to succeed" through "cooperative" behavior. We have seen the smallest possible unit of enregisterment so far—two conversations that presuppose each other and begin to establish a pathway across which Tyisha's social identity emerges.

We will offer two more brief examples of events along this pathway. The next occurred on February 7, during a discussion of Spartan infanticide. Lycurgus describes how ancient Spartans exposed sickly infants to the elements, reasoning that an infant too weak to survive would end up being a burden on the society and should be allowed to die of exposure. Tyisha was absent on the day this discussion occurred, but the teacher nonetheless mentioned her.

Segment 7: Positioning an absent Tyisha

	BRE:	they just put them out an- as a <u>test</u>. if it <u>lives</u> then it's strong. and if it <u>dies</u> then it dies.
	T/B:	I'm going to play Ty<u>i</u>sha. that's not <u>right</u>
	STS:	hahahahaha
250	T/B:	these people are <u>stupid</u>. that's not <u>right</u> we're[<u>missing</u>=
	STS:	[hnh haha
	T/B:	=her today.
	STS:	((7 seconds comments and laughter))
255	T/B:	she- you <u>know</u> that's what she'd say? what is your response to <u>that</u>?
	STS:	((unintelligible response)) hahahahaha
	T/B:	you'd never say that when she's in the <u>room</u>.

At line 248 the teacher characterizes Tyisha by creating a hypothetical narrated event in which she reacts to the practice of Spartan infanticide. She uses reported speech that might voice Tyisha as blunt, confrontational and perhaps unsophisticated. These utterances could also characterize her as an outspoken, no nonsense independent thinker willing to take chances, however. The term "stupid" in line 250 might index a lack of sophistication, and this seems to support the first reading. The teacher also presupposes that Tyisha intimidates other students at line 258.

The voice being assigned to Tyisha here is not fully clear from this short segment. But other events in the pathway provide relevant context that reduces the ambiguity. This brief hypothetical narrated event presupposes other events, like those on January 18 and 24, in which Tyisha has behaved in similar ways. It joins a pathway of linked events across which Tyisha's identity has been established—as a disruptive student who separates herself from others by taking contradictory positions and refusing to collaborate in productive classroom discussions. Figure 1.6 represents the parallelism and the accumulating presuppositions about Tyisha across the events of January 18, January 24 and February 7. These events provide cross-event context for each other, with the characterization of Tyisha as a disruptive outcast in the narrated events, and the positioning of her as an outcast in the narrating events, becoming more firmly established as the events presuppose each other.

By April 12 Tyisha's position had changed, however. On this day the class discussed John Steinbeck's story *The Pearl*. The story describes an indigenous person who finds a valuable pearl and must either accept an unfairly low price

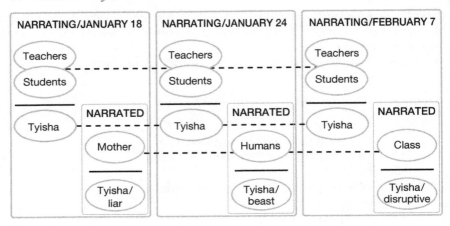

NARRATING/JANUARY 18	NARRATING/JANUARY 24	NARRATING/FEBRUARY 7

Figure 1.6 The pathway across three events

from the Europeans who dominate commerce in his town or risk a hazardous journey to the city to get a better price. Teachers and students discuss the question of whether one should accept unjust but familiar circumstances or risk more revolutionary changes. They do this by describing a second narrated event, in addition to the Steinbeck story—Jim Crow America, in which segregation laws disenfranchised African Americans, including family members of most of the students.

Segment 8: Tyisha is not content

	T/B:	okay, I, I, ex<u>cuse</u> me, I'm a <u>south</u>ern state. a:nd uh,
1180		I'll give you an <u>e</u>ducation <u>J</u>asmine. I'll give you an
		education in that building over <u>there</u>, with all these kids
		<u>crammed</u> in, with textbooks that are fifty years <u>old</u>. o:r
		(1.0) you can take a chance. and you can stand <u>up</u> to the
		power <u>structure</u>. and maybe even pull your kids out of
1185		school and <u>boy</u>cott <u>schools</u> for a <u>while</u>. and maybe not get
		any education at all for awhile because you want a <u>real</u>
		education and not this Jim <u>Crow</u> education.
	FST:	right.
	T/B:	what do you do?
1190	FST:	you stand <u>up</u> for what you be<u>lieve</u> in.
	T/B:	you <u>take</u> what you can <u>get</u>? <u>or</u> do you go after what
		is <u>real</u>ly what you <u>want</u>?
	STS:	((3 seconds of chatter))
	TYI:	because, if he had been <u>poor</u> for this <u>long</u>, and he had
1195		a chance to be <u>happy</u> with his <u>life</u>, why don't <u>give</u> it to
		someone you know that's not gonna be satisfied as you?

JAS: but, but in, in the long run, wait a minute, in the long run you <u>might</u> not even get <u>nothing</u>, so you <u>just</u> gonna <u>sit</u> there.

1200 *TYI:*   I'd <u>rather</u> go try, then just sit there and say this is about sitting down. I- I think I could have got <u>more</u> than <u>that</u>. I'm not gonna sit there <u>no</u> longer, I'm gonna go out and <u>search</u> for some <u>money</u>. I'm not gonna <u>be</u> like that.

Wortham (2006) analyzes the complex entextualization and enregisterment occurring in this and linked events. We do not have space for detailed analysis here, but one crucial element is a model drawn from the curriculum and used to position Tyisha in the narrating event. Both the Steinbeck story and Mrs. Bailey's example of Jim Crow America present a member of an exploited group, indigenous people or African Americans, who face a choice about whether to confront those in power.

In her example from Jim Crow America at lines 1179–1187, the teacher asks Jasmine whether she would confront racist educational disparities. Like the example of Tyisha and her cat, and Tyisha the courageous liar, this example places a student into the position of a person or topic from the curriculum. In those earlier cases teachers and students used the model from the curriculum—involving the distinction between humans and animals, or the distinction between moral and immoral acts—to position Tyisha as different from others in the class. But in this case the model incorporates Tyisha as a member of the classroom community. Figure 1.7 represents the two narrated events at this point in the conversation, with a member of an underprivileged group having to decide

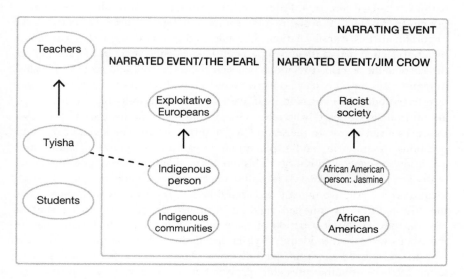

Figure 1.7 The final examples

whether to challenge the exploitative people in power. Wortham (2006) shows how, as the conversation proceeds, this model of social relations allows Tyisha herself to become a member of the students' social group, challenging people in power like the teachers.

By introducing the example of Jim Crow America—something that both teachers and students condemn on this and other days, and a topic that potentially marks Tyisha's similarity with many other students because they are seen as members of the same racial group—the teacher provides an opening for Tyisha to become less of an outcast. Tyisha's comments at lines 1194 and 1200 make clear that she would stick up for herself and work against those in power by, for instance, trying to sell the pearl for more money than the Europeans were offering. In this event and others from late February through May, Tyisha was identified by teachers and students more positively than before. She continued to defend unpopular positions and argue against teachers and other students. But they started to evaluate this behavior differently. Instead of treating it as a disruptive refusal to collaborate, they characterized it as a principled insistence on questioning authority. Before the passage above, Tyisha had argued that the indigenous protagonist should not accept exploitation by the Europeans and should instead demand fair treatment even if this required a risky journey. On other occasions in the spring she made similar arguments—for example, arguing that students should not uncritically accept historians' accounts of the past but should consult other sources. As described in Wortham (2006), these parallel narrated events helped establish a pathway across which an organized set of signs came to establish a different type of characteristic position for Tyisha.

From December through February several linked events established Tyisha as a disruptive outcast, including the examples on January 18 and 24. But then the pathway changed direction. From late February through May she turned into a principled dissenter. Wortham (2006) shows how one resource was particularly important to this transformation. The narrated events described in curricular materials shifted across these two parts of the academic year. In the first period the curriculum described relations between the individual and society, focusing in many cases on outcasts who were excessively individualistic. This model was transferred onto the classroom itself, with Tyisha often positioned in the role of an individualistic "beast" who refuses to collaborate, as we have seen in the two examples given above. In the second period, however, the curriculum addressed questions of authority and exploitation, foregrounding power relations and exploring resistance to authority. This model provided a different position for an outspoken participant like Tyisha, and she became a legitimate dissenter. Tyisha's identity as a disruptive outcast was established across a pathway of events, but then the pathway became less rigid and changed direction as other resources were introduced. After a period of some indeterminacy in which both charac- terizations were used to identify Tyisha, her pathway became more rigid again with her positioned as a principled dissenter. The voices or positions described as narrated events in the curriculum provided important resources for this change in Tyisha's identity.

Table 1.5 Cross-event discourse analysis of Tyisha across the pathway

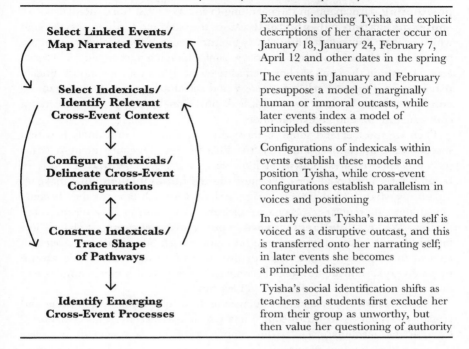

Select Linked Events/ Map Narrated Events	Examples including Tyisha and explicit descriptions of her character occur on January 18, January 24, February 7, April 12 and other dates in the spring
Select Indexicals/ Identify Relevant Cross-Event Context	The events in January and February presuppose a model of marginally human or immoral outcasts, while later events index a model of principled dissenters
Configure Indexicals/ Delineate Cross-Event Configurations	Configurations of indexicals within events establish these models and position Tyisha, while cross-event configurations establish parallelism in voices and positioning
Construe Indexicals/ Trace Shape of Pathways	In early events Tyisha's narrated self is voiced as a disruptive outcast, and this is transferred onto her narrating self; in later events she becomes a principled dissenter
Identify Emerging Cross-Event Processes	Tyisha's social identification shifts as teachers and students first exclude her from their group as unworthy, but then value her questioning of authority

Tyisha's pathway across events became rigid for a couple of months, then fluid for a short time, then rigid in a different direction for another couple of months. Table 1.5 represents this cross-event analysis. It took detailed empirical investigation to determine when and how the change in Tyisha's social identification occurred. The shape of pathways that emerges through enregisterment occurs at different spatial and temporal scales, and these pathways sometimes take unexpected turns. As Lemke (2000), Blommaert (2007) and Wortham (2006, 2012) argue, we must not let theoretical or political commitments predetermine the scales at which we expect social regularities to occur. It may be common for students from certain social groups to get increasingly identified as disruptive across their school careers, for example, but this does not occur in every case. The objects of discourse analysis are dynamic and heterogeneous in scale, and our approach must attend to this fact. We return to this issue of unpredictable pathways and heterogeneous scales, and the implications for social explanation more generally, in Chapter 6.

Discourse analysis across events

In order to do discourse analysis across speech events, we must first analyze discrete events—analyzing how **narrated events** and **indexical signs** establish

relevant context and provide resources for **voicing** narrated characters and **positioning** participants in the narrating event. We must trace the dialectic of **contextualization** and **entextualization**, the back-and-forth process through which relevant context establishes likely interpretations of the voicing, evaluation, positioning and **social action** occurring, while emerging interpretations of social action constrain the context construed as relevant. We must show how mutually reinforcing accounts of relevant context and social action solidify as organized **configurations** of signs are established, provisionally ending the dialectic of contextualization and entextualization.

Then we must extend some of these principles of discourse analysis within speech events to examine patterns across linked events. Discourse analysis across speech events requires analysis of individual events in a pathway, but it also requires three additional steps. We must **identify linked events** that make up a pathway, studying how events become relevant to each other as they become linked through reported speech, parallelism across narrated events or other devices. We must **delineate cross-event configurations**, studying how indexical signs across events come to presuppose each other and create relevant context that establishes more rigid pathways. And we must **trace the shape of pathways**, showing how they become rigid and establish more complex and durable processes like socialization and learning.

This book provides systematic guidance on how to combine within-event and cross-event analyses to do discourse analysis across speech events. Chapter 2 expands the accounts given in this chapter, providing a systematic overview of tools and techniques required to analyze discourse beyond the speech event. We present tools for doing discourse analysis within and across speech events through the five tasks of selecting linked events/mapping narrated events, selecting indexicals/relevant cross-event context, construing indexicals/tracing pathways, configuring indexicals, and inferring social action/broader social processes. Each component is illustrated through sample analyses.

Discourse analysis beyond the speech event has been done with several kinds of data. Although the approach presented in Chapters 1 and 2 applies to all discourse, somewhat different approaches are appropriate in different cases. Chapters 3–5 apply these tools and techniques to analyze three types of data: "ethnographic," "archival" and "new media." Ethnographic studies analyze living people and actions in context, typically at shorter timescales and within more limited spatial scales. Archival studies analyze historical processes, typically at longer timescales and broader spatial scales. Studies of new media analyze actions in mediated worlds, typically at shorter timescales but broader spatial scales. New media studies also often focus on highly interconnected messages that depend on each other for completion, whereas the documents, interviews and observations in ethnographic and archival studies are often less immediately interconnected. These are ideal types, and many research projects will involve more than one of these data sources.

Chapter 3 illustrates discourse analysis beyond the speech event using ethnographic data—face-to-face participant observation with living people in context.

We use examples from ethnographic discourse analyses that the two of us have recently done. Data from Wortham (2006) were introduced above, and the more extensive analyses in Chapter 3 trace a pathway of speech events across which one of Tyisha's classmates was socially identified. Reyes (2013) also examines classroom data over the course of a year. She shows how participants reject or support the use of student nicknames depending on the pathway along which a particular event of speaking is located. Chapter 4 shows how discourse analysis beyond the speech event can be done on archival data, in which researchers analyze discursive artifacts that illuminate broader sociohistorical processes. The chapter applies our approach to archival discourse analyses by Miyako Inoue (2006) on Japanese women's language and Robert Moore (2007, 2011) on Irish English accent. We focus on how the tools of voicing and reported speech facilitate cross-event archival analyses. Chapter 5 shows how discourse analysis beyond the speech event can be applied to new media data, in which researchers trace digital forms of communication that began emerging in the late twentieth century. We use recent work by Elaine Chun (2013) and Betsy Rymes (2014) to trace cross-event recontextualizations of media forms along pathways in digital space. Chun analyzes how a Chinese American, who deploys signs that are potential indexes of "blackness," gets identified across trajectories of YouTube commentaries. Rymes traces the recontextualization of music video genre elements in several videos that range from sincere to ironic performance.

Recent work in anthropology, linguistics and related disciplines has made clear that we must move beyond the speech event and examine pathways of linked events in order to understand how language helps constitute the social world. We now have a sophisticated theoretical account of this new approach to language and social life, and we have a growing body of quality empirical work that illustrates the productivity of the approach. But researchers interested in discourse need methodological guidance about how to study cross-event pathways empirically. This book provides such guidance. Chapter 6 closes the book by summarizing our approach and exploring the implications of cross-event analyses for common theoretical assumptions about the spatial and temporal scales of discursive action.

2   Central tools and techniques

Discourse analysis, whether within or across speech events, involves systematic investigation of signs that participants use to accomplish social action. If signs had univocal functions, discourse analysis would be easy—the analyst could simply consult a key that identifies what each type of sign means. But in fact any sign could signal many different types of social action. Signs only come to have clear meanings as relevant context emerges, and this happens as indexical signs come consistently to presuppose aspects of the context. Participants and analysts engage in a back-and-forth process of identifying the context that key signs index and adopting an interpretation of voicing, evaluation, positioning and social action that fits with this relevant context. Across an interaction or a pathway, relevant context and an interpretation of social action come to fit together such that participants and analysts can presuppose how participants are being positioned and what type of social action they are engaged in.

In Tyisha's case, as we saw in the last chapter, teachers and students use various signs that contribute to socially identifying her. Early in the interaction, for example, Tyisha says "my goal is to win in Nintendo." At the moment of utterance this could have meant several things: that Tyisha is trying to win an academic argument with the teacher by describing one of her activities, that she is just joking that video games are one of her primary interests, that she is interested in video games to the exclusion of other activities like schoolwork, or various other possibilities. Participants and analysts select from among these interpretations as other signs in the discursive interaction signal relevant context for interpreting the utterance about Nintendo. As described above, by the time the teacher says "so you *are* like an animal," it has become presupposed that Tyisha is more like her cat and less like other students who plan their activities systematically and pursue long-range goals. By the end of the interaction, it becomes clear that teachers and students have identified her as less diligent, as a disruptive and unpromising student. At this point indexical signs and an account of social action have come to reinforce each other and support a clear interpretation of what is happening in the narrating event.

We can use discourse analysis to study various aspects of discursive interaction. Halliday (1978) describes three "metafunctions," general types of social action that speakers accomplish. The "ideational" function communicates ideas. The "interpersonal" function establishes relationships. And the "textual" function creates coherence across segments of discursive interaction. Any stretch of discourse always accomplishes all three metafunctions. The metafunctions are also interdependent, with each one being accomplished in part through contributions from the others. Different approaches to discourse analysis focus on different metafunctions, however. Some study how signs communicate information, while others study how elements of discourse cohere into textual wholes. In this book we focus on the interpersonal metafunction—how participants establish relationships with others, how they position themselves interactionally, perform social actions and evaluate both others and the social world. Because participants accomplish the interpersonal functions of discourse in part through ideational and textual mechanisms, we provide some strategies for analyzing these metafunctions. For example, we show how the denotational content of narrated events (established through the ideational metafunction) serves as a resource for social action in the narrating event, and we show how indexical signs cohere into configurations (through the textual metafunction) that make robust interpretations of social action possible. But we study the ideational and textual metafunctions only for their contributions to the interpersonal functions of discourse, because our approach to discourse analysis aims to uncover the social actions accomplished through language use.

Our approach to discourse analysis

The first chapter introduced our approach to doing discourse analysis of discrete speech events. Our approach has three phases, and the second phase has three components. The first phase is **mapping narrated events**, using knowledge of semantic, pragmatic and grammatical regularities to describe the narrated content. Second, the analyst engages in the iterative process of selecting, construing and configuring indexicals. These three components are not linear. Discourse analysts start by **selecting indexicals**—identifying signs that might be important signals about the social action occurring, signs that could play a central role in contextualization. In this chapter we describe types of signs that often do this work, like deictics, in more detail. After selecting some potentially salient indexicals, analysts proceed to **construing indexicals**—inferring models of voicing, evaluation, positioning and social action that could fit with the relevant context signaled by salient indexicals. Selecting and construing indexicals together form the dialectic of contextualization and entextualization, as participants identify potentially relevant context and begin to construe the types of social action that might be occurring. This iterative process of identifying indexical signs and the relevant context they presuppose, then construing those signs and interpreting the social action occurring, stops when a configuration of mutually presupposing signs emerges and brings stability. From a discourse analytic point of view, this component of the analysis involves **configuring indexicals**—describing how groups of indexical signs cohere in configurations that solidify and thus establish relevant context and signal the social action being performed. After identifying such a

Table 2.1 The phases and components of discourse analysis

Phase 1: **MAPPING NARRATED** **EVENTS**	What characters, objects and events are referred to and characterized as the narrated contents of the discursive interaction (or of the several events forming a pathway of discursive interactions)?
Phase 2/Component 1: **SELECTING INDEXICALS**	Attending particularly to the types of signs that often signal the social action accomplished through discourse, which indexical signs become salient and signal relevant context within (or within and across) events?
Phase 2/Component 2: **CONSTRUING** **INDEXICALS**	Which accounts of voicing, evaluation, positioning and social action do participants use, explicitly or tacitly, to construe salient indexical signs and interpret narrated and narrating events?
Phase 2/Component 3: **CONFIGURING** **INDEXICALS**	How do salient indexical signs coalesce into stable configurations within (or within and across) events, such that relevant context and recognizable types of social action are established?
Phase 3: **INTERPRETING SOCIAL** **ACTION IN NARRATING** **EVENTS**	What account best explains the positioning and social action occurring in the narrating event (or across the pathway of narrating events)?

configuration, the analyst can proceed to the third phase, drawing conclusions about interactional positioning and **interpreting the social action** being accomplished in the narrating event.

In this chapter we illustrate each of these phases with an example, and in the next three chapters we use the approach to analyze six other examples. This chapter first applies our approach to a discrete speech event, then extends it to discourse analysis across events. Table 2.1 lists the questions addressed in each phase.

In Phase 1 the discourse analyst describes the narrated events that form the content of the discursive interaction(s). In Phase 2/Component 1 the discourse analyst identifies indexical signs that may be salient in the discursive interaction(s). Almost any sign could turn out to be salient in a given case. But particular types of signs are often important to accomplishing social action, and in this chapter we describe the most important of these. Discourse analysts attend to these types of signs in their initial pass through the data, because this often provides important clues about salient indexicals and relevant context. In Phase 2/Component 2 the discourse analyst construes the salient indexicals, inferring models of social action that may be signaled by key indexical signs. In Phase 2/Component 3 the discourse analyst examines how configurations of indexical signs come to presuppose each other, collectively establishing coherence within a discursive interaction or across a pathway of linked interactions.

In practice the three components of Phase 2 are not separable, because participants and analysts move iteratively through them. Analytically, however, it helps to separate them. In Phase 3, the discourse analyst provides an interpretation of the interactional positioning and social action occurring in the narrating event(s).

In Table 2.1, and in the sections below, it may seem that we have reversed components 2 and 3 in Phase 2, changing their order from what appears in Table 1.1 and other tables with the same format. These tables represent "configuring indexicals" on the third line, between identifying and construing, representing the iterative cycle of configuring and construing on the second and fourth lines with the process of configuring indexicals on the third line in between them. This is meant to represent the constraining force that configuring indexicals has on both selecting and construing indexicals, as the arrows in Table 1.1 indicate. In Table 2.1, which represents the phases discourse analysis proceeds through, we have reversed the third and fourth lines. When beginning a discourse analysis, construing indexicals happens before looking for configurations of indexicals. Identifying a stable configuration of indexicals ends the second phase, solidifying accounts of salient indexicals, relevant context and social action. In the midst of an analysis we move back and forth among selecting, construing and configuring, with the order depending on the details of the discourse being analyzed. But the first two components typically begin the analysis and the third typically ends it, and so in this chapter we discuss the components in this order.

Our model applies to the analysis of discrete speech events, and we extend it to analyze pathways of linked events. We introduce our model by analyzing a single speech event, one taken from a study by Reyes (2011). Later in the chapter, we extend the approach to analyze linked events along a pathway that includes this central example. Chapters 3–5 illustrate in detail how our approach can be applied to pathways of discursive interactions drawn from ethnographic, archival and new media studies.

The central example: Crying "racist" in classroom interaction

The example that we will use to illustrate our model comes from work by Reyes (2011) that analyzes classroom conversations among Asian American youth who cry "racist," presumably characterizing someone or something as racist. The data were collected as part of an ethnographic study of a fifth grade English language arts class that met Fridays after school in an Asian American supplementary school in New York City during 2006–2007. As was the norm in the school, this class had Korean American students and European American teachers.

In the following classroom interaction, recorded on December 8, the teacher (Mr. Bader) was trying to get the class back on task after a 10-minute break.

Segment 1: The sword of darkness

001	Mr. Bader:	I- I definitely want to- s- send somebody to the office to quiet
002		this crowd down, so, if- I see any twitches, or any, b- b- uh-
003		defiant behavior, I will-
004	Hyo:	send you to the office (just say it)
005	Mr. Bader:	take you to the office personally
006	Hyo:	no I will bring the hammer down
007	Mr. Bader:	bring the hammer,
008	Luke:	not- not bring-
009	Mr. Bader:	the hammer of Thor right coming down
010	Luke:	no not the hammer of Thor, the sword of- the sword of light
011	Mr. Bader:	da- da- Damo- Diocles Diocl-
012	Luke:	no the- no the sword of darkness
013	Mr. Bader:	the sword of darkness is coming to those who act in a, in
014		antisocial behavior
015	Joo-eun:	does that mean the sword is dark? [or does that mean-
016	Pete:	[you wish you were a little
017		boy again (don't you)
018	Joo-eun:	does that mean the blade is black?
019	Mr. Bader:	yes, this is black, this is- this is- carbon-
020	Pete:	racist! ((embedded in a cough))
021	Mr. Bader:	carbon- plated- steel. now, excuse me skateboard people, we are
022		recognizing the order of events or steps on page eleven

In this segment the teacher and students discuss how to eradicate disruptive classroom behavior with hammers and swords, using metaphors to describe the discipline the teacher threatens to impose. Then Pete cries "racist!" in line 020. How do we make sense of this utterance? The tools and techniques that we introduce in the following sections will help us analyze what is going on this segment. The tools and techniques allow us to address the key discourse analytic questions introduced in Chapter 1: What narrated events are described as the content of this interaction? Which indexical signs should we pay attention to? How are salient indexicals construed, yielding an interpretation of the social action occurring? How does a configuration of signs establish an account of the social action occurring?

Phase 1: Mapping narrated events

In the first step, a discourse analyst maps the narrated content of the discursive interaction. What narrated events do the participants describe as they speak to each other? In the example of Tyisha and her cat, from Chapter 1, these events included descriptions of Aristotle and his account of social outcasts, descriptions of what teachers and students were themselves doing in the narrating event, and the example of how Tyisha and her cat behave. We saw how narrated events can provide important resources that participants use to position themselves and others in the narrating event—as teachers and students transferred categories like "beast" from narrated to narrating events, using them to exclude and discipline Tyisha.

In the central example from Mr. Bader's classroom, lines 001–008 describe the classroom participants and the narrating interaction itself. Mr. Bader describes his inclination to enforce disciplinary rules, and Hyo appropriates Mr. Bader's voice, imagining him saying "bring the hammer down." Then from lines 009–019 teacher and students describe hammers and swords in a fantasy world, exploring their characteristics. At line 020 Pete seems to be calling the teacher a racist, although it will take further analysis to interpret this remark. In any case, at line 020 the narrated event shifts back to the classroom conversation itself. Then Mr. Bader returns to the substantive content of the lesson at lines 021–022.

In order to map narrated events, a discourse analyst must use knowledge about grammar, lexicon and sociocultural context. The goal is to identify the various narrated events—the characters, objects and actions described. In the example, the first narrated event about classroom behavior is marked in part by the use of deictics "I" and "you," which describe participants themselves, and in part through talk about classroom behavior management—which those with cultural knowledge recognize as a common topic for teachers and students. The second narrated event about fantasy objects is marked by talk about "Thor" and a "sword of darkness," which presuppose a realm of fantasy books, movies and games also familiar in the cultural context. The return to talk about curricular subject matter is marked by a change in aspect on the verb "we are recognizing" and by the reference to "page eleven" in their textbook. There exists no comprehensive list of cues or rules that a discourse analyst uses to identify the narrated contents of a discursive interaction—what Silverstein (1976) calls the "denotational text." The process of interpreting narrated events requires the same sort of context-dependent inference described in the last chapter, relying on what we know about grammar, lexicon and relevant background information to interpret indexes and symbols that communicate denoted content and build an account of what is being described.

Figure 2.1 represents the narrated and narrating events at this point in the interaction. The two central narrated events are represented in embedded boxes, showing relevant characters and objects. We leave out the third narrated event, the curricular topic introduced at lines 021–022, to save space. The teacher and students are represented in the narrating event, with Pete's puzzling accusation about "racist" off to one side because we do not yet know to whom or what this refers. It might refer to Mr. Bader, but that is not clear. As introduced in Chapter 1, such a diagram is a tool for spatially representing important information about narrated and narrating events, their elements and interrelations —not a precise representation of all possibly relevant elements. Wortham (2001) introduces such diagrams, with a few general conventions: the exterior rectangle represents the narrating event and the embedded rectangles represent narrated events; relevant characters and objects are represented as ovals in the appropriate space; relations among characters are either described in text or represented

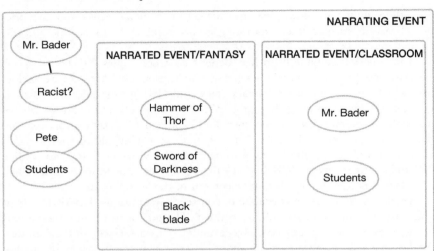

Figure 2.1 Narrated events in the central example

iconically—like the representation of hierarchical social relations represented with one character on top of another, or the representation of social relations or processes with a solid line connecting ovals; potential conceptual connections, like the possibility that Mr. Bader is racist, are also marked by solid lines; the mapping of parallel relations across narrated and narrating events is represented with dashed lines, as in Figures 1.2 and 1.6.

Phase 2/Component 1: Selecting indexicals

In the first component of the second phase, a discourse analyst looks for index-ical signs that often signal voicing, evaluation, positioning and social action. Although any sign can turn out to be pivotal in a given case, social action in most events will be signaled in part through a few recurring types of indexical signs. By focusing initially on these types of signs, discourse analysts are likely to uncover some of the indexicals that signal relevant context and support inferences about social action. Other relevant signs will often be linked to instances of the three types of signs we present here.

We recommend that discourse analysts initially look for three kinds of indexicals: **deictics**, **reported speech** and **evaluative indexicals**. These are not mutually exclusive categories, and a given sign or utterance can exemplify more than one type. For example, reported speech typically contains deictics, and reported speech can function as an evaluative indexical. It is nonetheless useful to separate the three types analytically, because it allows for systematic review of data and more efficient identification of potentially salient signs. In this section we define each type and the kinds of discursive work each often accomplishes.

Deictics

Deictics are denotational indexicals: they establish reference in the narrated event by indexically presupposing or creating an aspect of the narrating context itself. The grammatical structure of different deictics presupposes different aspects of the narrating event, ranging from participants (*I*, *you*) to spatiotemporal information (*here*, *now*) to discursive topics (*this*, *that*). We cannot know what deictics such as *here*, *now* and *I* refer to without information about where, when and by whom they are spoken. The referent of a deictic term thus "shifts" according to context (Jespersen, 1924; Silverstein, 1976). *I* refers to a different person when different people utter the word, *now* picks out a different time depending on the moment of utterance, and *they* refers to an indefinitely large group that does not include the speaker, a group that can only be identified if one knows information from prior conversation.

For example, when Mr. Bader says *you* in line 005—"take you to the office personally"—*you* likely refers to any one of the students who misbehaves. When Pete says *you* in lines 016–017—"you wish you were a little boy again"— *you* likely refers to Mr. Bader. English *you* can be used to refer both to plural addressees (i.e., "students") and to singular addresses (i.e., "Mr. Bader"). *You* can also be used as an indefinite pronoun to refer to people in general. Thus *you* can potentially refer to students, to Mr. Bader, or to any number of people or things, depending on context. Only by considering instances of *you* in an actual interaction can people begin to identify the referent of this deictic.

We will discuss four main types of deictics in this section: **spatial**, **temporal**, **person** and **discourse**. Spatial deictics presuppose information about place and location. They include words and phrases such as *here*, *around the corner* and *way over there*. When a speaker says "my family lives around here," we infer that family members live in some area centered around the speaker, wherever s/he is located at the moment of utterance. Like many deictics in English and other languages, *here* and *there* are radial—they presuppose an unspecified boundary around the speech event, with *here* describing things inside the boundary and *there* describing things outside. Exactly where that boundary is drawn varies from case to case and must be inferred from context-specific information.

Temporal deictics are concerned with past, present and future time. They include words and phrases such as *now*, *then*, *last month* and *a few years later*. Like spatial deictics, temporal deictics presuppose a radial geometry centered on the speech event, with some boundary determining where *now* ends and *then* begins. In lines 021–022, Mr. Bader uses *now* in a somewhat complex way, stating "(this is) carbon plated steel. now. excuse me skateboard people, we are recognizing the order of events or steps on page eleven." In this context *now* has the potential to establish the boundaries of the current event, marking the end of one phase of the activity and the beginning of another. This *now* may mark the start of a new event (one starting "right now," as it were), an event which will focus on "page eleven." In this context *now* marks the end of a previous narrated event in which Mr. Bader was describing "carbon plated steel."

Person deictics refer to speakers and those spoken to and about. They include words and phrases such as *I, you, she* and *them right here two weeks ago*, the last of which combines three types of deictics: *them* (person), *right here* (spatial) and *two weeks ago* (temporal). For example, in lines 021–022, Mr. Bader says *we* in "excuse me skateboard people, we are recognizing the order of events." It is not immediately clear whom *we* refers to in this case. There are at least four possibilities: an inclusive *we*, an exclusive *we*, a "royal *we*" and a "patronizing *we*." *We* might refer inclusively to Mr. Bader and all of the students in the room. *We* might refer exclusively to Mr. Bader and only some of the students in the room (for example, perhaps not the "skateboard people"). In its "royal" form, *we* might refer to Mr. Bader alone, speaking about himself in the plural because of his social status. In a "patronizing" form, *we* might function more like *you* and not include the speaker (as in an interaction where a doctor asks a patient "how are we feeling today?"), such that Mr. Bader would not be included with the students who are "recognizing the order of events."

Discourse deictics are words or expressions such as *this* or *that* which stand in for prior or future discourse, or refer exophorically to objects in the context. They are words used in place of other words or the topics referred to by other words. For example, when Joo-eun says *that* in line 015, "does that mean the sword is dark," *that* might refer back to the prior phrase, *the sword of darkness*, in lines 012 and 013. *That* may be a word standing in for *the sword of darkness*, thus making "does <u>that</u> mean the sword is dark" equivalent to saying "does <u>the sword of darkness</u> mean the sword is dark." Discourse deictics are flexible, able to refer to broad topics as well as specific utterances.

As discussed in Chapter 1, our approach to discourse analysis takes the distinction between narrated and narrating events as central. For discourse analysts to study the social actions accomplished through speech, a crucial task is to infer how participants' descriptions of narrated events have implications for their evaluations, positioning and social actions in the narrating event. Deictics are often important because they link narrated and narrating events, because their contributions to the narrated event (what they denote) depend on information they presuppose about the narrating event. Thus analysts can infer crucial information from deictics that may be relevant to understanding the positioning of interlocutors in the narrating event. For example, the distinction between *we* and *they* is often important to interpreting the relational functions of discourse. If a speaker systematically separates *us* from *them*, s/he may be giving participants and analysts crucial information about who is included in and who is excluded from some relevant group that includes the speaker.

When Mr. Bader says *I* in line 001—"I definitely want to send somebody to the office"—*I* surely refers to Mr. Bader. But when Hyo says *I* in line 006— "I will bring the hammer down" —does *I* refer to Hyo himself in the narrating event? It is more likely that Hyo is using reported speech and speaking as Mr. Bader. This introduces a more complex configuration of roles in both narrated and narrating events. We now have more than Mr. Bader the teacher interacting with a group of students. We also have at least one student (Hyo) speaking as a hypothetical Mr. Bader. This elaborates the narrated event that describes the classroom, the one represented on the right in Figure 2.1. We have Mr. Bader speaking as himself, saying what he would do to the students, and we have a student speaking as a hypothetical Mr. Bader and describing what Mr. Bader would do. By tracing the deictics, we can learn more about this narrated event and begin to identify its implications for the voicing, evaluation, positioning and social action occurring in the narrated and narrating events. The implications of Hyo's comment for the narrating event are not yet clear in the segment presented above. He might be teasing the teacher, implying that Mr. Bader is in fact a pushover and would never mete out such discipline. He might be criticizing the teacher for being a harsh disciplinarian. We can imagine other possibilities as well. The sections that follow elaborate the analysis to some extent, but our main purpose in this chapter is to use the example to illustrate the steps involved in our approach to discourse analysis. See Reyes (2011) for a fuller analysis of this discursive interaction.

Reported speech

Reported speech describes speech that is framed as occurring at some other time. Reported speech typically occurred in the past (e.g., "I told him, 'I'm busy'"), but it can also describe speech that will occur in the future (e.g., "I will tell him, 'I'm busy'"). By analogy, discourse analysts can also study reported thought, reported action or reports of any other performable display—"she said X," "she thought X," "she did X," where "X" can be any sign that is attributed to the actor referred to as "she." Reported speech marks a division between the narrating and narrated events in discursive interaction: the speaker who is reporting the speech is located in the narrating event, while the speaker whose speech is being reported is located in a narrated event, even if it is the same biographical person. Describing someone else's speech or action provides a powerful opportunity to voice or characterize them in the narrated event, and speakers often do this in ways that have implications for evaluation, positioning and social action in the narrating event. Reported speech is also a common means of linking speech events across pathways.

Reported speech is often divided into two main types: **direct** and **indirect**, although there are in fact intermediate forms like "indirect freestyle" (Fludernik, 1993). Consider the following ways that Mr. Bader could report to someone what Pete said:

"Pete said, 'you wish you were a little boy again'."
"Pete said that I want to be a little boy again."

In the first report Mr. Bader would be presenting reported speech directly, quoting the words that Pete uttered. In the second sentence, Mr. Bader would be presenting reported speech indirectly, summarizing Pete's utterance. The former claims to represent precisely what Pete said: "you wish you were a little boy again." The latter merely paraphrases what Pete said: "that I want to be a little boy again." Notice the shift in participant deictics used in the two cases. *You* refers to Mr. Bader when directly quoting Pete, and *I* refers to Mr. Bader when indirectly quoting Pete. In direct reported speech, deictics are used as if they were occurring in the narrated event (i.e., *you*/Mr. Bader who is narrated), whereas in indirect reported speech deictics are centered in the narrating event (i.e., *I*/Mr. Bader who is narrating).

In practice it is not always clear when speech is reported. For example, in line 004 Hyo says, "send you to the office," and in line 006, he says, "no I will bring the hammer down." Perhaps Hyo is reporting the (hypothetical or anticipated) speech of Mr. Bader, even though both utterances lack a clear framing (that is, Hyo does not explicitly say: "you should say, 'I will bring the hammer down'"). Hyo is apparently speaking as if he were Mr. Bader, such that *I* refers to Mr. Bader (not Hyo) and *you* in line 004 refers to students (perhaps including Hyo himself). Hyo is speaking as if he were Mr. Bader, appropriating his voice and elaborating his utterance as Hyo playfully imagines it should be.

Reported speech can be useful for discourse analysis in various ways. Reported speech creates or elaborates narrated events, and these events can be resources for performing social action. In Hyo's case, two events are in play: Mr. Bader describing what he might do to students and Hyo hypothetically describing what Mr. Bader might do to students. Depending on how it is formulated, Hyo's reported speech could have implications both for interpreting the first narrated event (perhaps implying that Mr. Bader would not actually do what he is describing, for example) and for the narrating event (perhaps characterizing Mr. Bader himself as harsh, or perhaps as lacking courage).

Reported speech also gives a speaker the opportunity to put words into the mouth of the quoted speaker, which allows the speaker to characterize that person. Reported speech often deploys **metapragmatic verbs**, "verbs of speaking," which are powerful ways of characterizing narrated speakers and positioning people in the narrating event (Silverstein, 1976). Compare the following ways that Mr. Bader could report what Pete said:

"Pete said, 'you wish you were a little boy again'."
"Pete insightfully remarked that I want to be a little boy again."
"Pete rudely interrupted me."

The metapragmatic verb that Mr. Bader chooses would position him with respect to the narrated event and with respect to Pete. *Said* is the most neutral of the three metapragmatic descriptions, while *insightfully remarked* and *rudely interrupted* make more presuppositions about the nature of the narrated event (e.g., it was rude) and about Pete's character. These characterizations also have implications for the narrating event. For example, Pete may be an undisciplined student who lacks academic promise. Metapragmatic verbs sometimes contrast with the content of reported speech, creating ironic and other effects. The second report above might have this form, if we presuppose that no reasonable person could claim that Mr. Bader wants to be a boy again.

Evaluative indexicals

By "evaluative indexical" we mean a very broad category of signs: indexes that point to relevant context in ways that potentially characterize and evaluate narrated characters and narrating participants. In the central example, what does it mean for Mr. Bader to say "quiet this <u>crowd</u> down" (lines 001–002), instead of "quiet this <u>class</u> down" or "quiet <u>you</u> down"? The different formulations presuppose different things about the group of students. Calling them a "crowd" might presuppose an evaluation of them, perhaps as disorganized or as vaguely threatening. As another example, consider the selection of "hammer" and "sword" from among all of the potential weapons that could have been referred to, and the depiction of those hammers and swords in terms of legends, colors and blades, as opposed to the various other ways hammers and swords could have been characterized. The following list sketches this progression of **reference** (underlined) and **predication** (bolded):

"<u>the hammer</u>" (line 006)
"<u>the hammer</u> **of Thor**" (line 009)
"<u>the sword</u> **of light**" (line 010)
"<u>the sword</u> **of darkness**" (line 012)
"<u>the sword</u> **is dark**" (line 015)
"<u>the blade</u> **is black**" (line 018)
"<u>this</u> **is black**" (line 019)

The types of people associated with these changing terms allow students to position Mr. Bader in a distinctive way. When we discuss the component "construing indexicals" below, we will see in more detail how attention to this progression of reference and predication can help us analyze the social action occurring in the speech event. For now, we emphasize simply that the different terms used to describe these objects are associated with different types of people and activities. Referring to a sword as a "blade," for example, is an expression that only certain kinds of people would unselfconsciously use—fans of movies and books from the fantasy genre, for instance.

When referring and predicating, speakers must select from among alternatives in paradigmatic sets. This applies to names, labels and descriptions. For example, what does it mean to refer to someone as an "attorney" as opposed to a "lawyer"? Both pick out the same group of professionals, but they presuppose different things about how much respect the speaker has for those people. "Ambulance chaser" is an alternative way of referring to the same group, one that has different presuppositions. Similarly, to describe someone as "assertive," as opposed to "aggressive" or "belligerent," presupposes different things about the character of the referent and the evaluation being made by the speaker. Evaluative indexicals are any signs that presuppose some evaluation of the people or objects being described, of the speaker, audience and others in the narrating event, or of relevant context—any signs that associate people or objects with some recognizable social type and evaluate that type.

An **emblem** is a particular kind of evaluative indexical, a sign or group of signs that presupposes and characterizes a recognizable social type (Agha, 2007). Take, for example, the term "little boy," which Pete uses in lines 016–017 when he says "you wish you were a little boy again." Various signs might be recognized as emblems of a "little boy" persona. If this is a social type that plays a significant role in the social action occurring in the classroom, we would expect other indexicals to presuppose it. It could be that Mr. Bader discussing hammers (lines 007, 009), Thor (line 009) and swords (line 013) also indicates "boyhood" to Pete—given widely circulating cultural associations between toy weapons, mythological superheroes and gendered childhood play. If this is in fact the case, we would have the three required elements of an emblem: (1) a sign or group of signs ("hammer," "Thor," "swords"); (2) a social type ("little boy"); and (3) a person for whom the sign is an emblem of the type (Pete and other participants who are familiar with this emblem).

Agha (2007) describes how emblems, and evaluative indexicals more broadly, fall on a continuum between **enregistered** and **emergent**. An enregistered emblem or indexical presupposes an established link between a sign and its social presuppositions. "Skateboard people" at line 021 presupposes a recognizable, largely male youth subculture that is associated with a constellation of features—people who ride skateboards like to hang out, are laid back, oppose themselves to mainstream culture in some ways, and so on. This set of associations, or the **voice** indexed by the term "skateboard people," has become enregistered for a large group of speakers in the U.S. Over several decades, more and more people have come to associate the riding of skateboards with this social type. An emergent emblem or indexical, on the other hand, has a more situation-specific meaning, with some important presuppositions having emerged recently in a given group or interaction. When Tyisha became a "beast," for example, teachers and students could subsequently presuppose that terms like "beast" and "animal" presupposed Tyisha herself. A comment like "some people behave like animals," in that classroom after the example described in Chapter 1, could be interpreted as a comment about Tyisha to people who participated in that classroom interaction—but it would not indicate that to someone familiar with more enregistered presuppositions but unfamiliar with that particular classroom conversation. Most discourse analyses rely more heavily on enregistered evaluative indexicals, but emergent meanings are often important as well.

Emblems and other evaluative indexicals can be linguistic or nonlinguistic signs. So far we have been concerned solely with linguistic signs. The words "hammer," "Thor" and "sword" might be emblems of the "little boy" persona. Evaluative indexicals can go beyond individual words as well. The use of a particular language, dialect or register can also be an emblem of a social type. For example, speaking a certain kind of French in a certain kind of place and time might be recognized as an emblem of a cosmopolitan persona. In addition, nonlinguistic signs, such as actions (e.g., gestures) or displays (e.g., clothing), can be read as indexes and sometimes evaluations of social types. Chapter 5 presents an analysis that focuses in significant part on nonlinguistic signs, when we discuss work by Rymes (2014) on pathways of events in new media.

Iteratively selecting indexicals

Deictics, reported speech and evaluative indexicals play important roles in discourse analysis that focuses on social action. We have sketched how each type of sign can communicate information about narrated and narrating events, about the types of social action occurring and about the social and interactional positions of participants. These three types of signs do not always play a crucial role in the social action accomplished through discourse, but we advise discourse analysts to start with these three types of indexicals because they often communicate important information about social action. We thus recommend that discourse analysts systematically identify the deictics, reported speech and evaluative indexicals in a text, picking them out before proceeding to further interpretation in components 2 and 3. Going systematically through a piece of discourse and identifying these three types of signs also establishes somewhat greater validity for the analysis, since systematic attention to all instances of these types makes an analyst less likely to seize on one interpretation and ignore other possibilities.

The three types of indexicals differ in one crucial respect. Deictics and reported speech are tokens of grammatical categories that can be identified relatively easily, without much dispute among analysts. Identifying evaluative indexicals requires more extensive knowledge of social context and cultural models, and different interpreters will sometimes disagree about what signs count as evaluative indexicals, what social type an evaluative indexical is indexing, and/or what evaluation is being made of that type. The class of evaluative indexicals is indefinitely large, because any sign could conceivably count as an index of a social type and an evaluation of that type, one that has implications for interpreting the social action in a discursive interaction. It requires substantial interpretation to identify an evaluative indexical, and multiple interpretations may be plausible in any given case. Thus the discourse analyst must have extensive experience with or ethnographic information about the relevant social group in order to identify and interpret evaluative indexicals.

This means that a first pass through a text in Phase 2/Component 1, identifying potentially relevant indexicals, will usually not capture all relevant evaluative indexicals. It is best to note as many as possible, but discourse analysts should not be overly concerned that some will be missed. As we have said, the process of discourse analysis is iterative. The analyst attends to salient indexicals and to the relevant context they index. By attending to deictics, reported speech and some evaluative indexicals, analysts can make inferences about contextualization, about aspects of the context that might be relevant to understanding the positioning and social action occurring. These inferences lead to provisional construals of the types of social action that salient indexicals and relevant contexts make plausible. Having construed social actions that might be occurring in the interaction, the analyst must then reconsider apparently salient indexicals, probably concluding that some are not so salient in this case and probably identifying others that had not been considered before. This latter group will most likely include indexes that did not appear to be important before a certain account of the narrating event became plausible. After reinterpreting salient indexicals, the analyst reconsiders whether these make certain types of social action more or less likely to be the ones occurring in the interaction.

This interpretive process often goes through several cycles, back and forth from part to whole, from particular salient indexicals to interpretations of the social action occurring across the whole discursive interaction. As analysis proceeds, there will be opportunities for analysts to notice relevant evaluative indexicals that might have been missed during the first pass. The first component in the second phase of our approach to discourse analysis, then, involves the systematic identification of potentially salient indexicals. The analyst should identify all deictics and reported speech, and as many evaluative indexicals as s/he can, expecting that other signs might become salient in future iterations of the analysis.

Phase 2/Component 2: Construing indexicals

In Phase 1 the discourse analyst describes the narrated events, identifying characters and models that might serve as resources for social action in the narrating event. In Phase 2/Component 1 the discourse analyst locates deictics, reported speech and evaluative indexicals that might signal the social action occurring. We focus on these three types of indexicals because of their potential to signal the social actions accomplished through discourse. But how do we know whether a given narrated pattern is in fact a resource for social action in the narrating event? How do we know whether an indexical sign is in fact important to signaling the social action occurring, and how do we know what it means? We can only answer these questions by, in Phase 2/Component 2, attending to **metapragmatic** processes (Silverstein, 1976, 1993). "Metapragmatics" refers to the signs and processes that describe how language performs action. "Metalanguage" is language referring to and characterizing language. "Metasemantics" is a more familiar subset of metalanguage, involving linguistic signs (e.g., explicit definitions) that describe the semantic meaning of linguistic forms. "Metapragmatics" is a less familiar type of metalanguage, describing linguistic signs that sometimes explicitly denote but more often implicitly organize the social action accomplished through discourse.

Metapragmatic models construe indexical signs. A given sign might have more than one potential implication for the social action occurring in the narrating event. In the example of Tyisha the beast in Chapter 1, her utterance "my goal is to win in Nintendo" could have had various implications. It could have pointed to potentially relevant contexts that supported more than one metapragmatic model of the interaction. Perhaps Tyisha just said that while trying to win an academic argument with the teacher, and it did not really matter whether or not she plays video games. Perhaps she was joking when she suggested that video games were one of her primary interests, and perhaps the teachers and students knew that she was in fact a diligent student. Or perhaps she is actually interested in video games to the exclusion of other activities like schoolwork. These are three possible models for construing that utterance and the indexical signs in it. As shown in Chapter 1, the evaluative indexical "Nintendo" in fact came to presuppose a model of intellectually deadening video game activities and students like Tyisha who allegedly favor such activities over intellectually productive activities.

In Phase 2/Component 2 the discourse analyst attends to salient indexicals and the context that they make salient, then infers which metapragmatic models might make sense of this context and describe the social action occurring in the discursive interaction. In other words, the analyst develops provisional accounts of the entextualization occurring in the discursive interaction. In this section we describe how metapragmatic discourse can be **explicit** or **implicit**. Then we describe two key processes for discourse analysts to focus on, as they identify the metapragmatic construals that participants make of salient indexicals. We introduced the first process in Chapter 1: through **voicing**, speakers identify narrated characters as having identifiable social roles. Through **evaluation**, speakers position themselves with respect to these voices, taking evaluative stances on the voiced characters, on other features of the social world and on other participants.

Explicit metapragmatic discourse

Metapragmatic discourse can be explicit. For example, if a speaker says "he speaks Korean too much," the speaker is explicitly characterizing someone's use of language. If a speaker says "you insulted me," the speaker is explicitly labeling prior discourse as an insult. Explicit metapragmatic discourse can be useful to a discourse analyst interpreting an interaction. At its most explicit, metapragmatic discourse can gloss the functions of specific talk—as in, "when I said 'my goal is to win in Nintendo,' I was just joking." If participants and analysts believe the speaker in such a case, they have a plausible account of what is occurring at that point in the discursive interaction, both the indexical signs that were salient and an account of the social action that occurred. Of course, speakers may be lying or they may be mistaken in their explicit metapragmatic accounts, so an analyst must continue to gather information about alternative interpretations despite the presence of such statements.

Explicitness is not a cleanly bounded category, and metapragmatic statements range from maximally explicit to less so. In the central example, Pete cries "racist" in line 020. Here the use of the word "racist" might overtly label prior language as "racist." But we do not yet know what language is being referred to or what precisely is racist about it. Pete does not give a full and explicit metapragmatic account of what the prior discourse was doing and what types of people other participants are, so full analysis of this example will also require examination of implicit metapragmatic processes. But through his use of that one explicit word, we do know that Pete is metapragmatically characterizing some segment of immediately preceding speech and evaluating it as "racist."

Implicit metapragmatic discourse

If a person says "he speaks Korean too much," after someone speaks in Korean, this explicitly characterizes the use of Korean negatively. But metapragmatic construal can also happen implicitly. Instead of saying "he speaks Korean too much," the subsequent speaker could have said "I'm getting dizzy" or could have rolled his or her eyes. These subsequent signs might tacitly construe the use of Korean negatively. Such tacit commentary often has implications for social action. For example, when Luke introduces "the sword of light" in line 010, we do not yet know what significance (if any) this phrase will have for the interaction. By looking for tacit metapragmatic commentary, we can begin to see how participants are construing this term. Rather than ignore Luke's contribution, Mr. Bader mentions the Roman figures of Diocletian and Damocles, central characters in stories that feature swords. Luke, although it is unclear whether he understands Mr. Bader's response, elaborates on his initial utterance by suggesting instead "the sword of darkness" in line 012. Mr. Bader then repeats "the sword of darkness" and continues by saying that it will be "coming to those who act in antisocial behavior." Joo-eun enters the discussion and asks if "the sword/blade is black" (lines 015, 018), after which Mr. Bader confirms: "this is black." Thus three participants take up the term "sword," making it increasingly central to the discussion, and together they make the sword seem increasingly dark and perhaps more menacing (going from "light" to "dark" to "black"). These are all instances of implicit metapragmatic commentary, which together make it more and more likely that the sword, its character and color will be relevant to some aspect of the discursive interaction. But its full implications are not yet clear.

Following the discussion about swords, Pete cries "racist" in line 020. Yet the term "racist" is not metapragmatically construed in any explicit way. There is no metapragmatic discourse after Pete's comment—such as "that's preposterous" or "stop calling Mr. Bader a racist"—no repetition or elaboration, such as "yes, that's obviously racist," and no implicit acts of acknowledgment, such as nervous giggles, head turns or audible inhalations of shock. Instead, Mr. Bader uses the deictic "now" to transition abruptly from the lengthy discussion about swords to the curricular task at hand: "we are recognizing the order of events or steps on page eleven." Is Mr. Bader's move in lines 021–022 implicit metapragmatic commentary on Pete's comment, or not? Was Mr. Bader's abrupt transition a response to Pete's racist accusation—perhaps trying to close off the possibility that something racist was said in their discussion—or was it a coincidence that Mr. Bader transitioned to another topic at that moment? Looking only at the segment provided above, we cannot answer with certainty.

Discourse analysis is an interpretive activity, not an algorithmic one in which correct answers can be derived. As described in the last chapter, there is no one-to-one correspondence between form and function, between a sign and the social actions that it signals. In some discursive interactions relatively univocal signs unproblematically signal the action occurring, but in general the signs that signal social action could support more than one interpretation. In order to figure out which indexicals are salient and what these indexicals signal, discourse analysts must select relevant context and infer appropriate metapragmatic models of the social action occurring. They do this in part by attending to voicing and evaluation.

Voicing

For discourse analysts interested in the social actions accomplished through language use, metapragmatic construal centrally involves the social identification of narrated characters and narrating participants. Participants and analysts identify the social action occurring, adopting a metapragmatic model of the discursive interaction, in significant part as they identify narrated characters and narrating participants as socially recognizable types of people who typically participate in some type of action. Mikhail Bakhtin (1935/1981) calls the establishment of such recognizable types "voicing." A "voice" (Wortham, 2001) or "figure of personhood" (Agha, 2005) is a recognizable social position. Take, for example, the "racist" voice (Hill, 2008). Many Americans today might associate this voice with certain kinds of racial identities (e.g., white), spatial locations (e.g., the American South), historical periods (e.g., before the Civil Rights Movement), musical tastes (e.g., country music), and so on. We can voice narrated characters or narrating participants as racists by drawing on the types of indexicals discussed in Phase 2/Component 2: spatial and temporal deictics (e.g., "racism was a big problem down South a while back"), reported speech (e.g., "racists say, 'I'm not a racist but...'" [Bonilla-Silva & Forman, 2000]), reference and predication (e.g., "those racists are uneducated") and other emblems of the racist voice (e.g., "they drive pick-up trucks").

For the racist voice to be recognizable to others, it must circulate across different temporal and spatial scales. The link between indexical signs and a social type or voice has what Agha (2007) calls a **social domain**, a social group within which this association circulates and is recognizable. Social domains can range from large to small, and they can expand and contract. For example, "jocks" and "burnouts" (Eckert, 1989) are social categories that circulate widely in American high schools, perhaps reaching their broadest social domain in the late twentieth century. Contemporary figures that circulate in more restricted domains might include "wiggers" (Bucholtz and Lopez, 2011), "fobs" (Reyes, 2007), and "model minorities," whether Asian American (Lee, 1996) or Latino (Wortham, Mortimer and Allard, 2009). Voicing also depends on **voicing contrasts** (Agha, 2005). For example, the racist figure is often positioned against the "liberal" figure and the jock against the burnout, with each voice emerging only as it is positioned relative to other voices.

As described in detail by Wortham (2001), after identifying central characters in the narrated events discourse analysts should look for salient indexicals that voice those characters. Tyisha had "the same goal my cat had, to go to sleep, and get up and eat" and "to win in Nintendo." These evaluative indexicals presuppose a voice—the lazy, intellectually unengaged teenager—that in fact ends up being assigned to Tyisha in the narrated event. The discourse analysis sketched in the last chapter (and described in detail in Wortham, 2006) presents many more indexical cues that together established this voice for Tyisha the narrated character. In the central example in this chapter, the teacher and students explicitly describe and implicitly presuppose the voices of "little boy" (lines 016–017), "racist" (line 020) and "skateboard people" (line 021). Pete accuses Mr. Bader of wanting to be a "little boy," for example, but in the short segment we have analyzed so far it is not yet clear whether this voice will become firmly established.

Once voices are established in the narrated event, they can have implications for the narrating event. Tyisha the narrated character is voiced as a "beast," and then she herself is positioned as an outcast in the narrating event, as less promising than the other students. In the example from this chapter, consider how Pete accuses Mr. Bader of wanting to be a "little boy" then quickly cries "racist." The juxtaposition of these two voices—the former potentially light-hearted, the latter potentially dangerous—might have implications for social action in the narrating event. The playful teasing through which the "little boy" accusation emerges might suggest that the "racist" accusation is playful as well. If the accusation of racism was made impishly, then it may not have serious implications for Mr. Bader himself.

Voices are central to discourse analysis that focuses on the social actions accomplished in discursive interaction. Characters that appear in narrated events are inevitably voiced, identified (clearly or ambiguously) as belonging to recognizable social types. Voicing is accomplished through signs like deictics, reported speech and evaluative indexicals. Analysts must attend to these signs and the context they make relevant, then infer the voices being assigned to narrated characters. Wortham (2001) describes a step-by-step procedure for analyzing voicing, and the examples in Chapters 3–5 illustrate our approach to uncovering voices. The process of voicing is important for two reasons: it gives the analyst a fuller picture of the narrated events, and it provides resources that speakers use to perform social action in the narrating events. In order to understand more fully how voicing contributes to social action, we need to explore how it inevitably involves evaluation.

Evaluation and positioning

Voicing always produces **speaker alignments** (Agha, 2005; Bakhtin, 1935/1981). When speakers presuppose a voice for a narrated character or narrating participant, they also position themselves with respect to that voice and evaluate it. When choosing between the terms "attorney," "lawyer" and "ambulance chaser," for example, a speaker communicates something about the character-istics of this group—perhaps that it is composed of high-status, respectable people or lower-status people who do not deserve respect—and simultaneously communicates something about his or her evaluation of the group. Discourse analysts study the complex ways in which participants position themselves with respect to the messages they deliver, the people they interact with and the larger social world.

Evaluation happens when participants position themselves with respect to voices deployed in narrated events. When Tyisha says "my goal is to win in Nintendo" and another student replies "that's your goal?" in an incredulous tone of voice, this other student negatively evaluates the voice of an intellectually unengaged video gamer. **Interactional positioning** happens when participants position themselves with respect to one another in the narrating event. When a student and then one of the teachers say to Tyisha "so you are like an animal," they are positioning themselves as fundamentally different from Tyisha, as more rational and civilized than she is. Evaluation and positioning happen simultane-ously, but it is useful to distinguish them for analytic purposes.

The central example from Mr. Bader's class involves both evaluation and interactional positioning. Evidence is relatively limited from the short segment given above, but Pete probably evaluated the racist voice negatively. In most mainstream institutions like schools, calling something racist also means evalu-ating it as immoral. We would normally presuppose that Pete is positioning himself against racism, and against whatever person or thing he is character-izing as racist in the classroom. Pete may be positioning Mr. Bader and his classmates (or at least their discourse) as racist, and positioning himself as morally superior to them because he is not racist and because he is able to detect covert racism.

There is another possibility, however. It may be less that Pete is evaluating the racist voice negatively in order to position himself as nonracist, and more that he is constructing a clever persona by presupposing a humorous meta-pragmatic model that has become prevalent in recent years. A decade or two ago calling someone a racist was normally a serious accusation, in most main-stream settings, and it is of course still serious in many contexts. But crying "racist" has become a joke as well. In other words, a robust branching pathway of speech events has developed, in which accusations of "racist" have become more and more likely to be a joke than a serious description of morally offensive behavior. There are other pathways of speech events in which accusations of racism remain serious and should be considered as such. But popular discourse also contains this new way of using and construing the accusation, and the metapragmatic model of crying "racist" circulates densely in certain kinds of popular culture that is avidly consumed by people like Pete and his friends. In order to explore how this dense pathway of crying "racist" events might help us construe Pete's utterance, we need to go beyond this one speech event. We do this in the next major section below, after we discuss the third component of configuring indexicals.

In Phase 2/Component 1, the discourse analyst identifies potentially salient signs—like deictics, reported speech and evaluative indexicals—that might signal the social action occurring. These signs point to potentially relevant context. In Phase 2/Component 2, the discourse analyst makes inferences from this potentially relevant context. Some of these inferences involve voicing, identifying the types of people and events being described in the narrated events. Some inferences are about the narrating event, inferring how speakers evaluate those voices and position themselves with respect to each other. These inferences are provisional, however, because newly salient indexicals and relevant context can emerge, as the iterative process of selecting and construing indexicals takes place. In the next section we discuss the discursive mechanisms through which this dialectic of contextualization and entextualization eventually ends, such that participants and analysts know what type of action is occurring, as a configuration of indexical signs solidifies.

Phase 2/Component 3: Configuring indexicals

Explicit or implicit metapragmatic discourse indicates how participants and analysts should interpret key indexicals, making certain metapragmatic models the most plausible ones for construing the social action occurring in a discursive interaction. As we have described, however, the process of interpreting a discursive interaction is not unidirectional. There are no unequivocal indexical signs that indicate how participants and analysts must understand the social action occurring. Neither do metapragmatic models have priority over indexicals, determining the meaning of an event regardless of the indexicals present. Instead, there is a back-and-forth, part–whole interpretive process, what (following Silverstein, 1992, 1993) we called in Chapter 1 the dialectic between contextualization and entextualization. Indexicals indicate which metapragmatic models are most likely in play, then those models organize the indexicals—making some of them appear more salient and making clear what context they index. But then these indexicals and newly relevant context lead participants and analysts to reconsider appropriate metapragmatic models, and so on.

This is a familiar interpretive process, the "hermeneutic circle" (Heidegger, 1927/1962). Construal of a whole text depends on interpretations of individual parts, but those parts are selected and construed based on a presupposed account of the whole. In theory, there is no end to this circle. In practice, people interpret their discursive interactions, most often unproblematically, all the time. How do they do it? Stated in abstract terms, unproblematic interpretation of a discursive interaction happens as a configuration of mutually presupposing indexical signs emerges and solidifies, locking into place a mutually reinforcing construal of key indexicals and a metapragmatic model of the overall social action—a process described by Silverstein (1992, 1993). In Phase 2/Component 3, discourse analysts trace these emerging and solidifying configurations.

This section describes how discourse analysts do it. In Phase 2/Component 3 we examine how indexicals are configured in ways that make entextualization possible. The process of entextualization describes how an account of social action emerges over the course of an interaction, as indexical signs and metapragmatic models come to buttress each other. Entextualization involves solidification, as the meaning of an event—the voices in the narrated events, the evaluation, positioning and social action in the narrating event—becomes more robust and more highly presupposable over time. We will illustrate this process by describing the textual parallelisms created in Mr. Bader's class above, in which, as weapons become increasingly dangerous, they become increasingly dark.

Entextualization

As described in Chapter 1, we adopt a "consequentialist" view of meaning in discourse. Some elements of meaning are decontextualizable, with a linguistic form having in some respects the same meaning in whatever setting (Putnam, 1975). Grammatical categories capture some such elements—"boy," for example, is a count noun, and it can be the subject of mental state verbs, among other enduring properties. Thus we know that, whatever context we utter the word "boy" in, the entity thus denoted is expected to be physically discrete and capable of human mental activities. But in most respects meaning is context dependent or indexical. The meaning of an utterance depends in significant part on how it is taken up by subsequent utterances. The concept of **uptake** is central to a consequentialist view of meaning (Garfinkel, 1967). Rather than understand meaning as fully locatable in preexisting definitions or speaker intentions, the meaning of a sign depends in substantial part on how it is taken up by subsequent speakers and utterances, on how it is metapragmatically construed, explicitly or implicitly, in subsequent discourse. This brings us to "entextualization," as described in the last chapter, the process through which signs are recontextualized such that an account of social action emerges to organize the discursive interaction.

Most discursive interactions could be interpreted in more than one way. What sounds like a compliment can turn out to be an insult ("Wow, you're on time today!"). What seems to be lunch with a friend can become a therapy session. What starts as routine classroom management can end as racist discourse. Entextualization is the process through which an interaction with indeterminate meaning comes to be recognizable as one type of event or another, as having been a recognizable type of social action (Bauman and Briggs, 1990; Silverstein, 1976; Silverstein and Urban, 1996). Without entextualization there could not be a recognizable event apart from the stream of discursive activity. Entextualization establishes an event, its boundaries and its meaning. Entextualization is somewhat like the gelling of Jell-O, as it transitions from a liquid to a solid state. When Tyisha was talking about playing Nintendo, sleeping and eating, it was still not clear what implications this might have for her position in the narrating classroom interaction. But around the moment when the teacher said "you are like an animal," her position as a disruptive outcast, as someone less worthy than the other students and teachers, became more solid and presupposable.

We can recast our question about Mr. Bader's class in these terms. The utterance "racist" at line 020 is a sign that needs interpretation. It is not explicitly metapragmatically framed, so we need to identify the implicit metapragmatic construal that indicates what sort of social action it helps to signal. This construal would normally occur over time, as other signs come to presuppose a convergent interpretation. The back-and-forth, part-and-whole circle of interpretation, from indexical signs to metapragmatic construals and back, comes to a provisional end when a set of indexical signs locks together in what Silverstein (1993) calls a **poetic structure**. Poetics in this sense involves the recurrent patterning of indexicals. This "text-metricality," as Jakobson (1960) calls it, emerges from textual parallelisms in which similar linguistic forms recur. In our terms, speakers create **configurations** of mutually presupposing indexicals.

When analyzing the discourse immediately preceding Pete's utterance, we asked whether Hyo was reporting the speech of Mr. Bader in line 004 when he says "send you to the office" and in line 006 when he says "I will bring the hammer down." By looking at an emerging configuration of indexical signs, we can begin to answer this question:

"I definitely want to **send somebody to the office**" (Mr. Bader in line 001)
"I will . . . **send you to the office**" (Mr. Bader and Hyo in lines 003–004)
"I will . . . take you to the office personally" (Mr. Bader in lines 003, 005)
"I will bring the hammer down" (Hyo in line 006)

There are two overlapping poetic patternings across these text segments. One is "send [pronoun] to the office," and the other is "I will [verb phrase]." After Mr. Bader says "send somebody to the office," Hyo repeats this phrase—changing only one word, "somebody" to "you." Mr. Bader also uses an "I will" sentence structure, and Hyo echoes with threats that adopt this structure. These two parallelisms, in which Mr. Bader leads and Hyo follows, provide more evidence that Hyo is, in fact, speaking as if he were Mr. Bader in lines 004 and 006. Hyo may be reporting anticipated speech of Mr. Bader or reformulating and suggesting new threats for Mr. Bader to use.

The progression of reference and predication about hammers and swords, described above, also involves poetic parallelism, a configuration of mutually presupposing indexical signs:

"the hammer" (line 006)
"the hammer **of Thor**" (line 009)
"the sword **of light**" (line 010)
"the sword **of darkness**" (line 012)
"the sword **is dark**" (line 015)
"the blade **is black**" (line 018)
"this **is black**" (line 019)

Several parallelisms occur in these segments. There are repetitions of the head of the noun phrase, "the [hammer/sword/blade]," and the two characterizations of this noun, "of [Thor/light/darkness]" and "is [dark/black]." The poetic progression involves shifts in both slots. In the head of the noun phrase, the weapon becomes increasingly dangerous, changing from "hammer" to "sword" to "blade." In the characterizations of this object, the weapon becomes increasingly dark: from "light" to "dark" to "black." These configurations will help us interpret the social action occurring in Mr. Bader's classroom.

Let us return to Pete's puzzling utterance about racism. This utterance takes up the emergent configurations just described. That is, as the unfolding discourse links increasing forms of violence (from "hammer" to "sword" to "blade") to the darkening of those forms (from "light" to "dark" to "black"), Pete seems to presuppose wider U.S. racial ideologies that link blackness—as an emblem of a racialized identity—to negative qualities like danger and brutality. Pete construes the configuration of implicit indexical links between "black" and violence and characterizes the preceding discussion as racist. His crying "racist" entextualizes the preceding discourse as racist, presupposing an ideology that associates violence with blackness.

Our analysis so far has focused on the discourse in Mr. Bader's classroom, using it as an example to illustrate the various components of our approach to discourse analysis within the speech event. Table 2.2 summarizes the steps in our approach.

The final step is to identify the positioning and social action occurring in the narrating event. We have argued that Pete is probably crying "racist," making a joke by accusing Mr. Bader of using the word "black" inappropriately. In order to understand this construal of the narrating event more fully, however, we need to examine other speech events in the branching pathway across which people cry "racist."

Table 2.2 The components of our approach to within-event discourse analysis

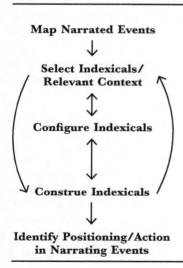

Map Narrated Events ↓	Describe the characters, actions and events in the various narrated events, perhaps representing them visually
Select Indexicals/ Relevant Context ↕	Attend initially to deictics, reported speech and evaluative indexicals
Configure Indexicals ↕	Identify configurations of indexicals that emerge and collectively presuppose relevant context and support some model of the social action occurring
Construe Indexicals ↓	Through an iterative process, infer construals of social action that could explain the salient indexicals, then reconsider which indexicals might be salient, then infer a revised account
Identify Positioning/Action in Narrating Events	Draw conclusions about the social action occurring in the narrating event

Across events

Our model for discourse analysis of discrete speech events—which involves the mapping of narrated events and then the selection, construal and configuration of indexicals—shows that individual events can never be understood in isolation. Reported speech, to take one of our central types of indexicals, depends on links across quoted and quoting events, and so it cannot be understood without reference to at least two linked events. Emblems presuppose associations between indexical forms and social types, associations that are established through branching chains of events that extend far beyond any individual speech event. So even discourse analysis of discrete events must extend beyond a focal event, relying on knowledge of specific other events (like those quoted or presupposed in other ways) and background knowledge about signs and social types from the larger social world which have been established across many events.

When we say "discourse analysis beyond the speech event" we mean more than this type of cross-event dependence, however. As described in Chapter 1, this book applies discourse analysis to an object more extensive than a discrete discursive interaction or a repeated type of interaction. We focus on **pathways** of linked speech events, a series of events that presuppose each other and have some temporal direction. Many important social processes involve such pathways. Socialization and ontogenetic development necessarily involve individual change across a series of events (Wortham, 2005). The historical emergence of social types, together with habitual evaluations of those types, necessarily involves linked series of events (Agha, 2007). In this section we further develop our approach to discourse analysis, sketching how the tools we have described can be used to study trajectories of events.

In the second section below we illustrate discourse analysis beyond the speech event by introducing more interactions, from the fifth grade classroom at the Asian American supplementary school and from television comedies, in which people cry "racist" and by considering mass media discourses about what crying "racist" means. We show how a discourse analyst can trace cross-event linkages that are established across such events. Thus we explore how racist discourse becomes **enregistered** and widely recognized in contemporary U.S. society. Before moving to this illustration, we review the concept of enregisterment and the three additional components required for discourse analysis across speech events.

Enregisterment

As described in Chapter 1, Agha (2007) defines "enregisterment" as the process through which signs come reliably to signal certain social types, for some group of speakers, over time. Enregisterment is analogous to the process of entextualization in many ways, except that it occurs across events. As an example of enregisterment Agha (2007) describes how the association between the phonological regularities described as British "Received Pronunciation" and a speaker of Standard English did not exist at the beginning of the nineteenth century, but was well established a century later. He shows how the change occurred through a linked series of speech events in which the hearer in one event circulated a sign or model when speaking in a subsequent event. Hearing someone associate a phonological regularity from Received Pronunciation with educated, refined character, a hearer might presuppose the same association in subsequent speech. As more hearers and speakers did this, the sign–identity linkage circulated more widely. Agha describes how readers of prescriptivist works that specified "correct" pronunciation in nineteenth-century Britain sometimes wrote novels that circulated Received Pronunciation more widely as an index of refined social identity. Over time, as links between pronunciation and models of personhood traveled across branching pathways, more people recognized and accepted the association between these phonological forms and personal characteristics like "educated" and "refined."

Enregisterment involves the creation of links across pathways of events, through which a larger social process occurs—like the establishment of a social type (refined, educated Britons) and the linguistic signs that index it (the phonological regularities of Received Pronunciation). For smaller scale cross-event processes, too—like the emergence of a social identity for someone like Tyisha across weeks or months in classroom discourse—the appropriate metapragmatic model for understanding the student's identity may not solidify in one speech event or one class session. Instead, as illustrated in Chapter 1, it may take several linked events for an identity to emerge, and that identity might subsequently shift across a pathway of subsequent events. Discourse analysis across speech events traces the linked events across which enregisterment occurs.

As described in Chapter 1, the solidification of cross-event pathways is similar in many respects to within-event entextualization, the gelling of indexes and metapragmatic models that buttress each other within an event. Early in a pathway, like Tyisha's pathway through the classroom discussions across that academic year, the nature of an emerging identity might be ambiguous. More than one model might conceivably describe the focal person's identity or the ongoing type of social action occurring. Just the discussion of Tyisha the courageous liar, taken by itself, could have merely involved teachers and students teasing Tyisha, or it could have been an aberration. Across events, however, as teachers and students continued to talk with and about Tyisha, a clearer identity emerged for her. The discussion of Tyisha the beast reinforced Tyisha's status as an outcast, as someone different from the other students who was likely to disrupt classroom activities and did not follow mainstream social norms. The pathway became more rigid, as it were, and subsequent events were increasingly constrained by the mutually reinforcing models of identity that had been applied to her in earlier events.

Pathways become more rigid in this way as a set of mutually presupposing indexicals emerges across events. Within an event, the cycle of iterative part–whole interpretation comes to an end when a set of indexicals and the metapragmatic models they make salient come to buttress each other, as a configuration of indexical signs gels and presupposes relevant context that supports consistent inferences about the types of social action occurring. Across events, something similar happens. Indexicals across several events come to presuppose each other and to presuppose certain models of social identity and social action, thus making the pathway more rigid and the metapragmatic model more easily presupposable across events.

Discourse analysts must do three things to trace cross-event pathways, in addition to analyzing contextualization and entextualization within discrete events. First, we must **identify linked events** that make up a pathway. We do this by describing how quotation, parallelism across events and other devices establish linkages and thus create **cross-event context**—linked events across a pathway that become a special kind of context crucial to enregisterment. In the case of Tyisha from Chapter 1, for example, Figures 1.5 and 1.6 represent the parallel narrated voices, narrating positions and narrating evaluations across the events of Tyisha the courageous liar and Tyisha the beast. The robust parallels across both narrated and narrating events on these two days indicate that the events are linked as part of a pathway. They form cross-event context for each other, context crucial to interpreting the emergence of Tyisha's social identity across these and other events in the pathway.

Second, we must **delineate cross-event configurations** of signs, describing how indexical signs from more than one event come to presuppose each other and create relevant context for interpreting both individual events and pathways across them. In Chapter 1, for example, we described various signs that helped characterize Tyisha as an immoral, disruptive outcast. In the discussion of Tyisha the courageous liar, the expressions "lie to her face," "lying in another person mother face" and "tell her this big bold-faced lie" accumulate to voice Tyisha as unethical. In the discussion of Tyisha the beast that occurred a week later, "play Nintendo" and "go to sleep, get up and eat" presuppose a related voice of someone wasting her life and refusing to participate in socially valued pursuits. In the courageous liar discussion, the teacher implies that Tyisha is not cooperating with others to move the conversation forward, saying "I know you never bought into it, but the rest of us seem to be using this as a definition." In the beast discussion, the teacher says "you throw out seventeen things and then nobody can even begin to address any of these things." These claims presuppose similar models of Tyisha's disruptive behavior in the narrating events, and they thus form cross-event configurations that hold these events together and collectively presuppose a narrated voice (immoral and beast-like), a narrating position (outcast from the core group of teachers and students) and a consistent type of social action (exclusion) across the pathway.

Third, we must **trace the shape of pathways**, showing how they become rigid and thereby accomplish processes like socialization and learning. This requires inference from cross-event configurations, in which participants and analysts construe a cross-event process like the social identification of Tyisha. As sketched in Chapter 1 and described in detail by Wortham (2006), Tyisha becomes a disruptive outcast across several classroom conversations from December through February. Her pathway shifts from the direction it was going early in the academic

Table 2.3 The phases and components of discourse analysis beyond the speech event

Phase 1: **IDENTIFYING LINKED EVENTS AND MAPPING NARRATED EVENTS**	What events are linked in a pathway, through reported speech, parallelism, shared referents or other devices, such that the events might together accomplish some social process? What characters, objects and events are referred to and characterized in the narrated events of these linked discursive interactions?
Phase 2/Component 1: **SELECTING INDEXICALS AND IDENTIFYING RELEVANT CROSS-EVENT CONTEXT**	Attending particularly to types of signs that often signal the social action accomplished through discourse, which indexical signs become salient both within and across events? What context do these signs make relevant—attending both to larger social context and to cross-event context, to how signs index other events in the trajectory?
Phase 2/Component 2: **CONSTRUING INDEXICALS AND TRACING SHAPE OF PATHWAYS**	Which accounts of voicing, evaluation, positioning and social action make sense of salient indexical signs and allow participants and analysts to interpret narrated and narrating events? How do these accounts organize both individual events and the pathway across events?
Phase 2/Component 3: **CONFIGURING INDEXICALS AND DELINEATING CROSS-EVENT CONFIGURATIONS**	How do salient indexical signs coalesce into stable configurations within and across events, such that relevant context, recognizable types of social action and more rigid pathways are established?
Phase 3: **INTERPRETING SOCIAL ACTION AND IDENTIFYING CROSS-EVENT PROCESSES**	What account best explains the positioning and social action occurring in the narrating event (or across the pathway of narrating events)?

year. She stops being another good student and becomes identified as disruptive. Later in the spring her identity changes again, and she becomes a reasoned dissenter instead of a disruptive outcast.

We illustrate these three components of discourse analysis across speech events briefly here, with more data from the Asian American supplementary school classroom and short examples from more widely circulating media discourse. Table 2.3 describes the steps in discourse analysis beyond the speech event. The next three chapters illustrate our approach in more detail.

A second example: Crying "racist" in classroom interaction again

The following excerpt comes from a conversation that occurred two months after the central example from Mr. Bader's classroom. It was recorded at the same school, and contained most of the same students, but took place in a different classroom with a different teacher. Here again a student cries "racist" during a classroom conversation. In this interaction the teacher, Mrs. Turner, is explaining a homework assignment on gun control. Mrs. Turner and the students are discussing the Columbine shooting—an event in which two students shot many people at their school in 1999—as a sample topic for their essay.

Segment 2: Goths with guns

030	*Mrs. Turner:*	these were not your (2.0) typical high school students, s- th- the
031		rest of the students at school were not like that. it was this
032		isolated group that unfortunately turned on their own, yes.
033		((calling on Dan whose hand is raised))
034	*Dan:*	maybe it was like- like jealousy
035	*Mrs. Turner:*	well whatever the case they were fr- members of a group, i- it
036		was very much like the gothic- groups, that wear the black
037		clothes and the- y'know- the- the black makeup and-
038	*Ike:*	Men in Black ((several students laugh))
039	*Chul:*	racism
040	*Mrs. Turner:*	th- the point is these kids got a hold of their parents' guns, now
041		out west, where you can easily get a gun like this, and shop at a
042		local Walmart

We will begin by sketching how we might analyze this as a discrete discursive interaction, using the approach we have outlined. The main narrated event involves the students who shot people at Columbine High School in 1999, but there is another narrated event that describes "Goth" people more generally. Figure 2.2 represents these narrated events.

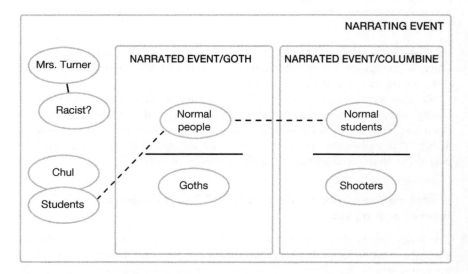

Figure 2.2 Narrated events in the Columbine example

In Phase 2/Component 1, we would select indexicals that might be salient, point to relevant context and support some account of the social action occurring. Exploring the voicing, we would note that the shooters are characterized, using evaluative indexicals, as "not . . . typical" (line 030), "isolated" (line 032), "turn[ing] on their own" (line 032) and "jealous" (line 034). The teacher also compares the shooters to "gothic groups" (line 036). "Goth" is a widely recognized subcultural movement, identifiable through various emblems of the Goth persona—which often include black hair, dark eyeliner, black nail polish, black period clothing and use of pagan or occult symbolism. The color black is central, and the teacher mentions it twice in her description of Goth clothes and makeup (at lines 036–037). After Ike shouts out the title of a Hollywood movie, "Men in Black" (line 038), Chul cries "racism" (line 039). This accusation is not picked up in subsequent discourse, and Mrs. Turner immediately uses the deictic "now" (line 040) and changes the topic back to gun control and the academic task.

In Phase 2/Component 2 of a more extensive analysis of this discursive inter-action, we would explore the metapragmatic construals participants make of salient indexicals. In this case speakers presuppose a recognizable voice for the Columbine shooters, characterizing them as deviant. The teacher establishes a voicing contrast between two types of students: the deviant shooters, who are "not your typical high school students" (line 030) and "the rest of the students" (line 031). She evaluates the Goth voice negatively and positions herself and the students as normal people who differ from this deviant group. But then Chul goes in a different direction. Like Pete in the discursive interaction described earlier, Chul apparently positions himself as a morally superior decoder of covert racism. But from this brief excerpt it is not yet clear how this voice relates to the teacher and students themselves and to the social action occurring in the narrating event.

Chul's and Pete's comments share at least three features. First, the cries of "racist" in both interactions immediately follow descriptions of violence that are linked to the term "black." Crying "racist" in these cases is triggered by associations between blackness and deviance or violence. Second, in both cases the teachers react quickly and abruptly, transitioning back to academic topics immediately after the comment. They both use the deictic "now" to recenter the interaction on official classroom business. Third, we argue that both are best read as jokes. The teachers apparently sense some danger in these comments about racism, which explains their abrupt transitions. But both instances belong to a dense, branching pathway of events in contemporary American society in which people cry "racist." In order to understand this event, and the earlier one in Mr. Bader's classroom, we need to examine this pathway. Reyes (2011) provides a detailed analysis of how these students draw on other events in this broad pathway in order to make jokes and unsettle white teachers. Here we will briefly sketch some other events in the pathway.

Other examples: Crying "racist" in mass media

Reyes (2011) describes examples of crying "racist" from the mass media. Consider examples from two situation comedies on network television: *30 Rock* and *Parks and Recreation*. In a 2006 episode of *30 Rock*, a white character (Liz) believed her black co-worker (Tracy) when he told her that he could not read in order to get out of work. When the truth comes out, they have the following confrontation:

Segment 3: 30 Rock

050	*Liz:*	you are unbelievable
051	*Tracy:*	I'm unbelievable? what about your racist mess. thinking a grown
052		man is illiterate. that's the subtle racism of lowered expectations.
053		Bing Crosby said that.
054	*Liz:*	no, Bill Cosby said that
055	*Tracy:*	that's racist
056	*Pete:*	look, we can all agree Liz is generally pretty racist, the point is
057		you have people counting on you, you can't be finding excuses
058		not to be here
059	*Tracy:*	but this job is hard

The first accusation of racism here, at lines 051–052, is more substantial. But "that's racist" at 055 is less clear. In line 052, Tracy loosely cites a quote, whose popularity is often attributed to George W. Bush: "the soft bigotry of low expectations." But Tracy attributes the quote to Bing Crosby. Even though Tracy delivers the line with a straight face, this is surely a joke to the show's producers and audience, because Bing Crosby was not known for his anti-racist consciousness. Liz then attributes the quote to Bill Cosby. Bill Cosby has in fact said things like this, and so her correction is at least reasonable. But Tracy accuses her of racism, perhaps because she corrected him for confusing similar sounding names: Bing Crosby and Bill Cosby.

In another example, from *Parks and Recreation* in 2011, a character (Ben) moves in with his married co-workers (April and Andy) and tries to teach them how to do laundry:

Segment 4: Parks and Recreation

060	*Ben:*	okay, so you always separate your lights from your darks
061	*April:*	that's racist
062	*Ben:*	and then you get your laundry- where's your laundry detergent

This is also clearly a joke, because distinguishing between "light" and "dark" clothing does not in this case seem to have anything to do with racism. The two examples of crying "racist" in classroom interactions participate in a broad, branching pathway that includes clearly humorous instances like these.

Instances of crying "racist" have become so established that mass media discourse now contains many explicit metapragmatic commentaries on the phenomenon, as described in Reyes (2011). For example, the website *Know Your Meme* created a webpage in 2010 that defines the phrase, "that's racist," as "an expression often used in jest to point out the politically incorrect or racially insensitive nature of a post or comment online." *All Things Considered*, a news program on National Public Radio, did a story in 2011 on how the phrase "that's racist" has shifted from a "serious accusation" to a "commonplace quip." Moreover, animated memes have been widely distributed in online communication that present crying "racist" as a joke.

So the classroom instances of crying "racist" discussed above can be linked to these and other instances of the phenomenon that appear in the mass media. Pete and Chul are most likely trying to link their comments in a pathway with other instances of crying "racist," ones that they and their peers—but perhaps not their teachers—are familiar with from mass media. Reyes (2011) argues that these instances form a pathway because they share the three features described above: they respond to some comment about blackness, they are short and dropped quickly from subsequent conversation, and they are probably best construed as jokes. This constitutes a cross-event configuration, a set of indexical signs that establish these three features in each event, in parallel fashion. These and many other events constitute a broad, branching pathway of discursive interactions in which some accusations of racism have shifted over the past decade or two from being serious to being humorous.

This pathway is in some respects different from the pathway of events across which Tyisha's identity developed. That pathway included a dozen or so individual events, in a circumscribed spatiotemporal location. The pathway of crying "racist" events contains thousands of such events, branching widely across virtual and real time and space, accelerated by mass media and social network distribution. As Agha (2007) argues, such robust and branching pathways are similar in principle to more localized pathways. But discourse analysts must adopt somewhat different approaches to collecting data on these different types of pathways. The next three chapters apply our approach to three types of pathways: less dense, more temporally and spatially localized pathways like the one that involved Tyisha, which are most appropriately studied through ethnographic approaches; more dense, longer timescale pathways that emerge across historical time and are best studied through archival approaches; and more dense but shorter timescale pathways created in new media discourse. The next three chapters apply the tools and techniques developed in this chapter to ethnographic, archival and new media data, illustrating in more detail how our approach to discourse analysis can document how social processes are accomplished across pathways of speech events.

3 Discourse analysis of ethnographic data

Discourse analysis beyond the speech event has been done with several kinds of data. The concepts and the methodological tools and techniques developed in Chapters 1 and 2 apply to all discourse, but analysts will use these somewhat differently when working with different types of data. In Chapters 3–5 we apply our approach to analyze three types: "ethnographic," "archival" and "new media." Ethnographic studies analyze living people and actions in context, typically at shorter timescales and across more limited spatial scales. Archival studies analyze historical processes, typically at longer timescales and broader spatial scales. Studies of new media analyze actions in mediated worlds, typically at shorter timescales and broader spatial scales. New media studies most often focus on highly interconnected messages that depend on each other for completion, whereas the documents, interviews and observations in ethnographic and archival studies are often less immediately interconnected. These three categories are ideal types, and many research projects will involve more than one of them. Analysts will nonetheless apply our concepts and methods somewhat differently when working with the three types of data, and it is useful to illustrate discourse analysis on each separately.

This chapter applies discourse analysis beyond the speech event to ethnographic data—face-to-face participant observation with living people in context. We use examples from ethnographic discourse analyses that the two of us have done. Wortham (2006) analyzes a pathway of speech events that took place in one high school classroom across an academic year. The analysis in this chapter picks up the example that opened Chapter 1, following one of Tyisha's fellow students and illustrating how tools and techniques from Chapter 2 can be used to trace how he was positioned in increasingly uncomfortable ways across the academic year. Reyes (2013) also examines classroom data across a year, from the Asian American supplementary school introduced in Chapter 2. We use concepts from Chapter 1 and analytic tools from Chapter 2 to show how teachers and students in one classroom deployed nicknames in ways that accomplished social action.

Both of these analyses draw on year-long ethnographic projects in individual classrooms, in which the researcher was physically present with participants. As

Hammersley and Atkinson (1995) and many others describe, ethnography involves at least three data sources: field notes and/or recordings drawn from participant observation, interviews and documents. Ethnography is designed to understand people's activities from their own point of view, uncovering the concepts and models that they use to make sense of experience. This does not mean that ethnographers never use outsider categories in their analyses. But they only do so if they have evidence that participants themselves tacitly presuppose these categories.

Ethnographic research is an excellent complement to discourse analysis. As described in Chapter 2, discourse analysts must know two kinds of things about participants' understandings. First, they must know what relevant indexical signs point to. For example, in order to understand Tyisha's use of the term "Nintendo," and other participants' construals of this sign, a discourse analyst must know something about video games and the types of people who stereotypically play them. Second, discourse analysts must recognize the cultural models that participants use to construe indexical signs. In Tyisha's case, for example, a discourse analyst must know about norms of classroom behavior, like the model of a "disruptive" student. Analysts who are already familiar with a setting may have knowledge of indexical signs, relevant contexts and cultural models. But in most cases analysts need to learn at least some of these signs, contexts and models, and this involves participant observation, interviewing and analysis of documents.

Discourse analysis of ethnographic data typically focuses on relatively local, shorter-term processes. It analyzes recordings of naturally occurring events, interview transcripts and/or documents in order to understand how groups of people make sense of their experiences in one or a few settings. Unlike archival data, most ethnographic data come from participant observation and interviews in which an ethnographer records actual people interacting. Unlike new media data, most ethnographic data come from face-to-face interactions in which the ethnographer participates or observes. In order to study pathways of events using ethnographic data, an ethnographer has to record potentially linked events within and across settings, over time, and then identify which events are in fact linked into pathways through which consequential social action occurs.

Example 1: Maurice

Maurice the beast

On January 24, as we have seen in Chapter 1, Tyisha and her classmates discussed selections from Aristotle's *Politics* in which he argues that "the state is by nature clearly prior to the individual since the whole is of necessity prior to the part" and that "he who is unable to live in society, or who has no need because he is sufficient for himself, must be beast or god." Discussion focused on a "beast in the woods," a term that they interpreted to mean a person who refuses to make the sacrifices necessary to live successfully with others. Before discussion of the example that included Tyisha and her cat, Mrs. Bailey nominated another student, Maurice, as a hypothetical beast in the woods.

Segment 1: Maurice in the woods

315 *T/B:* I mean think of what- he's saying
there. he's saying if Maurice went <u>out</u> and lived in
the <u>wo:ods</u> (4.0) ((some laughter))
   FST: °they're talking about you°
   T/B: and <u>never</u> had any <u>contact</u> with the <u>rest</u> of us,
320 he would be- uh- like an <u>animal</u>.

The example of Maurice the beast disappeared from the discussion relatively quickly at this point. Much later, a few minutes after the discussion of Tyisha and her cat, Mrs. Bailey returned to the example of Maurice as a beast.

Segment 2: Maurice the beast in the woods

   T/B: now we put Maurice out in the woods. Maurice,
when would you get up? and go to bed.
915 *MRC:* <u>when</u> I was ready to.
   T/B: when you were ready to. Maurice, if you had
your <u>dru</u>thers what would you be eating all day
long, [liver=
   MRC: [whatever I want.
920 *T/B:* =or ice cream? you going to eat liver? or are
you going to eat ice cream.
   STS: ice cream.
   MRC: with what?
   FST: I eat liver.
925 *STS:* <u>ice cream</u>. ((students echo ice cream and
comment on the choice of ice cream or liver))
   MST: druthers
   T/B: you have a choice.
   FST: °every day°
930 *MRC:* ice cream.
   T/B: ice cream. ummm.
   FST: °be healthier if you ate the liver°
   T/B: shhh. (2.0) the- the water where you <u>are</u> is
very, very <u>cold</u>. and it's [not very warm outside.=
935 *MRC:*   [((3 unintelligible syllables))
   T/B: =how often are you going to- to- to clean
yourself off? ((laughter))

FST: Right Guard
MRC: depends when we're talking about.
940 T/B: okay, so you might go the <u>whole</u> winter and
well into the <u>sum</u>mer, right? without ever getting
<u>clean</u>.

By making Maurice an example at line 913, Mrs. Bailey may be putting his actual identity in play. With Tyisha, we saw that discussion of the example about her and her cat had implications for her own position in the narrating event. The same thing might happen with Maurice. Teachers and students could infer something about Maurice himself from their discussion of him as a hypothetical beast in the woods. Is Mrs. Bailey implying that there is something beast-like about Maurice?

Figure 3.1 represents the discussion of this example, mapping the narrated events early in the conversation. In the first narrated event, Aristotle makes the distinction between gods, beasts and humans—with humans living together in society and beasts unable to do so. In the second narrated event, the example, Maurice is a hypothetical beast who lives apart from the teachers, students and other humans who live in society, and he does not follow social norms like bathing. In the narrating event, teachers and students are discussing Aristotle. We have separated girls from boys in the figure because, as described more extensively below, in this classroom the split between girls and boys is especially salient. The girls dominate conversation throughout the year, and Maurice is the only boy who willingly speaks. We have separated out Maurice in the

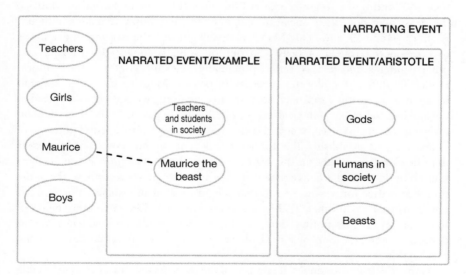

Figure 3.1 The example of "Maurice the beast"

narrating event, because the example with him as a character turns out to have specific implications for Maurice himself. Focusing for the moment on this discrete speech event, our discourse analytic question is: what implications does discussion of these narrated events have for the positioning and social action occurring in the classroom interaction? Figure 3.1 represents this as yet undetermined relationship as a dashed line between the narrated character Maurice the hypothetical beast and Maurice himself, the student participating in the narrating event.

The next step is selecting indexicals. We must identify salient indexicals and the relevant context they presuppose and then construe those indexicals, inferring what types of action may be taking place through the discourse. Mrs. Bailey describes the hypothetical Maurice not eating liver (line 918) and not bathing (line 936). Both of these are stereotypical caricatures of American children and youth, who are often seen as picky about food and resistant to their parents' desire that they eat healthy foods and bathe regularly. By choosing topics that are likely to elicit laughter from teenagers, the teacher may be signaling that she is joking, while also pursuing the academic discussion. Other students act as if they and the teacher have in fact been joking with Maurice, when they laugh at line 937 and a student makes another joke by referring to a brand of deodorant at line 938.

So far, it seems that the teacher is jokingly putting Maurice into the role of a hypothetical beast, at the same time as she explains Aristotle's argument to the students. But the characteristics that Mrs. Bailey attributes to Maurice the beast are not merely funny. They also index typical behaviors of what we might call "difficult" children. Such children stereotypically want to eat only ice cream, refuse to eat healthy food (lines 917–921), resist bathing (lines 933–937) and refuse to go to bed on time (line 914). The hypothetical Maurice the beast does not follow social norms, and this may imply that he is difficult. At lines 915, 919 and 930, Maurice readily makes the appropriate choices to take on the role of a beast. So our question becomes: do teachers and other students index this other potentially relevant context—the cultural model of "difficult" children—in order to positon Maurice himself as difficult in some way? In our approach to discourse analysis, we answer this question by looking for other indexical signs that might make the model of difficult children salient. We ask whether other signs cohere into a configuration of indexicals that establishes this model as relevant, or not. We cannot answer the question based only on the segment given above. We must examine signs that come later in the conversation, to see whether they presuppose the same things and thus form a more robust configuration of indexicals that supports one construal or another. Table 3.1 represents the different components of our analysis so far, noting that we do not have sufficient evidence yet to describe a configuration of indexicals or to determine the social action being accomplished.

As the discussion continues, it seems as if the teachers are not in fact positioning Maurice himself as difficult in the narrating event.

Table 3.1 Analysis of "Maurice the beast" early in the example

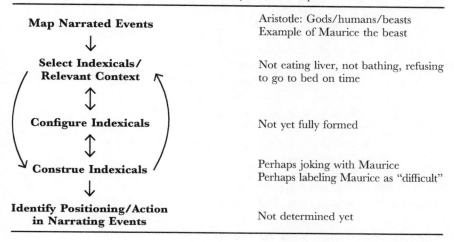

Map Narrated Events ↓	Aristotle: Gods/humans/beasts Example of Maurice the beast
Select Indexicals/ **Relevant Context** ↑↓	Not eating liver, not bathing, refusing to go to bed on time
Configure Indexicals ↑↓	Not yet fully formed
Construe Indexicals ↓	Perhaps joking with Maurice Perhaps labeling Maurice as "difficult"
Identify Positioning/Action **in Narrating Events**	Not determined yet

Segment 3: Maurice is civilized

```
990   T/B:   what's- what's the difference between the two
             aspects. Maurice in the forest and the Maurice that
             we know in this classroom, who doesn't scratch
             when he itches.
      FST:   he's civilized.
995   MRC:   that's what I said.
      T/B:   umm, he's civilized. what did you say
             Maurice?
      MRC:   that's what I said.
      T/B:   you're civilized.
```

At lines 990–993, Mrs. Bailey distinguishes between Maurice "in the forest" and Maurice "in this classroom." Unlike the Tyisha case discussed in Chapter 1, in which the boundary between Tyisha the beast and Tyisha the student blurs, here Mrs. Bailey explicitly separates Maurice the beast from the real Maurice and positions Maurice himself as "civilized," as part of society like the other students in the narrating event.

The teachers and students discuss this example for a few minutes, and they mostly maintain this clear separation between Maurice the narrated character and Maurice himself in the narrating event. There are only a few minor indications that Maurice himself might also be getting positioned negatively. At the end of the class, Mrs. Bailey characterizes Maurice as perhaps even more dangerous than a beast when she tries to explain another of Aristotle's points. Aristotle says:

Segment 4: Quoting Aristotle

```
         T/B:   for man, when perfected,
                is the best of animals, but when separated from law
1145            and justice, he is the worst of all, since armed
                injustice is the more dangerous. and he is equipped
                at birth with arms meant to be used by intelligence
                and virtue, which he may use for the w- worst ends.
                wherefore if he have not virtue, he is the most
1150            unholy and most savage of animals and the most
                full of lust and gluttony. but justice is the bond of
                men and states.
```

For Aristotle, the teacher explains, a self-centered human can be even more dangerous than a beast. Mrs. Bailey uses Maurice to illustrate this point.

Segment 5: Maurice could be sneaky

```
         T/B:   what
                happens if you take someone like Maurice out in the
1105            forest is doing what he wants to do, for the
                immediate pleasure of what he wants to do and then
                you add on to it the component that he can also
                think about future pleasures, doing what he wants to
                do. and he can have some planning mechanism
1110            there, to think in terms of the things in the future
                that he can plan to do that will make him feel good.
                what happens to him? a lion is dangerous, but what
                about a Maurice?

. . .

1125            Maurice is somebody maybe you
                don't even see and you know, he can be doing
                what?
         FST:   ((2 unintelligible syllables))
         T/B:   the lion you see, you know he's dangerous.
1130            Maurice you can see- °let me put it this way°
                Maurice you can see now (1.0) and don't perceive
                him as being dangerous, but what else could be
                happening?
         FST:   he could be sneaky.
1135 T/B:       he could be plannin' how to get somethin' or
                do somethin' that makes him feel good
```

This new hypothetical, narrated Maurice is a beast in some ways but not in others. The stereotypical beast is self-interested but unable to reason in complex ways. But this hypothetical Maurice is both self-interested and intelligent. Mrs. Bailey

Table 3.2 Initial elaboration of the "Maurice the beast" example

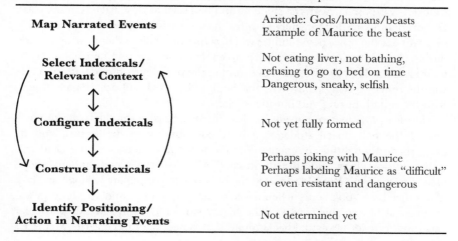

Map Narrated Events ↓	Aristotle: Gods/humans/beasts Example of Maurice the beast
Select Indexicals/ Relevant Context ↕	Not eating liver, not bathing, refusing to go to bed on time Dangerous, sneaky, selfish
Configure Indexicals ↕	Not yet fully formed
Construe Indexicals ↓	Perhaps joking with Maurice Perhaps labeling Maurice as "difficult" or even resistant and dangerous
Identify Positioning/ Action in Narrating Events	Not determined yet

uses indexicals that presuppose the hypothetical Maurice is "dangerous," out to get people and sneaking around unseen in a menacing way. He is intelligent, but he pursues what makes him "feel good."

Table 3.2 is similar to Table 3.1, but it adds the new indexicals the teacher uses in this last segment. These signs presuppose a different voice for the narrated Maurice, the hypothetical beast. Early in the example, Maurice the beast was self-centered and apart from human society. But teacher and students quickly made clear that this voice does not characterize Maurice the student himself. As Mrs. Bailey voices the narrated Maurice not only as selfish and anti-social, but also as sneaky and dangerous, a discourse analyst might ask whether this new characterization of Maurice's narrated character has implications for his position in the narrating event. We note this in the "construing indexicals" line of the table. But no robust configuration of indexicals has emerged to support this interpretation yet, so we cannot conclude that the "dangerous" narrated voice has any implications for Maurice's position in the narrating event. In order to discover whether he is in fact being positioned in some negative way, we need to consider other speech events he participated in across the year. By making him a participant example of a "beast in the woods," the teacher has raised the possibility that Maurice is an uncooperative outcast like Tyisha, or perhaps even dangerous to the social order in the classroom. But based only on the conversation in this one speech event, this possibility is not realized.

The girls against the boys

Maurice was a 14-year-old African American boy. Like most of the students in Mrs. Bailey and Mr. Smith's class, he had scored in the third quartile on the assessment test for eighth graders. Like Tyisha and many of his other peers, he was verbally skilled and seemed more intelligent than his test scores indicated. Maurice was popular with the students and had several close friends in the class. He joked and wrestled playfully with his male friends before and after class. He also sat near the other boys, and he would sometimes talk to them surreptitiously during class. Maurice was physically larger than average, and he played on the football team. He was also attractive, and many of the girls flirted with him. He was interested in the girls as well, and he flirted, teased and occasionally fought with them both during and outside of class.

Maurice participated actively in class discussions all year. He was routinely one of the half dozen students actively contributing to discussions, and he often made thoughtful comments. For the first three months of the academic year, both teachers and students treated Maurice as a good student and a valued participant. But Maurice was the only boy to participate willingly in class. The other boys spoke only when asked a direct question, and so Maurice was an unusual boy in this context. The highly gendered nature of this particular classroom provides essential background that is necessary to construe Maurice's emerging position.

Wortham (2006) describes a somewhat distinctive local model that emerges in this classroom: both teachers and students habitually presuppose that girls are less troublesome, smarter and more promising than boys. This model circulates widely in American society and many American schools, increasingly in recent decades. But teachers and students developed a specific local version of this model that emerged over the first two or three months of the academic year, with teachers and students positioning boys and girls differently. They presupposed that girls cooperate more with teachers, are more intelligent and will more likely succeed in life. Boys, in contrast, supposedly resist classroom expectations, are less intelligent and are less likely to succeed. More than any other category of identity, gender became relevant to the social identification of these students in this particular classroom. By the middle of the year, many students were routinely identified according to these gendered models—as "promising girls" and "unpromising boys"—and these categories of identity could easily be presupposed in almost any interaction.

By the end of November, Mrs. Bailey had articulated the model of promising girls and unpromising boys explicitly, and several girls were beginning to treat the boys as if they were unpromising. The teachers often referred to the class in gendered terms, especially when making comments about discipline. On November 30, for instance, Mrs. Bailey characterized girls and boys this way: "Okay, that's one meaning of 'discrimination.' I look and I see differences. . . . I see that Katrina is a girl and William is a boy and I discriminate against William because he's a boy and girls are much easier to deal with." This comment was not tongue in cheek—she said it with a straight face, and it fit with similar comments that she made. The teachers and the vocal girls often excluded the boys from the classroom conversation, treating them as third-person objects of discussion and legitimate targets of the girls' teasing. The boys, except for Maurice, did not say anything and kept their heads down.

Maurice's classroom identity emerged in this context. The other boys rarely contributed to class discussion, but Maurice participated actively and successfully throughout the year. He almost always answered questions willingly, articulated his own arguments about the subject matter and engaged in constructive discussion with the teachers and other students. Despite his gender, Maurice began the year being treated by teachers and students as a typical promising student. In the first two or three months, the teachers and many female students accepted and even praised his regular contributions. After a few months, however, the vocal female students and sometimes the teachers began to identify him in a less flattering way—not as the same sort of disruptive outcast that Tyisha became, but as an outcast nonetheless.

The first extended example of the vocal girls picking on Maurice occurred on December 17. They are discussing "The Sniper" by Liam O'Flaherty, a short story in which a soldier for the Republican side unwittingly shoots his brother during the Irish Civil War. In the following segment they define "civil war," and the girls jump in quickly when it looks as if Maurice is about to make a mistake.

Segment 6: Maurice makes a mistake

```
    T/B:      what kind of war do you get family on opposite
              sides? (2.0) civil war. what's a civil war?
    FST:      °a wa[r°
    FST:          [a war
40  MRC:          [a war against- one country against-
    FST:      no:
    FST:      no
    FSTS:     ((2 seconds of overlapping chatter))
    T/B:      okay, a war within the country. a war with- shhh
45  FST:      ((6 unintelligible syllables))
    T/B:      a wa:r within the country. so brother fights against
              brother. neighbor fights against neighbor. is there any
              outside invasion going on here, am I protecting my home
              against a bunch of foreigners?
50  MRC:      no
    FST:      no:
    FST:      no
```

At line 41, a female student says "no" with noticeable stress and elongation of the vowel (similar to the fall-rise intonation contour as one would find with "duh," often meaning "how could you be so stupid as to say that?"). Another student repeats "no" at line 42. Maurice had only begun to make an error, but the girls quickly jump on him. At line 50, Maurice says "no" himself, perhaps attempting to preempt the girls' criticism. But the girls repeat "no" at lines 51 and 52, with the same intonation contour at line 51, reminding everyone of Maurice's earlier mistake.

As the conversation proceeds, the girls continue to object to Maurice's comments. This pattern recurs from December through the end of the year: girls often tease or disagree with Maurice, and the teachers do not intervene.

Segment 7: Maurice makes another mistake

	T/B:	you don't know who you're fighting a<u>gainst</u>? you <u>do</u>
		know who ((3 unintelligible syllables)) you're fighting
90		a<u>gainst</u>, don't you?
	FST:	right=
	FST:	yeah
	T/B:	who's that?
	FST:	((4 unintelligible syllables))
95	MRC:	same people in the=
	FST:	<u>no</u>
	T/B:	the <u>peo</u>ple that are <u>like</u> you. people in your <u>coun</u>try.

At line 95, Maurice begins to answer Mrs. Bailey's question. His truncated response may well have been correct, but at line 96 a female student cuts him off with another "no." The teacher steps in immediately and gives the correct answer, without commenting on whether Maurice might have been correct and without intervening in the developing conflict between Maurice and the girls.

Table 3.3 represents our cross-event discourse analysis at this early stage. So far we have the events from December 17 and January 24, together with several others which we do not have space to present in detail—events in which the girls tease or exclude Maurice (cf. Wortham, 2006). We select these two focal events because in both of them Maurice is positioned in unexpectedly negative ways, as making a stupid mistake and perhaps as an outcast, even a dangerous outcast. The second line mentions a few indexicals across the two events that could presuppose these construals. These indexicals have not yet come together into a solid configuration that would support some reading of the pathway Maurice is traveling over time, however. We have seen a few indications that Maurice is not a typical good student. And we know that, as a male in a classroom with a strong model of "unpromising boys," he is anomalous. But his pathway could still go in several directions. He could end up being an exception to the rule, accepted as a good student despite his gender. He could give up his attempt to be a good student and join the boys sitting silently at the back of the room. There are various other possibilities as well. We need to trace his participation across other events to see if more dense cross-event indexical configurations emerge and establish a clearer pathway.

On February 18, the class discussed the scene from the *Odyssey* in which Odysseus encounters the Sirens. The Sirens were female creatures who lured sailors with enchanting songs and then killed them. Having been warned, Odysseus makes his men plug their ears and tie him down, so that he is able to enjoy the Sirens' song while his men keep the ship safely away. The class explores

Table 3.3 Initial cross-event analysis of Maurice's pathway

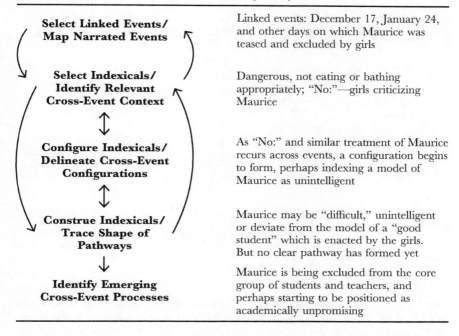

Select Linked Events/ Map Narrated Events	Linked events: December 17, January 24, and other days on which Maurice was teased and excluded by girls
Select Indexicals/ Identify Relevant Cross-Event Context	Dangerous, not eating or bathing appropriately; "No:"—girls criticizing Maurice
Configure Indexicals/ Delineate Cross-Event Configurations	As "No:" and similar treatment of Maurice recurs across events, a configuration begins to form, perhaps indexing a model of Maurice as unintelligent
Construe Indexicals/ Trace Shape of Pathways	Maurice may be "difficult," unintelligent or deviate from the model of a "good student" which is enacted by the girls. But no clear pathway has formed yet
Identify Emerging Cross-Event Processes	Maurice is being excluded from the core group of students and teachers, and perhaps starting to be positioned as academically unpromising

the implicit messages of this episode, like the representation of women as seductive but dangerous. In the discussion Mrs. Bailey makes Maurice himself an example, a victim of the girls.

Segment 8: Maurice victimized by the girls

```
        CAN:    think you like somebody else on purpose. pretend to
                like somebody else on purpose.
     90 T/B:    okay, that could hurt Maurice, that kind of thing. They
                could play with his affections and then toss him overboard.
                okay, what else c- could the ladies in the room do?
        FST:    we can become obsessed
        T/B:    not, not the women being obsessed with him, wh-
     95         what might happen to Maurice? I want your opinion. what,
                what might happen to you, Maurice? (10.0) Maurice, is
                this thing in this classroom full of women a distraction?
                ((female laughter)) would you do better in a classroom full of
                boys? (4.0)
    100 MRC:    °I don't know°
        T/B:    Maurice, I'm asking you a question.
        MRC:    I don't know.
        T/B:    you don't know.
```

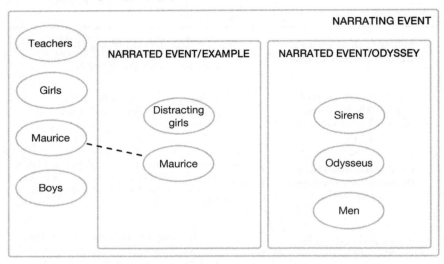

Figure 3.2 The example of the Sirens

Candace describes a generic male who might be hurt by dangerous girls. At line 90, Mrs. Bailey explicitly introduces Maurice as the subject of discussion. This adds Maurice as a character in an example, with Mrs. Bailey and the girls voiced as potentially dangerous females and Maurice as their potential victim. Figure 3.2 represents the narrated and narrating events at the point, with the relationship between the girls and Maurice in the example potentially having implications for Maurice's actual position in the classroom.

Mrs. Bailey refers to Maurice in the third person at line 91, making him an object of discussion for the moment. Mrs. Bailey also makes him the object of the girls' actions—they could hurt him, "play with his affections and then toss him overboard." Maurice has thus become an object in two ways: a few lines earlier in the conversation he refused to participate, and now the females have excluded him interactionally; Mrs. Bailey has also described him, within the example, as an object of the girls' actions. As shown at line 93, the girls continue to position themselves as first-person participants, referring to themselves as "we."

In her comments at lines 94–99, however, Mrs. Bailey makes it clear that she does not want to focus on the women's "obsessions." She wants to focus on Maurice. She turns to him at line 95, referring to him again as "you" and inviting him to be a participant in the conversation. But Maurice, uncharacteristically, does not respond at all. At lines 95–101, Mrs. Bailey increases the pressure on Maurice to respond, escalating to the explicit statement, "Maurice, I'm asking you a question." The teachers often spoke like this to other boys when they refused to participate, but I had never observed them talking like this to Maurice. Maurice responds with "I don't know," twice, which is the only thing he says in this whole discussion.

By focusing on the gendered dimension of the Sirens myth, and by using Maurice as an example, Mrs. Bailey presupposes the separation between boys and girls in the classroom. This opens up the possibility that she might apply gendered categories of identity from the curriculum to students themselves, positioning Maurice and perhaps others in the narrating event. Because Mrs. Bailey and the girls were teasing him, Maurice likely suspected that this would not be a dispassionate academic discussion of subject matter. Mrs. Bailey thus put Maurice in an awkward position. He generally cooperated with the teachers and participated willingly in class, but he may have known that this particular topic would be dangerous, an opportunity for Mrs. Bailey and the girls to tease him or position him in unflattering ways. So it is likely that he chose to act like a stereotypical male student and refused to participate.

Mrs. Bailey and the girls responded by explicitly characterizing the boys as unpromising.

Segment 9: Boys are stupid

JAS: you <u>would</u> because they are able to take ((4
105   unintelligible syllables)) stupid things because if more <u>boys</u>
     than girls
T/B: <u>oh</u> the place would get <u>stup</u>ider.
     ((laughter from female students))
T/B: that's how boys are, they're kind of <u>stupid</u>. maybe,
110   maybe the boys in this room are a little bit ((2 unintelligible
     syllables)). <u>o</u>kay, ahh, (6.0) I am going to have to ask this
     question to the girls because the boys aren't very
     <u>forth</u>coming. any<u>bo</u>dy in here ever have a <u>crush</u> on
     somebody?

At line 105 Jasmine seems to be saying that a predominantly male class would produce more "stupid" comments. Mrs. Bailey echoes this at lines 107 and 109, characterizing boys as stupid. She may be teasing here, trying to entice the boys to participate. Wortham (2006) shows, however, that she has articulated this negative evaluation of boys on several other days, without apparent irony. Thus her blunt statement here is probably not just teasing. The message about the boys' identities in the narrating event is clear: they are uncooperative and unpromising students. Mrs. Bailey then directs her instruction exclusively to the girls at lines 111 and beyond. Thus she not only *describes* but also *enacts* the difference between promising girls and unpromising boys, acting as if it is not worth teaching the boys because they do not respond anyway.

Table 3.4 represents our emerging cross-event discourse analysis of the three events on December 17, January 24 and February 18. These three events are linked because in each Mrs. Bailey and the girls position Maurice as marginal. On December 17 the girls gang up on him in the narrating event, acting as if he is stupid. On January 24 Mrs. Bailey creates the example of Maurice the

Table 3.4 Emerging pathway for Maurice

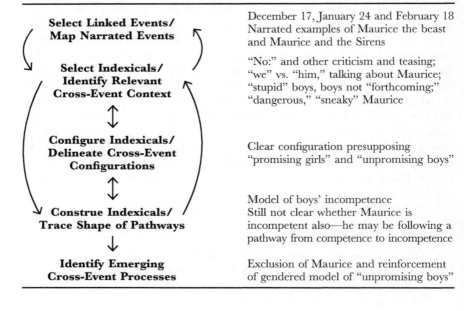

Select Linked Events/ Map Narrated Events	December 17, January 24 and February 18 Narrated examples of Maurice the beast and Maurice and the Sirens
Select Indexicals/ Identify Relevant Cross-Event Context	"No:" and other criticism and teasing; "we" vs. "him," talking about Maurice; "stupid" boys, boys not "forthcoming;" "dangerous," "sneaky" Maurice
Configure Indexicals/ Delineate Cross-Event Configurations	Clear configuration presupposing "promising girls" and "unpromising boys"
Construe Indexicals/ Trace Shape of Pathways	Model of boys' incompetence Still not clear whether Maurice is incompetent also—he may be following a pathway from competence to incompetence
Identify Emerging Cross-Event Processes	Exclusion of Maurice and reinforcement of gendered model of "unpromising boys"

beast, which might imply that he is an outcast, maybe even a dangerous one. Neither of these events in itself establishes an enduring position for Maurice, but—together with other events in which the girls pounce on his mistakes— these events form a potential trajectory across which Maurice may be getting positioned as an unpromising boy and something of an outcast. The example of the Sirens on February 18 makes clear that Maurice is male and different from the vocal, cooperative, intelligent girls who dominate classroom conversation. Mrs. Bailey and the vocal girls foreground gender as a salient dimension and clearly apply the local classroom model of promising girls and unpromising boys to Maurice.

With the February 18 discussion, a more rigid pathway began to form. Across several events, Maurice's competence was questioned. Mrs. Bailey and the girls reminded him that boys are not good students and that he is a boy. Thus they foregrounded a central tension in Maurice's position, his desire to be a good student in a context where boys are not supposed to be good students. A configuration of indexicals across events emerged, presupposing that he was marginal. Maurice's position in the classroom thus began to solidify across a pathway of linked events. In the early months of the year he was just another good student. But starting in December Mrs. Bailey and the girls placed increasing pressure on him, foregrounding the tension in his position as the one boy who wanted to succeed academically. The example discussed in the next section crystallized the choice teachers and students were forcing on him, a choice between being a promising student and being one of the boys.

Maurice in the middle

Maurice went from being just another good student in the fall, to being the only vocal boy and an outcast whom the vocal girls marginalized in class discussion. In the spring the teachers sometimes joined the vocal girls in treating Maurice as an outcast and in pressuring him to choose between his identity as a good student and his identity as a male. On May 10, for example, the class read Cicero's letter to Atticus. In this letter Cicero ponders what he should do about the tyranny of Caesar and the plot by Cassius and Brutus to overthrow him. Should he tell Caesar? Should he join the plotters? Or should he just keep quiet? The text describes three central characters: Caesar the tyrant, those plotting against him, and Cicero caught between the two. Mr. Smith makes Maurice an example, to illustrate Cicero's dilemma.

Segment 10: Maurice would not tell the teacher

```
        T/S:    Maurice let's give a good example, you'll love this.
                suppose this dictator, me. there was a plot going on.
150             and you found out about it. and you knew it was gonna-
                it's existing (3.0) among the people you knew. would
                you tell me. (5.0)
        MRC:    you said they know about it.
        T/S:    the plotters, against me. they're planning to push me
155             down the stairs. [and you know about it
        STS:                     [hnhhahahaha
        T/S:    now we all know Maurice and I have ha(hh)d
                arguments all year. would you tell me about it.
        MRC:    well- I might but uh what if they- what if they found
160             out that I told you then they want to kill me. (5.0) so I'm
                putting myself in trouble to save you, and I'm not going to
                do it.
        STS:    hnh hahahaha
```

The example describes a role structure analogous to that in Rome: Mr. Smith the hypothetical tyrant, the plotters planning to push him down the stairs and Maurice the potential informer caught between the two.

Figure 3.3 represents the analogy among the roles described in Cicero's text, the roles described in the example and the positions enacted in the narrating interaction itself. The first narrated event is described in Cicero's letter, with Caesar opposed to the plotters and Cicero caught in between these two groups. The second narrated event has three analogous characters, in Mr. Smith's example of himself as a hypothetical tyrant, hypothetical student plotters and Maurice hypothetically caught in the middle. The outer rectangle represents the interaction between teachers and students in the classroom. At this point in the conversation, Mr. Smith and Maurice occupy conventional positions as teacher

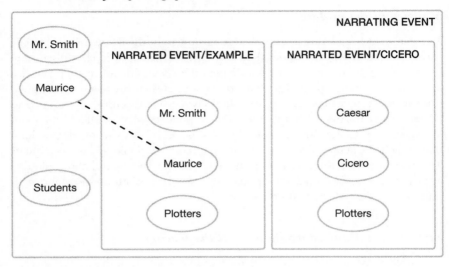

Figure 3.3 Maurice caught in the middle

and student discussing the curriculum. But Mr. Smith's comment at lines 157–158 indicates that their own relationship may also involve tension that would predispose Maurice to join the plot against him.

The dashed line in the figure represents potential implications that the example might have for Maurice and Mr. Smith themselves in the narrating interaction. By asking whether Maurice would side with him against the student plotters, in the hypothetical example, Mr. Smith may be asking Maurice a question that has consequences for Maurice himself: is Maurice on the teachers' side or not? If we were just doing within-event discourse analysis, we could not draw conclusions about the potential parallel between Maurice's hypothetical position as someone caught between a tyrant and the plotters and his actual position as a boy caught between his desire to succeed in school and his male peers' refusal to participate in class. But the cross-event configuration of indexicals described above has already established this position for him. As the latest linked event in this pathway, the example of Maurice caught in the middle presupposes and reinforces Maurice's position caught between the promising girls and the unpromising boys.

As they continue discussing the example, Maurice's hypothetical decision about whether to side with Mr. Smith has increasingly clear implications for Maurice's own position.

Segment 11: Maurice would not get involved

T/S:	then what's his <u>prob</u>lem. if the man- <u>you</u> just told me
190	point <u>blank</u> [that we could be pushed down stairs=
MRC:	[so.

T/S:	=and you wouldn't feel a <u>thing</u> about it. what's his big deal, if he believes Caesar is a <u>ty</u>rant, so what.
MRC:	well- he- if u:h he ((4 unintelligible syllables)) that they're
195	making some kind of plot a<u>gainst</u> him, but he doesn't want to get in<u>volved</u>. he doesn't know if he <u>should</u> get involved, he could get himself in more trouble. since he's already ((3 unintelligible syllables))=
T/S:	well if <u>Caesar</u>'s a <u>ty</u>rant why <u>should</u>n't you get involved. tyrants are generally <u>dict</u>atorial <u>nast</u>y people

When Mr. Smith says, "<u>You</u> just told me point <u>blank</u> that we could be pushed down stairs and you wouldn't feel a <u>thing</u> about it" (lines 189–192), both the volume and tempo of his speech increase, as if he is angry. This contrasts with his lighthearted tone and laughter at line 157 above, where he seemed to be teasing. By line 192, Mr. Smith has escalated his emotional involvement. It used to be a joke, but now he may be taking Maurice's choice more seriously. Even though they are just speaking about the hypothetical example, Mr. Smith treats Maurice's choice not to tell him as a betrayal. Maurice tries to distance himself at this point, referring to "he," Cicero, and not to his own hypothetical character in the narrated example, but this strategy does not work.

Table 3.5 represents both the early stages of our within-event discourse analysis on the May 10 event and the solidifying cross-event analysis including

Table 3.5 Maurice's pathway, including preliminary analysis of May 10

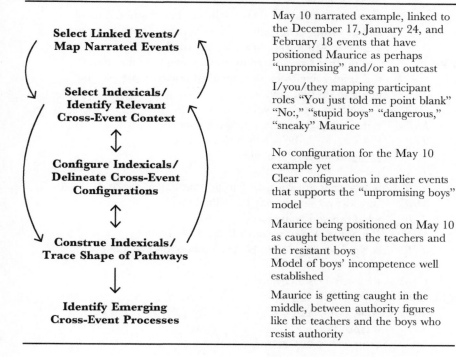

Select Linked Events/ Map Narrated Events	May 10 narrated example, linked to the December 17, January 24, and February 18 events that have positioned Maurice as perhaps "unpromising" and/or an outcast
Select Indexicals/ Identify Relevant Cross-Event Context	I/you/they mapping participant roles "You just told me point blank" "No:," "stupid boys" "dangerous," "sneaky" Maurice
Configure Indexicals/ Delineate Cross-Event Configurations	No configuration for the May 10 example yet Clear configuration in earlier events that supports the "unpromising boys" model
Construe Indexicals/ Trace Shape of Pathways	Maurice being positioned on May 10 as caught between the teachers and the resistant boys Model of boys' incompetence well established
Identify Emerging Cross-Event Processes	Maurice is getting caught in the middle, between authority figures like the teachers and the boys who resist authority

the events described above from earlier in the year. Salient indexicals in the example of Mr. Smith the tyrant include the personal pronouns *I*, *you* and *they*, which map out the opposed groups represented in Figure 3.3, as well as Mr. Smith's anger ("you just told me point blank"). These indexicals could be construed to indicate that Mr. Smith is questioning Maurice's own loyalty to the teachers and the academic mission of the school. When we add relevant cross-event context from earlier events like those on December 17, January 24 and February 18, this construal becomes more likely.

As the discussion proceeds, a configuration of indexical signs emerges within the May 10 event and more firmly presupposes the tension in Maurice's position as the only potentially promising boy. This configuration connects to the cross-event configuration of indexical signs that has already presupposed similar positioning in the earlier events, such that a pathway of linked events becomes more rigid and establishes Maurice's predicament more firmly.

Segment 12: Maurice would stay away

	T/S:	gee you sound terribly con<u>fus</u>ed Maurice. sort of like <u>C</u>icero here.
	T/B:	what w- if you knew that they <u>ac</u>tually- you know there's a group of kids that are <u>ac</u>tually going to do: this
225		<u>das</u>tardly deed. and you <u>know</u> that there's going to be some re<u>ac</u>tion. what might you do th- and you kn- you know basically wh:ile you might not be- <u>en</u>amored totally of Mr. Smith or myself you- basically: don't wish that we were crippled for <u>life</u> or whatever, what might
230		you <u>do</u> that day. you know that's going to come- that this is all going to happen on <u>Wed</u>nesday. what are you going to <u>do</u> that day.
	CAN:	<u>I</u> would try to warn you.
	FSTS:	right. I would [((overlapping comments))
235	T/B:	[he's- he's not- he's not going to warn us though.
	T/S:	no.
	T/B:	what- what are you going to <u>do</u> that day Maurice. (1.0)
	MRC:	stay away. ((2 unintelligible syllables))
240	T/B:	<u>what</u> are you going to do?
	MRC:	I'm going to <u>stay</u> away so I won't be- be:
	T/B:	so you're not going to come to school on Wednesday.
	MRC:	°no°
	CAN:	that way he's a <u>cow</u>ard.
245	FST:	what would <u>you</u> do.
	MRC:	what would <u>you</u> do.
	T/S:	a <u>cow</u>ard.
	CAN:	yeah 'cause he's <u>scar</u>ed.

This segment further connects the narrated example and the classroom inter-action itself. Teachers and students repeatedly start making a point in the con-ditional, or with a modal that indicates the example is hypothetical (lines 223, 229, 233, 245)—saying "if he knew," he "might" and he "would." But then they use the present indicative, talking about Maurice's actions as if they are happening in the here and now—"there's a group of kids" (line 224), "he's not going to warn us" (lines 235–236) and "he's scared" (line 248). Maurice himself describes his hypothetical narrated actions in the present ("I'm going to stay away" [line 241]).

The girls' appearance in the example raises the question of how this narrated content helps position the girls and Maurice in the narrating event. At lines 233–234, Candace and other female students indicate that they would join the teachers. This adds another group to the example: loyal subjects. But it also reinforces the girls' position as students loyal to the teachers' agenda and opposed to the boys' resistance in the classroom. The girls intensify Maurice's predicament here. When Candace and Mr. Smith call Maurice a coward at lines 244 and 247, Candace begins to speak as Candace herself, in the narrating event, and not as a hypothetical Roman. She is not only elaborating the example but also challenging Maurice himself. Like their characters in the example, the girls affiliate with the teachers and exclude Maurice in the narrating interaction.

When the girls enter the example as loyalists, the local classroom model of promising girls and unpromising boys becomes more readily available as a resource for positioning students in the narrating event. The teachers and the girls use the curricular distinction between the powerful, the loyal and the resistant to reinforce Maurice's awkward dual identity. Insofar as he wants to be a good student, Maurice might want to affiliate with Mr. Smith the tyrant and thus, by implication, with Mr. Smith the teacher. But once the girls enter the example, Maurice would have to affiliate with both the girls and the teachers. This would damage his standing with the boys. Mr. Smith and Candace thus put Maurice into a Cicero-like predicament, caught in the middle and unsure what to do.

Figure 3.4 represents the analogy among (1) Caesar, Cicero and the Roman plotters; (2) Mr. Smith the tyrant, Candace the loyalist, Maurice the potential informer and the student plotters; and (3) the teachers, the "loyal" girls, Maurice and the "resistant" boys. The figure represents the analogy with dashed lines across the three realms. Teachers and students intensify Maurice's predicament by using a model of identity borrowed from the curriculum, one that represents Cicero caught in the middle between those in power and those who resist. Like Maurice the hypothetical informer, and like Cicero, Maurice himself gets excluded from the classroom interaction as he thinks about what to do. The teachers and the vocal girls accomplish this marginalization in part through pronoun usage. For much of the remaining discussion after line 244, other speakers exclude Maurice from the conversation, referring to him as *he*, whereas before they had referred to him as *you*. Immediately after Candace has said that she, unlike

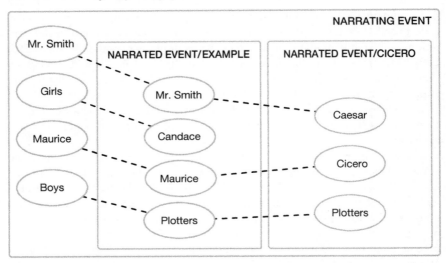

Figure 3.4 Parallelism across narrated and narrating events

Maurice, would warn the teachers about the plot, the teachers and girls start to exclude Maurice as *he*, positioning him as an outcast who no longer belongs to the group that dominates classroom discussion.

Later in the conversation Mr. Smith speaks about Maurice's interactional position in the past tense, as if Maurice has made a final decision to betray him.

Segment 13: Maurice would be an accomplice

	T/S:	you told <u>us</u> you wouldn't tell us <u>anything</u>.
	FST:	haha
	FST:	°<u>I</u> wouldn't.°
	T/S:	you'd rather see our mangled <u>bo</u>dies at the bottom of
365		the staircase.
	MRC:	I: told you I wouldn't be coming to <u>school</u> that day.
	T/S:	does that mean you're not part of the plot.
	FST:	yeah
	MRC:	I'd <u>still</u> be part of it. I- [if I
370	*T/B:*	[if you- if you <u>know</u> about it=
	T/S:	if you <u>know</u> about it that's: an ac<u>com</u>plice. you <u>knew</u>
		about it. you could have <u>stopped</u> it. all you had to do is say-
		it shouldn't be done, it's wrong.

Note the use of reported speech in lines 361 and 366. "You told us you wouldn't tell us anything" contributes to the voicing of Maurice's hypothetical narrated character as morally questionable. Maurice uses a parallel construction at line 366 to try to change the implications. Maurice must decide whether to accept Mr. Smith's description of the evils that Maurice's hypothetical actions have caused, or whether to change course and affiliate with the teachers in the classroom. In his response, Maurice tries to cast himself as a potential victim of the plotters, just as the teachers are. But he does not succeed. Candace and the girls have labeled him a coward. And Mr. Smith accuses Maurice of wishing for the teachers' violent demise. Mr. Smith's colorful comment at lines 364–365 might be a joke, but Maurice's tone at line 366 is earnest. Mr. Smith speaks in an angry tone again at line 371. By using the word "accomplice" to refer to Maurice, Mr. Smith further voices Maurice's hypothetical character as morally questionable.

Maurice says that his hypothetical character will stay away, and then he withdraws from the conversation in the narrating event. After line 373 the teachers and students consistently refer to Maurice as *he* for about six minutes. Maurice can still be a member of the boys' group, but the other boys almost never participate in class. He tried to maintain his position both as a student who makes valuable contributions in class and as an adolescent male respected by his peers. But through the example Mr. Smith and the girls made this difficult, and for the moment they have forced him to choose one position over the other.

Table 3.6 summarizes the cross-event discourse analysis we have given of Maurice from December 17 to May 10. A cross-event configuration of indexical

Table 3.6 The full cross-event analysis of Maurice's predicament

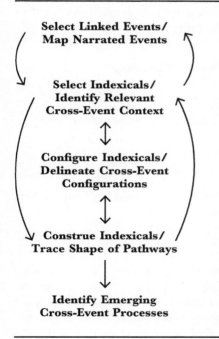

Select Linked Events/ Map Narrated Events	December 17, January 24, February 18, May 10. Examples of Maurice the beast, Maurice and the Sirens, Maurice in the middle
Select Indexicals/ Identify Relevant Cross-Event Context	On May 10, Maurice called a "coward," refusing to defend the teachers, as an "accomplice" who "wouldn't tell us anything;" Maurice as "he," excluded from the narrating conversation
Configure Indexicals/ Delineate Cross-Event Configurations	Robust cross-event configurations presuppose the "unpromising boys" model. Also configurations presupposing the tension in Maurice's position as a promising boy
Construe Indexicals/ Trace Shape of Pathways	"Promising girls" and "unpromising boys." Maurice caught between teachers/girls and boys. Pathway from good student to questions about intelligence to caught in the middle
Identify Emerging Cross-Event Processes	Maurice pressured to choose whether to be a good student or a male, reminded that boys are not supposed to excel in school

signs has solidified, establishing a robust construal of relevant indexicals. We can now describe the interactional positioning and social action occurring in the various events along the pathway, as well as the overall shape of that pathway. Maurice began as just another good student. When the local model of promising girls and unpromising boys became robust in October and November he was the one boy who acted like a promising student, and no one challenged him. But starting in December the vocal girls questioned his academic contributions and worked to marginalize him. In January teachers and students made Maurice a "beast," which reinforced his awkward position as the only boy who participated in class discussions. Then in the spring, the teachers joined the vocal girls and forced Maurice to choose between the loyal, promising girls and the resistant, unpromising boys. Our approach to cross-event discourse analysis has allowed us to uncover the mechanisms teachers and students used to establish this pathway and pressure Maurice in this way. Now we move on to our second example of discourse analysis beyond the speech event using ethnographic data.

Example 2: Nicknames

A 10-year-old boy raises his hand and informs the teacher that he prefers to be called by his first name instead of the name of a corporation. The teacher refuses. In this after school program the student, Samuel Jung, was sometimes referred to as "Samsung," but on this day Samuel attempted to change that. As the teacher, Mrs. Turner, was asking the class for sample sentences for their assignment, Samuel raised his hand and she called on him:

Segment 14: Student resists the nickname "Samsung": March 9, 2007, 4:33 pm

	Mrs. Turner:	yes?
	Samuel Jung:	from now on I'm Sam, he's Sam P. ((referring to Sam Park))
	Mrs. Turner:	you're Samsung.
	Sam Park:	Electronics
5	*Mrs. Turner:*	Samsung
	Sam Park:	Electronics
	Mrs. Turner:	in your case it ((Samuel Jung's sentence)) might be "help me Sam my circuit breakers are going"
	Sam Park:	Electronics
10		((Sam Park, Chul laugh))

At line 2 Samuel explicitly states his desire to be referred to in a different way: "from now on I'm Sam, he's Sam P." Mrs. Turner rejects this, reiterating his established nickname by saying "you're Samsung." The deictics "I" and "you" organize the narrating event as a conversation between Samuel and Mrs. Turner. Samuel positions others—like "he," referring to fellow student Sam Park—

as overhearers, not direct participants. Sam Park nevertheless inserts himself into the conversation, supporting Mrs. Turner's continued use of the nickname "Samsung" by interjecting "Electronics" each time she says "Samsung," thus completing the full name of the corporation.

Mrs. Turner also uses reported speech to suggest that Samuel is connected to Samsung Electronics and should be referred to in these terms. At line 7 she returns to the academic task at hand. She constructs a hypothetical sentence Samuel could use in the class assignment: "help me Sam my circuit breakers are going." The deictics "me" and "my" presuppose Samuel Jung as the speaker of the direct quote. She also makes Sam Park the addressee of this quote. The sample sentence has the format required for the assignment, but the content returns to the presupposition that Samuel is connected to electronics. Sam Park and another student, Chul, treat this as a joke by laughing, thus ratifying Mrs. Turner's refusal to give up the link between Samuel Jung and his nickname Samsung. Thus a configuration of indexicals has emerged—the continued use of "Samsung," the use of "electronics" immediately following these uses, "circuit breakers" and the laughter—and this configuration supports our interpretation that Mrs. Turner and the other students are rejecting Samuel's bid to change his nickname.

As an ethnographer in this classroom, Reyes (2013) had been witnessing the playful use of corporate names as student nicknames for over a month in her fieldwork. But she was troubled by this moment. She wrote in her field notes that day: "Samuel cannot control how he is referred to. Mrs. Turner won't allow it. Granted, she's doing it in a joking manner, but it still seems coercive." Why did Mrs. Turner reject Samuel's request to change his nickname? Why did she insist on referring to her student with the name of a corporation? In what ways does and should the teacher control the forms of address? Reyes had been observing this classroom every week for nearly seven months. One might think, after such extended ethnographic observations, she would have had a clear sense of how the nickname "Samsung" was being used. But these questions could only be answered by adding discourse analysis to her ethnography. It was only after she started doing discourse analysis across speech events, reviewing video recordings of the classroom in which the nickname "Samsung" was used, that she began to understand the social actions being accomplished through these acts of naming.

The following interaction took place on February 9, 2007, the first day that the nickname "Samsung" was used in the classroom and exactly one month prior to the interaction above. Mrs. Turner was handing out papers to students, and she called "Samuel" as the name of the student whose paper she was holding. But Samuel Jung indicated that it is not clear to whom she is referring:

Segment 15: Teacher resists the nickname "Samsung": February 9, 2007, 4:28 pm

Mrs. Turner:	Samuel
Samuel Jung:	me?
Chul	Samsung ((laughs))
Bill:	Samsung
5 *Samuel Jung:*	Samsung- ((smile, waves hands in air))
Mark:	Samsung
Mrs. Turner:	Sam Jung, not Samsung
Samuel Jung:	but I prefer Samsung
Mrs. Turner:	well
10 *Mark:*	Samsung
Samuel Jung:	I used to let people in my school call me that
Bill:	Samsung?
Samuel Jung:	yeah Samsung

On the first day that the nickname "Samsung" was used, it was Samuel himself who accepted and promoted its use. Mrs. Turner resists the nickname at line 7, asserting that his name is "Sam Jung, not Samsung." After Samuel Jung responds "but I prefer Samsung," Mrs. Turner replies not with agreement but with an ambivalent "well." Samuel and his classmates seem to enjoy the nickname and treat it as appropriate, repeating it several times while laughing and smiling. Samuel both implicitly and explicitly gives reasons why "Samsung" is an appropriate nickname. At line 2 he says "me?" after Mrs. Turner calls "Samuel," presupposing that his first name results in confusion because other children in the classroom are also named Samuel. At line 11 he explicitly says "I used to let people in my school call me that," trying to establish the nickname's appropriateness in a school context.

Something clearly happened between the interactions in February and March. In February Samuel insisted on "Samsung" and Mrs. Turner resisted it. In March Samuel resisted "Samsung" and Mrs. Turner insisted on it. Did the nickname mean one thing in February but something else in March? How did the meaning of the name solidify or transform over time? These questions can only be answered by doing discourse analysis across speech events. First, we have to find other interactions along the pathway, other events in which the nickname Samsung appeared. Then we have to analyze both within-event and cross-event patterns, analyzing the social actions accomplished through use of this name and the pathway across which Samuel went from embracing to rejecting it.

Background on the students and the school

In order to understand the emerging meaning of "Samsung" in this classroom, we need some background information that Reyes (2013) gathered in her year-long ethnographic and discourse analytic study at "Apex," an Asian American supplementary school (sometimes called a "cram school") in New York City in 2006–2007. Apex is located in a middle-class Queens neighborhood in which Asian Americans—primarily Korean Americans and Chinese Americans—comprise about a quarter of the population. Across the year, Reyes gathered video recordings of classroom interaction among Korean American fifth graders and European American teachers in an English language arts class that met on Fridays after school, and she did participant observation inside and outside of class with teachers, students, staff and administrators. Students were very sensitive to issues of race, class and gender, which they frequently discussed in classrooms, hallways and elsewhere.

Asian American supplementary schools are private educational institutions that offer additional academic instruction during nonschool hours. These schools are often established by Asian immigrants in urban ethnic enclaves in the U.S., and they primarily serve Asian immigrant communities. Asian American supplementary schools often also act as sites of ethnic community formation and urban immigrant support, in addition to their function of academic enrichment, particularly for parents with concerns about navigating American educational institutions and raising children in the U.S. (Zhou, 2009).

In interviews with administrators and teachers at Apex, as well as at other Asian American supplementary schools throughout New York City, Reyes was told that Asian immigrant parents typically prefer the following school organization: the director is an Asian immigrant like themselves, the teachers are "American" (which usually means native English-speaking European American), and the students are children of Asian immigrants. Immigrant parents reportedly want to have their children taught by those whom they consider most familiar with the American educational system. Apex reflected this preferred organization for the administration, staff and students—with the exception of one native Spanish-speaking teacher and one American-born Korean American teacher out of the dozen teachers employed.

Nicknaming in the class

On January 12, 2007, the spring semester began at Apex. The fifth grade class Reyes had been following since September was assigned to a new classroom and a new teacher. The class had 11 students, three girls and eight boys, all of whom had emmigrated from Korea as children or were born in the U.S. to Korean immigrant parents. The European American teacher, Mrs. Turner, realized that there were two "Sams" in the class—Samuel Jung and Sam Park—and she commented on this while taking attendance. Samuel Jung offered a solution, asking to be called by his initials, "S.J." Mrs. Turner sternly replied, "I don't do nicknames." Having two students with the same first name created problems for Mrs. Turner. During an interview toward the end of the semester she said: "One of the Sams, I don't remember which one. I forget which one. I just don't remember the last names. I get them confused." Despite this difficulty, she did not accept Samuel's suggested nickname. Already on the first day of class, she asserted that only she had authority to establish legitimate naming practices in the classroom.

Despite her claim not to use nicknames, however, Mrs. Turner proceeded to assign several nicknames over subsequent months. In some ways this change ran parallel to a shift in her teaching style and the classroom atmosphere, which gradually changed from strict and conventional to more relaxed and informal. She dubbed one boy "Freckles," because he had many freckles. She called another boy "Billy Goat," apparently because his name was Bill. And she called a third boy "Patricia." His name was Pat, but one day he said he was a girl, in response to Mrs. Turner saying that the girls' essays were better, and at that point she dubbed him "Patricia."

Nicknames for Samuel Jung and Sam Park

Although Samuel Jung offered the nickname "S.J." for himself on January 12, as a solution to the problem of differentiating between the two Sams, Mrs. Turner rejected this. Instead she tried to use "Samuel" for Samuel Jung and "Sam" for Sam Park. As time went on, she used other nicknames as well. On February 9, as we have seen, Samuel embraced the nickname "Samsung," a Korean electronics corporation, and Mrs. Turner started using this nickname shortly thereafter. A few days later, she began using "LG," another Korean electronics corporation, as a nickname for Sam Park. She also occasionally used "Sam's Club," an American corporation, as another nickname for Sam Park. "Samsung" and "LG" are in many ways comparable corporate brands—both large, successful Korean electronics corporations, often associated with advanced levels of knowledge, state of the art technology, sleek design and upscale markets. Sam's Club, by contrast, is an American corporation often associated with bulk products, overconsumption, discount items and bargain hunters.

Although both students could be mischievous, Samuel Jung and Sam Park came to be positioned in different ways across the semester. Samuel Jung was more outspoken, often bragged about his academic achievements, and was repeatedly labeled "smart" and a "genius" by his classmates. Sam Park had a lower profile and—though not timid—he was more deferential to the teacher and no one remarked about his intelligence one way or the other. Although the two boys expressed different views about their nicknames on different occasions, during one interview Samuel Jung had this to say about being called Samsung: "I don't really care. People used to call me Samsung a lot. People used to call me that in school sometimes, so I'm not that unused to it or anything." Reyes asked him if people used the nickname "in a mean way." Samuel replied: "No, in a funny way, fun."

Tracing nicknames in the classroom

The following excerpt contains the first use of "Samsung" in the classroom. This occurred just a few minutes earlier than the excerpt given above, on February 9.

Nearly a month into the semester, Mrs. Turner was handing out copies of the homework assignment. On each sheet of paper an office administrator had written the name of a student. As Mrs. Turner was calling student names, she paused, looked at the paper in her hand, then asked:

Segment 16: First use of the nickname "Samsung": February 9, 2007, 4:04 pm

Mrs. Turner:	Samuel, what is your last name?	
Jeff:	Jung	
Samuel Jung:	J, U, N, G.	
Mrs. Turner:	I asked him	
5 *Samuel Jung:*	J, U, N, G.	
Mrs. Turner:	okay they wrote down Sam Sung	
	((Pat, Chul, Bill laugh; Samuel Jung shrugs then smiles))	
Chul:	ha ha ha Samsung	
Samuel Jung:	yeah, people used to call me that in my old- in my real school	
10 *Chul:*	Samsung	
Samuel Jung:	Samsung	
Bill:	Samsung? uh Samsung, oh it's supposed to be a "j"	
Samuel Jung:	yeah	
Bill:	Sam Jung	
15 *Samuel Jung:*	it's just one letter difference	

At line 6 Mrs. Turner informs the class that the name written on the paper is not "Sam Jung" but "Sam Sung." Several students laugh, enthusiastically repeat "Samsung" and discuss the similarity between Samuel's surname and the corporate name. Samuel Jung then says at line 9 that Samsung was his nickname at his "real school," differentiating his "real" public school from the supplementary school, which is perhaps "pretend" or "unofficial."

The use of the deictics "your," "I" and "him" position participants in the narrating event, with the conversation occurring between Mrs. Turner ("I") and Samuel Jung ("your," "him"). But the terms "they" and "people" suggest that others outside of the classroom are responsible for creating the nickname "Samsung." The nickname has a longer pathway of usage behind it, which might give it more weight than other possibilities suggested by participants in this classroom, like the "S.J." suggested by Samuel Jung.

Figure 3.5 represents the narrating and narrated events in this brief interaction so far. In the narrating event, the teacher, Samuel Jung and other students are interacting. There is not yet evidence that any distinctive social action is occurring, other than routine classroom administrative business and some joking about a potentially humorous nickname. In the narrated event, they are discussing "Samsung" as a variation on Samuel Jung's name and as a potential nickname for him. It is too early to tell whether this nickname will recur or whether it will facilitate more complex social action.

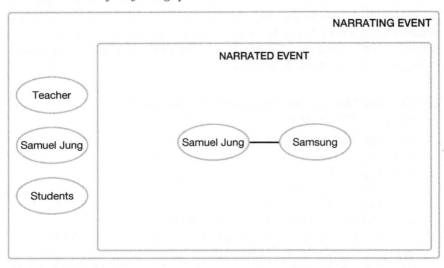

Figure 3.5 "Samsung" as potential nickname for Samuel Jung

About a month later, the nickname LG was first used for Sam Park. In the following excerpt, students are discussing their next essay topic, which is about an "evil twin." Sam Park tells the class that his evil twin is Samsung Electronics, presupposing that "Samsung" is the nickname for the other "Sam" in the class (i.e., Samuel Jung). Then a classmate assigns the nickname LG to Sam Park, a move that is quickly ratified by Mrs. Turner and another classmate.

Segment 17: First use of the nickname "LG": March 16, 2007, 4:22 pm

Sam Park:	my evil twin is um Samsung Electronics
Bill:	why are you pointing to me
	((Jeff, Chul laugh))
Mrs. Turner:	okay he's not-
5 *Mark:*	Samsung's evil twin is LG
Mrs. Turner:	yes LG Electronics
Jeff:	L- LG is Sam ((pointing to Sam Park))

Here the students presuppose the nickname "Samsung" for Samuel, presupposing a pathway of linked events and drawing this locally established nickname from some of those previous events. They contrast Samsung with its business rival LG, and they use this opposition to map out the contrast between Samuel Jung and Sam Park.

Less than an hour later, Sam Park acquires a second nickname: "Sam's Club." In the following excerpt, Mrs. Turner calls on one of the Sams to read. As noted above, Mrs. Turner has sometimes differentiated between the two Sams by calling Samuel Jung "Samuel" and Sam Park "Sam." In this passage she first says "Sam," then after a pause adds "-uel," which causes some confusion.

Segment 18: First use of the nickname "Sam's Club": March 16, 2007, 5:14 pm

Mrs. Turner:	who would like to begin reading? okay Sam. -uel
Sam Park:	okay
Samuel Jung:	((looks up)) huh? Samuel's me
Mrs. Turner:	I don't know, you're Samsung, that's Sam something.
5 *Sam Park:*	Sam
Mrs. Turner:	Sam's Club. Samsung, Sam's Club. go ahead

When her awkward pause between "Sam" and "-uel" causes confusion, Mrs. Turner turns to Samuel Jung's nickname, Samsung. She then seems to feel a need for a parallel construction, but at line 4 she just says "Sam something." Sam Park suggests simply "Sam," but Mrs. Turner makes the construction more parallel by filling in a corporate name. For some reason she chooses "Sam's Club."

These excerpts represent the baptismal events in which the nicknames "LG" and "Sam's Club" were first used for Sam Park. After only these brief mentions on March 16, we cannot yet know whether the nicknames will recur or have more serious implications for social action in the narrating event. But there are some clues already. First, both excerpts show that "Samsung" has become a presupposable nickname for Samuel Jung, established across a pathway of events. Second, even in these few excerpts there have been several potentially salient indexicals. After "Samsung" was first introduced in response to a typographical error that administrators made on the attendance sheet ("Sam Sung" instead of "Sam Jung"), Samuel Jung quickly offered his history with "people" using that nickname at his "real school." "LG" emerged as a "twin" corporate nickname, giving Sam Park a parallel nickname from a corporation with similar scale and prestige. "Sam's Club" emerged in response to a need for differentiation between the two Sams. The poetic parallelism with "Samsung" created a slot that Mrs. Turner filled with "Club" to complete another corporate name. As they move forward in a pathway of linked events it may come to matter that Sam's Club provides relatively inexpensive items to lower-status customers, in contrast with the relatively high status objects made by Samsung and LG. But this presupposition is not yet salient. In none of these three cases does anyone object to the introduction of corporate names as student nicknames. In fact, the nicknames inject some humor into the discussion that both teacher and students seem to appreciate. So far, then, the use of the nicknames seems to create a more casual classroom atmosphere in which teacher and students engage in playful banter.

Figure 3.6 represents the narrating and narrated events, combining the several interactions we have discussed so far. In the narrated event, Mrs. Turner,

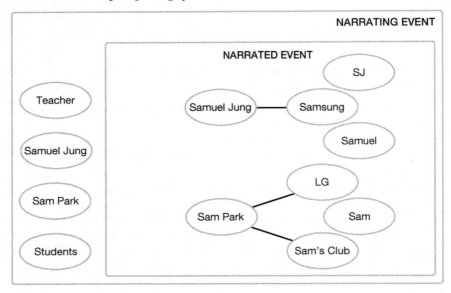

Figure 3.6 Potential nicknames for Samuel Jung and Sam Park

Samuel Jung, Sam Park and other students are discussing the nicknames they
might use for Samuel Jung and Sam Park—both because they need to distinguish
between the two and because the proposed nicknames are amusing. We do not
yet know if these nicknames will be used consistently. There is some evidence
that Samsung is already established, because it has been used for more than
a month. But it remains to be seen whether "LG" or "Sam's Club" will recur.
The other nicknames that have been suggested—"S.J.," "Samuel" and "Sam"
—also remain possible names for the two students, although "S.J." has not
recurred and ends up fading away. In the several narrating events the teacher
and students are discussing these possible nicknames, and they are also joking
with each other.

Table 3.7 describes the various elements of our cross-event analysis so far.
We have discussed four narrated events in which potential nicknames are
suggested for Samuel Jung and Sam Park. Teacher and students have created
a poetic parallelism between Samuel Jung's nickname "Samsung" and Sam
Park's potential nicknames "LG" and "Sam's Club." The phrase "real school"
and various other potentially relevant indexicals have occurred, but none of
these have recurred or become particularly salient. It may be that "Samsung,"
"LG" and "Sam's Club" are emerging as viable nicknames for Samuel Jung
and Sam Park, while others (e.g., S.J., Samuel, and Sam) are not. It may be
that nicknames are one way to establish a casual, more entertaining classroom
atmosphere. From looking only at these four events, we do not yet have enough
evidence to draw firm conclusions about the social actions being accomplished
across this pathway.

Table 3.7 Initial analysis of the nicknames across events

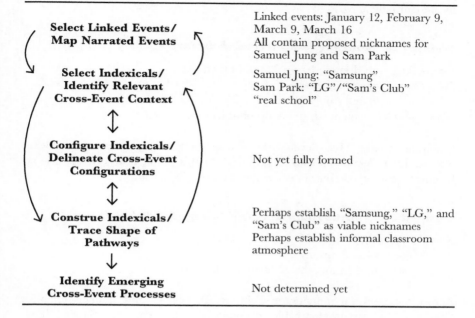

Select Linked Events/ Map Narrated Events	Linked events: January 12, February 9, March 9, March 16 All contain proposed nicknames for Samuel Jung and Sam Park
Select Indexicals/ Identify Relevant Cross-Event Context	Samuel Jung: "Samsung" Sam Park: "LG"/"Sam's Club" "real school"
Configure Indexicals/ Delineate Cross-Event Configurations	Not yet fully formed
Construe Indexicals/ Trace Shape of Pathways	Perhaps establish "Samsung," "LG," and "Sam's Club" as viable nicknames Perhaps establish informal classroom atmosphere
Identify Emerging Cross-Event Processes	Not determined yet

Establishing "Samsung"

Across several events, the nickname "Samsung" changes from being something Mrs. Turner resists—saying "I don't do nicknames"—to something that teacher and students presuppose as a normal term of address. On February 9, a few minutes after the nickname "Samsung" was introduced, we saw in the passage above that Samuel said "I prefer Samsung" and "I used to let people in my school call me that." Although the teacher initially used "Samsung" herself in this passage, she ended up resisting the nickname, saying "Sam Jung, not Samsung." About five minutes later, Mrs. Turner was handing out a different set of papers. She initially called "Samuel" but abruptly stopped and used "Samsung" instead. This was followed by laughter and repetitions of the nickname by students, as well as verbal and physical displays of triumph by Samuel Jung.

Segment 19: Samsung marked: February 9, 2007, 4:33 pm

Mrs. Turner: Samuel- Samsung
Chul: Samsung ((laughs))
Samuel Jung: whoo ((smiles, raises arms sharply into a V-shape))
Bill: Samsung

Two minutes later, Mrs. Turner asks a question to the class and then calls on Samuel Jung. Previously, when she used the nickname "Samsung" she always preceded it with "Samuel." Here she uses only "Samsung," and this is followed by student laughter.

Segment 20: Samsung less marked: February 9, 2007, 4:35 pm

Samuel Jung:	oh, I know I know ((hand raised))
Mrs. Turner:	okay Samsung
	((Chul, Bill, Pat laugh))
Samuel Jung:	a sentence is made up of at least one noun

One minute later, Mrs. Turner asks another question to the class and calls on Samuel Jung. Again she uses "Samsung." At this point, however, there is no laughter, echoing or other responses to the use of Samsung.

Segment 21: Samsung unmarked: February 9, 2007, 4:36 pm

Samuel Jung:	((hand raised))
Mrs. Turner:	okay Samsung
Samuel Jung:	um, I think this is right- I don't know

Across these several minutes on February 9, teacher and students establish "Samsung" as an unremarkable, presupposable nickname for Samuel Jung. Using "Samsung" avoids confusion between the two Samuels, and by the final excerpt it has become unproblematic and no longer causes commentary.

One construal of the social action here would be: in getting the teacher to accept this nickname students are overcoming her initial resistance to nickname use and enjoying a small act of defiance. Using the nickname loosens the formality of the classroom that Mrs. Turner tried to create in the first few weeks of the semester. As the teacher gradually surrenders and comes herself to use "Samsung," she weakens a bit. Table 3.8 represents our analysis at this point. The conversations about nicknames on February 9 and March 16 are linked events in which Samuel Jung is called "Samsung." Within the event on February 9, and across these events on February 9 and March 16 (as well as intervening events recorded by Reyes), a cross-event indexical configuration emerges, more and more robustly establishing "Samsung" as an unremarkable nickname for Samuel Jung. The students take some pleasure in getting their way on this issue, on convincing the teacher to use the nickname and act less formally in the classroom.

Nicknames as tools for targeting students

Let's return to the puzzle we started with. Why did Samuel Jung ask to be called "Samsung" on February 9, and accept the nickname on several other occasions, but then resist it on March 9? Here we reproduce the relevant transcript from March 9, introduced above.

Table 3.8 Cross-event establishment of "Samsung" as an unremarkable nickname

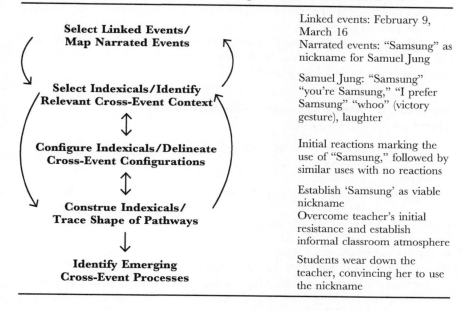

Select Linked Events/ Map Narrated Events	Linked events: February 9, March 16 Narrated events: "Samsung" as nickname for Samuel Jung
Select Indexicals/Identify Relevant Cross-Event Context	Samuel Jung: "Samsung" "you're Samsung," "I prefer Samsung" "whoo" (victory gesture), laughter
Configure Indexicals/Delineate Cross-Event Configurations	Initial reactions marking the use of "Samsung," followed by similar uses with no reactions
Construe Indexicals/ Trace Shape of Pathways	Establish 'Samsung' as viable nickname Overcome teacher's initial resistance and establish informal classroom atmosphere
Identify Emerging Cross-Event Processes	Students wear down the teacher, convincing her to use the nickname

Segment 22: Student resists the nickname "Samsung": March 9, 2007, 4:33 pm

	Mrs. Turner:	yes?
	Samuel Jung:	from now on I'm Sam, he's Sam P. ((referring to Sam Park))
	Mrs. Turner:	you're Samsung.
	Sam Park:	Electronics
5	*Mrs. Turner:*	Samsung
	Sam Park:	Electronics
	Mrs. Turner:	in your case it ((Samuel Jung's sentence)) might be "help me Sam my circuit breakers are going"
	Sam Park:	Electronics
10		((Sam Park, Chul laugh))

At line 2 Samuel explicitly calls for a new naming practice: "from now on I'm Sam, he's Sam P." Mrs. Turner directly refuses, asserting "you're Samsung." Even though the deictics "I" and "you" suggest that this is a conversation between Samuel and Mrs. Turner, Mrs. Turner and Sam Park override Samuel and work as a team to maintain "Samsung Electronics" as Samuel Jung's nickname. In lines 7–8, Mrs. Turner uses reported speech to position Samuel Jung in an unusual way. Her hypothetical sentence for Samuel, "help me Sam my circuit breakers are going," characterizes Samuel as a faulty piece of electrical equipment. It is not yet clear what implications this might have for his position in the narrating event. Sam Park and Mrs. Turner seem just to be joking, with their use of the nickname continuing the more lighthearted tone.

As we move across the trajectory of linked events in which "Samsung" occurs, we find more jokes, with a mildly negative tone. In several interactions following March 9, Samuel Jung was absent but nonetheless became a topic of conversation. In these interactions, "Samsung" is used not to address Samuel Jung directly, but instead to talk about him. In the first excerpt, Mrs. Turner provides an explanation for Samuel Jung's absence.

Segment 23: "Samsung" deals with complaints: March 16, 2007, 4:18 pm

Mrs. Turner:	all right. we're still missing two people, we're missing Samsung and Mi-
Sam Park:	Electronics
Mrs. Turner:	yes and Mike. Samsung probably went to Sony, that's why he's not
5	here today
Mark:	Sony's there to complain

In this interaction, Samuel Jung is "he," separate from "we" (Mrs. Turner and the rest of the class). Sam Park interjects "Electronics," in the familiar way that we have seen before, and then Mrs. Turner and Mark continue the joke by mentioning another large electronics corporation and suggesting that Samsung has to deal with complaints.

About a month later, Samuel Jung was absent again.

Segment 24: "Samsung" went bankrupt: April 20, 2007, 4:22 pm

Jeff:	where's Sam Jung
Mark:	Samsung went out of business
Mrs. Turner:	((laughs)) he went bankrupt

Here Samuel Jung is jokingly referred to less as a student and more as a corporate entity, in this case a bankrupt corporation. This joke is similar to the others, which cast him as a corporation that had to deal with complaints and a faulty piece of electrical equipment. In this last case a student initiates the joke, then Mrs. Turner laughs and contributes. By this point she has clearly accepted the use of nicknames and allows the students to create a more informal tone in the classroom.

About a month later, Samuel Jung was absent again.

Segment 25: "Samsung" went abroad: May 18, 2007, 4:07 pm

Mark:	what happened to Samsung
Min:	yeah he never comes anymore
Mrs. Turner:	he- he is- he went abroad to Hitachi ((laughs))
Chul:	Hitachi
5	((Mrs. Turner laughs))
Chul:	Hitachi yeah

Table 3.9 The cross-event analysis of "Samsung"

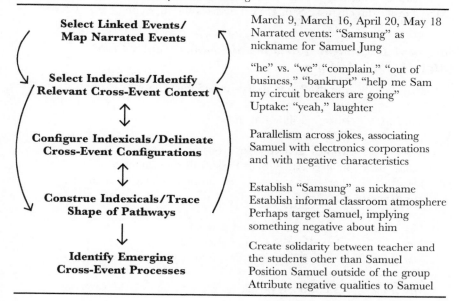

Select Linked Events/ Map Narrated Events	March 9, March 16, April 20, May 18 Narrated events: "Samsung" as nickname for Samuel Jung
Select Indexicals/Identify Relevant Cross-Event Context	"he" vs. "we" "complain," "out of business," "bankrupt" "help me Sam my circuit breakers are going" Uptake: "yeah," laughter
Configure Indexicals/Delineate Cross-Event Configurations	Parallelism across jokes, associating Samuel with electronics corporations and with negative characteristics
Construe Indexicals/Trace Shape of Pathways	Establish "Samsung" as nickname Establish informal classroom atmosphere Perhaps target Samuel, implying something negative about him
Identify Emerging Cross-Event Processes	Create solidarity between teacher and the students other than Samuel Position Samuel outside of the group Attribute negative qualities to Samuel

Here Mrs. Turner accepts Mark's use of the nickname "Samsung," and she makes a familiar joke with the name of yet another Asian electronics corporation. Chul appreciates the joke, ratifying her contribution through repetitions and an affirmative "yeah."

Table 3.9 represents our analysis of the linked events in March, April and May in which the narrated events include references to Samuel Jung as "Samsung." All of the events include jokes, which are parallel with one another, inducing laughter by associating Samuel initially with Samsung Electronics and then with other well-known electronics corporations. They all include mildly negative characterizations. They all position Samuel Jung apart from the teacher and his classmates, as someone talked about and not with. Collectively, these events accomplish several social actions. They establish Samsung as a viable nickname. They establish an informal classroom atmosphere. They also target Samuel Jung, as an electronic or corporate object that has more negative qualities than positive ones. He is portrayed as an entity with faulty circuit breakers that receives complaints and has financial problems—all of which contrasts with the actual Samsung, which is a prosperous corporation creating desirable technology. These negative characterizations of Samuel also contrast with his more common position as an unusually intelligent and industrious student. The teacher and other students establish solidarity at the expense of Samuel Jung, positioning him outside of the group and making veiled criticisms of him.

A similar thing happens to Sam Park on May 18. In the following excerpt, Mrs. Turner directly asks Sam Park if he likes the nickname Sam's Club.

Segment 26: Student resists the nickname "Sam's Club": May 18, 2007, 4:24 pm

Mrs. Turner:	you like being called- um- Sam's Club?
Pat:	no
Sam Park:	I like it a little but then-
	((Min laughs))
5 Jane:	who cares if you like it or not
Samuel Jung:	he likes Amy ((Sam Park's other nickname))
Sam Park:	there's no point- there's no point of saying Sam's Club
Mrs. Turner:	why not
Sam Park:	I don't have a club
10 Mrs. Turner:	there is a store called Sam's Club
Jane:	what about LG, what about LG
Sam Park:	yeah but then it's- it's a poor club then, a poor club
Min:	what?
Mrs. Turner:	it's not poor. people go there to buy wholesale goods

In this passage they explicitly discuss the nickname "Sam's Club" that was first used for Sam Park on March 16 and recurred occasionally throughout the semester. Unlike "Samsung," the nickname "Sam's Club" was not used often. But here and on another occasion in April analyzed in Reyes (2013), Sam Park resists the nickname "Sam's Club" just like Samuel Jung resists "Samsung." Furthermore, in the May 18 discussion the teacher and students used the nickname to exclude, tease and negatively characterize Sam Park just as they had treated Samuel Jung. The teacher and other students united in using a nickname to associate Sam Park with a negative aspect of a corporation—in this case the low-status goods and customers associated with Sam's Club.

If we examined only this brief event, it might seem a stretch to conclude that teacher and students exclude and negatively characterize Sam Park. But if we examine it within the trajectory of events about "Samsung" described above, the parallelism is clear. The cross-event context of the other events about "Samsung" has established a robust pattern in which teachers and students associate a corporate nickname with negative connotations and attach it to a student, both excluding and teasing him. Both Sams are characterized in comparable ways, as corporate entities that have negative qualities. Both Sams become the target of jokes and are positioned outside of the unified group of teacher and other students. Both Sams resist this use of the nickname, but are unsuccessful. The discussion of Sam Park and Sam's Club follows the same pattern as the one established for "Samsung," even though it is less extensive, and the other events along the pathway provide structure that helps establish similar exclusion and teasing even in this brief interaction on May 18.

This example of nicknaming, together with the example of Maurice's emerging identity that we analyzed above, illustrates how to do discourse analysis beyond the speech event on ethnographic data. The analyst must record many events in the settings being studied, across an extended period of time. We cannot tell in advance which events will be linked into pathways that accomplish social actions of analytic interest, although we can predict that perhaps certain individuals or topics might form the basis for relevant pathways. Ethnographic research necessarily takes place over more limited temporal and spatial scales, because of limitations on ethnographers' time. But discourse analysts should gather as much data as possible in relevant settings. Analysis then proceeds by identifying pathways of linked events that together accomplish social actions.

4 Discourse analysis of archival data

Chapter 3 showed how discourse analysis beyond the speech event can be applied to ethnographic data. We presented two ethnographic case studies, each of which involved analysis of several events over time, and we showed how configurations of indexical signs across pathways of events helped establish social action. In this chapter and the next we apply discourse analysis beyond the speech event to two other kinds of data: archival material and new media. Ethnographic, archival and new media data are not mutually exclusive, and many research questions will require analysis of two or all three types. In the example of students crying "racist" described in Chapter 2, in fact, Reyes (2013) supplements her ethnographic study by analyzing both new media data in which crying "racist" circulates as a comedic genre as well as archival material that shows what it has historically meant to cry "racist" in the U.S. at different points. Both examples we describe in this chapter focus on archival material, but they also draw on ethnography and new media data to some extent. We separate the three, as ideal types, because there are some differences in how to apply our approach to the three kinds of data.

In this chapter we apply our approach to archival data, focusing on analyses of discursive artifacts. We describe work by Miyako Inoue (2006) on "Japanese women's language" and Robert Moore (2007, 2011) on "Irish English accent." Each of these studies stands on its own, and we make no claim to reanalyze their data or draw different conclusions than the authors. We use our terminology and diagrams to present their discourse analyses, borrowing their compelling accounts to illustrate how our methodological concepts, tools and techniques can be applied to archival data.

The studies by Inoue and Moore are similar in several ways. They both investigate how ways of speaking become linked to types of people over time— kinds of Japanese women and girls in the case of Inoue, and kinds of Irish people in the case of Moore. They both focus on reported speech, as a key discursive tool for signaling social action. The studies also diverge in two important ways. First, their data come from very different sources. Much of Inoue's data come from print media, such as magazine advertisements, and many incorporate visual images. Moore focuses on three books, one of which emerged from a collaborative blog. Second, Inoue describes more dramatic change, while Moore describes stability and change. Both describe how a set of emblems marks a certain kind of speaker across a century or more—women being marked by a certain style of speech in Japan and Irish speakers being marked by a stigmatized way of using English—and how the presupposed identity of this kind of speaker shifts in more or less dramatic ways over time. We have chosen examples that diverge in these two ways in order to demonstrate how our approach to discourse analysis can be used with a wide range of data sources and contribute to various kinds of archival projects. Any analysis of discursive data from historical materials, drawn from longer temporal and broader spatial scales, can benefit from discourse analysis beyond the speech event.

Example 1: Japanese women's language

Segment 1: Speech from the geisha house

> As to the question of how such private speech used in the geisha house came to permeate the upper-class family and became the common speech of respectable mothers and daughters: there are a number of former geisha among the wives of now powerful people who became influential as meritorious retainers at the time of the Meiji Restoration. Many other women with whom such women (former geisha wives) interact and closely socialize also have the same previous occupational [geisha] background. . . . They use such speech as *ii(n)-dayo* ["It is okay"] or *yoku-(t)teyo* ["That's fine"], even to their children. Then, those children acquire such speech and start using it outside their home. That's how speech such as *atai* ["I"] and *yoku-(t)teyo* ["That's fine"] became common usage today. I think this observation would probably not prove wrong. In support of my theory, it was around the time when the offspring of "the ex-geisha-now-upper-class wives" started going to school that such speech became prevalent.
>
> (Takeuchi, 1907, pp. 24–25)

In this excerpt, Kyuichi Takeuchi, a famous Japanese sculptor, connects categories of persons and categories of speech. In the narrated event, Takeuchi describes "former geisha" and "respectable mothers and daughters." He discusses how geisha "permeate the upper-class family" both physically and linguistically. Physically, geisha took up positions in upper-class homes as "the wives of now powerful people." Linguistically, the "private speech" of geisha became the "common speech" of upper-class women and girls.

Figure 4.1 represents the narrating and narrated events in this excerpt. The narrating event involves Takeuchi writing to people who will read his work. In archival work narrating events are somewhat different than the narrating events described for ethnographic work in the last chapter. The narrating event involves on the one hand the act of writing, with Takeuchi writing to an imagined audience of possible readers and aiming for certain effects on that audience. On the other hand, the narrating event includes many events of reading in which

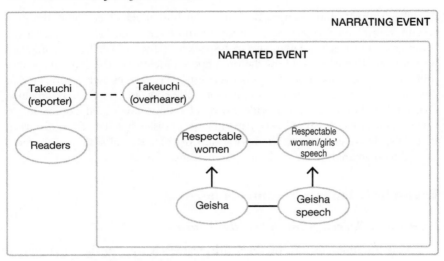

Figure 4.1 Geisha speech

people interpret Takeuchi's writing in various contexts—often privately while reading, but sometimes in conversation with other readers. Narrating events in archival studies are more obviously cross-event phenomena, because they involve linked events of production and reception.

In the figure we present Takeuchi as an overhearer of women and girls in the narrated event, as well as a reporter in the narrating event, because he presumably knows about the narrated events he describes through personal experience. Takeuchi's narrated event describes "geisha" and "respectable women and girls." He claims that these two social categories have distinct styles of speech. We represent this with lines that connect person categories to speech categories. Takeuchi describes a social change: geisha come to populate upper-class society, becoming respectable women themselves, and over time this changes how respectable women and girls speak. The lines with arrows represent this historical change and the supposed influence that geisha had on respectable women and girls.

Note the reported speech that Takeuchi uses to characterize geisha—sentence-final particles *-teyo* and *-dayo*, and the first-person pronoun *atai*. To a speaker of Japanese at the time, these forms indexed a recognizable style of speaking, one linked both to "the geisha house" and to "today's" respectable mothers and daughters. He can take for granted that his intended readers will be able to infer the kinds of people and types of speech events he is describing. He goes on to explain his "theory": women and girls came characteristically to speak this way because geisha married powerful men during the Meiji Restoration (1866–1869) and brought their ways of speaking with them. As these former geisha became

Table 4.1 Initial analysis of Takeuchi's text

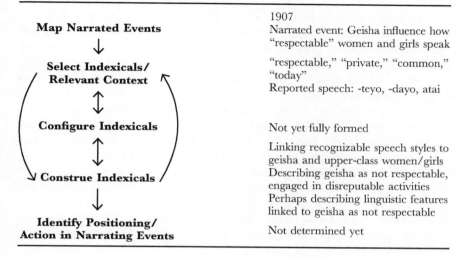

	1907
Map Narrated Events ↓	Narrated event: Geisha influence how "respectable" women and girls speak
Select Indexicals/ Relevant Context	"respectable," "private," "common," "today" Reported speech: -teyo, -dayo, atai
Configure Indexicals	Not yet fully formed
Construe Indexicals	Linking recognizable speech styles to geisha and upper-class women/girls Describing geisha as not respectable, engaged in disreputable activities Perhaps describing linguistic features linked to geisha as not respectable
Identify Positioning/ Action in Narrating Events	Not determined yet

mothers, they transmitted "private" geisha speech to their daughters. When these daughters used it at school, elements of geisha speech became part of a new way of speaking—common "schoolgirl speech." At this point we will merely note two other potentially salient indexicals in the excerpt. Takeuchi's use of the evaluative indexical "respectable" may presuppose that geisha speech is not respectable, and his use of the term "private" to describe geisha's activities may presuppose their potentially disreputable activities with men.

Table 4.1 represents our brief analysis of this single speech event. The narrated event provides an account of geisha speech becoming common among upper-class women and girls. We have described two evaluative indexicals that might establish geisha as disreputable, although we would need more evidence to draw this conclusion authoritatively. We also described Takeuchi's quotation of the linguistic features linked to geisha (e.g., *-teyo*, *-dayo*). No configuration of indexicals has emerged yet to presuppose definite voicing, positioning or social action. Such a configuration of indexicals could emerge across this one text, if Takeuchi had written a more extensive account that established some definitive social action. But with archival data it is often the case that configurations of mutually presupposing indexicals emerge across temporally distant events as broader social processes take hold. An analyst must explore whether descriptions like this one also appeared, before or after this publication, and how readers interpreted those texts. Takeuchi may be positioning himself and others in ways that have implications for important social processes in Japanese history. But this one event by itself does not suffice to draw any conclusions about the social action or these broader processes.

Background

Miyako Inoue (2006) describes how gendered speech types became linked to gendered types of people at the turn of the twentieth century in Japan, and how this discursive work contributed to broader sociohistorical processes. Her work illustrates how discourse analysis beyond the speech event can be productively applied to archival data. "Women's language," according to Inoue, "is a set of linguistic beliefs about forms and functions of language used by and associated with (Japanese) women" (2006, p. 13). In the United States linguistic features that can be associated with certain types of women and girls include tag questions (ending statements with questions, as in "that movie was great, wasn't it?") and uptalk (ending statements with rising intonation, as in "I live in Brooklyn?"). In a similar way, the sentence-final particles -*teyo* and -*dayo* are linguistic features associated with certain kinds of women and girls in Japan. As Inoue argues, these features do not necessarily describe the actual speech of women, but most people believe that they do. Inoue focuses not on women's speech itself, but on speech about women's speech, on how people describe the supposed characteristic speech of women.

Inoue argues that the variety known as "Japanese women's language" has not always had the same social value. Through her analysis of discursive materials from the 1800s to the present, she identifies three main phases in which "Japanese women's language" has been understood in different ways: first, as vulgar "school-girl speech" in the late 1800s, then as urban middle-class "women's language" in the early 1900s, and finally as gentle and refined "women's language" in the late 1900s. Her analysis shows how contemporary discourse on women's language, which bemoans the loss of a beautiful and sophisticated feminine style, forgets that these gendered linguistic forms were initially considered obscene, associated with the "private" activities of geisha.

In this chapter, we present a few pieces of data from the first two phases of "Japanese women's language," enough to show how Inoue applies discourse analysis beyond the speech event to reveal interesting patterns in her data. See Inoue (2006) for the detailed presentation of her argument. Inoue relies on two main sources of archival data to build her arguments about the first two phases. First, she examines commentaries on the speech of schoolgirls that appeared in Japanese print media from the 1880s through the early 1900s. She focuses on how male intellectuals reported the "strange" sounds of schoolgirls that they allegedly overheard. In these materials readers encountered "schoolgirl speech" as reported by male "listening subjects." Second, Inoue examines images of women speaking in women's magazines from the early 1900s through the 1930s. She focuses on how photos and illustrations of urban middle-class women were accompanied by captions that claimed to represent their typical speaking voices. In these materials readers encountered "women's language" as allegedly spoken by women themselves. In this second phase, "schoolgirl speech" gradually becomes understood as "women's language," as gendered linguistic features become associated with a more universal urban middle-class female speaker. Inoue uses discourse analysis beyond the speech event to trace the solidifying pathways across which this historical change occurred.

Inoue emphasizes a distinction between what she calls "quoted speech" and "quoting speech." She uses "quoted speech" to describe speech that is presented as occurring outside of the immediate moment of speaking. For example, in the excerpt above Takeuchi writes: "They use such speech as *ü(n)-dayo*." The use of "they" seems to indicate that "*ü(n)-dayo*" is the speech of "them," the "former geisha" which took place in some other time and place. Male authors in print media used quoted speech to characterize "schoolgirl speech" around the turn of the twentieth century. "Quoting speech" describes speech that is presented as occurring within the moment of speaking. This often occurs when print media juxtaposes an image of a person with a piece of text such that the person is understood as the speaker of that text. To use an example that we will discuss below, the use of the first-person pronoun "I," in "I used to have frizzy hair," suggests that the person pictured next to these words is the speaker of these words. Quoting speech was more typical in the second phase, when "women's language" was animated by images of female bodies in women's magazines.

Phase 1: "Schoolgirl speech" from the 1880s to the early 1900s

The following excerpt appeared in 1888 in a piece called "Vogue speech," by the well-known Japanese writer Koyo Ozaki. It was published in a women's magazine, *Kijo no tomo* [*The lady's friend*]. Inoue identifies this as one of the earliest commentaries on "schoolgirl speech." It thus stands near the beginning of the trajectory of events across which this form of "Japanese women's language" was identified and characterized. All discourse segments in this section were originally written in Japanese. Our transcripts draw on the English translations that appear in Inoue's publications.

Segment 2: Speech from daughters of low-class samurai

> I do not remember when, but for the last eight or nine years, girls in a primary school have been using strange language in their conversation among themselves. . . . In the last five or six years even those girls in the girls' high school have acquired such speech, and it has even reached the society of noblewomen. . . . The strange speech that schoolgirls use today was formerly used by the daughters of the low-class samurai [*gokenin*] in the Aoyama area before the Meiji Restoration. . . . Thoughtful ladies must not let a beautiful jewel become damaged or a polished mirror become clouded by using such language.
>
> (Ozaki, 1994 [1888], pp. 4–5)

In this excerpt Ozaki refers to several types of women and girls. There are "girls in a primary school," "girls in the girls' high school," "noblewomen," "schoolgirls," "daughters of the low-class samurai" and "thoughtful ladies." Some of these "schoolgirls" are using "strange" speech—with "strange" an evaluative indexical that voices these speakers negatively. He uses several temporal cues to suggest that "strange" schoolgirl speech is a recent, emergent phenomenon that is in danger of spreading. He says that "strange" speech was "formerly" used by daughters of the low-class samurai but is "today" used by schoolgirls. "Strange" speech is spreading as girls age—from primary school where it has been used for "the last eight or nine years," to high school where it has been used for "the last five or six years" and now even to the "society of noblewomen." If they use "strange" speech with "low-class" origins, Ozaki claims that girls and women will turn from "a beautiful jewel" to a "damaged" one, and from a "polished mirror" to a "clouded" one. The use of such evaluative indexicals—"strange" to describe speech, and "damaged" and "clouded" to describe what the use of that speech does to women and girls—clearly attributes a negative voice to such speakers and communicates Ozaki's negative evaluation of this linguistic corruption.

Figure 4.2 maps the narrated and narrating events in this excerpt. In the narrating event, Ozaki writes for his readers. As in the excerpt from Takeuchi above, the author imagines an audience and projects an image of the narrating event. Given that his commentary appears in a women's magazine, Ozaki writes as if he is addressing "thoughtful ladies," giving them stern, avuncular advice about their linguistic habits. Because of the mass mediated nature of Ozaki's message, there are many narrating events of reading in which others interpret his writing. We have limited information about these events. In the narrated

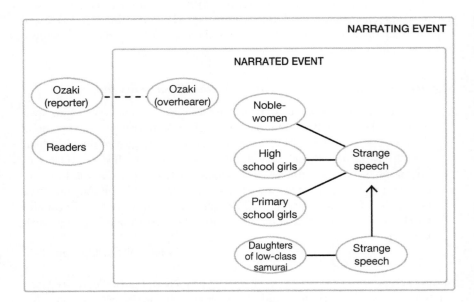

Figure 4.2 Strange speech

event, Ozaki is tacitly an overhearer, acting as if he knows about this form of speech because he has supposedly heard it himself. The narrated event focuses around the daughters of low-class samurai, schoolgirls and noblewomen, all of whom are using "strange" speech. Ozaki gives an account of how this speech emerged historically, migrating from daughters of low-class samurai to schoolgirls and then to noblewomen. He does not explain how schoolgirls began speaking like daughters of low-class samurai.

With the historically earlier excerpt from Ozaki as background, let us return to the excerpt from Takeuchi presented above. It was published in 1907, nearly twenty years after Ozaki's piece. Takeuchi titled his essay "The common language among women in Tokyo" (*Tokyo fujin no tsuuyoogo*). Figure 4.1 and Table 4.1 present our analysis of the narrated events, the salient indexicals and possible construals of these indexicals in Takeuchi's piece. We noted the presupposition that this form of women's speech is not "respectable," because of its association with geisha, and the historical account of how this form of speech came to be used by upper-class women. By considering Ozaki and Takeuchi's pieces as events in the same pathway, we can begin to see a configuration of indexicals emerging across the two events. Both pieces discuss how schoolgirls speak. Both characterize this speech in derogatory ways, as "strange," "private," "low-class," and "damag[ing]." Both describe the historical spread of this speech, with some alarm, as it has moved from low-class origins ("samurai" and "geisha") to upper-class society ("noblewomen" and "respectable women and girls"). Ozaki described "daughters of low-class samurai," while Takeuchi focused on "former geisha" or "ex-geisha-now-upper-class wives," a rich combination of reference (geisha, wives), predication (upper-class) and temporal markers (ex-, now). The parallels between the pieces clearly make it plausible that both appear in a pathway of events that characterize "schoolgirl speech" at a particular moment in Japanese history.

Before pursuing these cross-event linkages further, let us consider one more excerpt, from a 1908 piece titled "The reform of teyo-dawa speech" by Yoshimitsu Yanagihara. "Teyo-dawa" are two sentence-final particles that were considered a central part of this distinctive female way of speaking. By 1908, both "teyo-dawa speech" and "schoolgirl speech" (*jogakusei kotoba*) had emerged as recognizable labels for this type of speech, which was increasingly associated with schoolgirls.

Segment 3: Speech from the pleasure quarters

The recent speech of Tokyo has spread from the pleasure quarters to the upper class and has become habitual. For example, as with *iyada-wa*, *ikenai-wa*, or *nani-nani-shi-teyo*, etc., girls heavily abuse *wa*, *teyo*, and so on. What is even more outrageous is that they use *nasu(t)te* when they mean to say *nasaru-ka* [Are you going to do such-and-such?], and thus they shamelessly mistake the past tense for the future tense (and this is called 'low-class language').

(Yanagihara, 1908, p. 14)

As in the other two events in this pathway that we have reviewed, Yanagihara links ways of speaking to types of people. He uses reported speech to identify several linguistic forms that characterize the way of speaking: *-teyo*, *-wa* and various others. Yanagihara goes into more linguistic detail than Ozaki and Takeuchi, identifying a characteristic "mistake" in verb tense as "low-class language." He associates this way of speaking with an undesirable kind of woman in the "pleasure quarters." Given the context provided by earlier events in the pathway, we can conclude that this probably includes geisha houses. As Ozaki and Takeuchi did, Yanagihara gives a historical account of how this speech style came to be used by schoolgirls. It has "spread" from "the pleasure quarters" to influence the "recent" and "habitual" speech of "girls" in "Tokyo."

Table 4.2 presents our account of this pathway so far, across the three events from 1888 (Ozaki), 1907 (Takeuchi) and 1908 (Yanagihara). We argue that these events form a pathway, despite their historical distance, because they share several features: they all describe "schoolgirl speech," mentioning several of the same linguistic forms as markers of this way of speaking; they all characterize women and girls who speak this way in negative terms; and they all offer similar historical accounts of where this way of speech originated and how it has spread. All three narrated events describe two kinds of women and girls. On one side there are "low-class" women and girls, like geisha and daughters of samurai. On the other side are "upper-class" women and girls, like noblewomen and schoolgirls

Table 4.2 Cross-event analysis of commentaries on "schoolgirl speech"

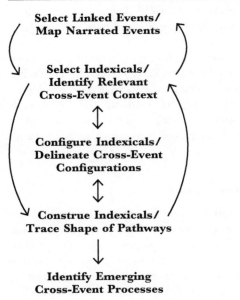

Select Linked Events/ Map Narrated Events	Linked events: 1888, 1907, 1908 Low-class women's speech transforms upper-class women's and girls' speech
Select Indexicals/ Identify Relevant Cross-Event Context	Geisha, pleasure quarters, daughters of samurai, schoolgirls, upper-class respectable, outrageous, strange Reported speech: -teyo, -dayo, atai, dawa
Configure Indexicals/ Delineate Cross-Event Configurations	The indexicals come to presuppose each other, such that the speech is "strange" and the historical change is corrupting
Construe Indexicals/ Trace Shape of Pathways	Denigrating "low-class" women's speech Lamenting and warning against upper-class women's and girls' new form of speaking
Identify Emerging Cross-Event Processes	Identifying schoolgirls as a problem for Japan Expressing Japanese male intellectuals' anxiety about modernity

from "respectable" families. The narrated events describe how the speech of low-class women has corrupted the speech of upper-class women and girls. An emerging cross-event configuration of indexicals voices these two groups of women as disreputable and respectable, as corrupting and in danger of being corrupted.

At the end of the nineteenth and beginning of the twentieth centuries in Japan, "schoolgirl speech" was enregistered—it became a recognizable way of speaking that was associated with identifiable types of people. It was a "strange" language with low-class origins, one that disturbingly began to corrupt "respect-able" women and girls. The three male writers, who position themselves as overhearers in the narrated events and as cultural critics in the narrating events, lament the adoption of supposedly low-class and immoral language by "thought-ful" and "respectable" women and girls. They warn their readers about how women are becoming corrupted by this new way of speaking. Inoue argues that these views of "schoolgirl speech" participate in broader Japanese male anxieties about modernity that developed at the time. Ozaki, Takeuchi, Yanagihara and men like them were anxious about the blurring of social distinctions, as happened, for example, when geisha married upper-class men. They were also anxious about shifting gender roles, as more girls began to attend school. At this historical moment, such men used their commentary about women's language as part of a broader attempt to contain the female subject in the face of social upheaval.

Phase 2: "Women's language" from the early 1900s to the 1930s

The three events described above form part of a pathway across which "schoolgirl speech" was codified as a recognizable way of speaking and associated with the social types of "respectable" women and girls who were supposedly becoming corrupted by disreputable, "low-class" people. Inoue (2006) describes other events along this pathway from the same time period. As we mentioned above, she also shows how this pathway changed direction in some respects as it continued into the twentieth century. In this section we sketch her account, offering a few examples of the next phase in the pathway.

By the early 1900s, Japanese schoolgirls were understood to speak a common language called "schoolgirl speech" or "teyo-dawa speech." Linguistic forms such as *-teyo* and *-dawa* had become established as what Agha (2007) calls "enregistered emblems" of this form of speaking. That is, the use of these forms could index the speaker as a member of the social group described by Ozaki, Takeuchi and Yanagihara—women and girls who had been corrupted by strange, outrageous and vulgar speech that came from lower-class, disreputable origins and had lamentably spread to more respectable females. But in the early 1900s many Japanese began to evaluate this way of speaking differently. Within a decade or two, "schoolgirl speech" came to be understood as "women's language" (*onna no kotoba*). It was no longer a vulgar language associated with schoolgirls, but a way of speaking linked to the middle-class urban woman.

In this section we analyze a few discourse segments from archival data that Inoue presents in her account of the shift from "schoolgirl speech" to "women's language" that occurred between the 1900s and the 1930s. These data come from two women's magazines: *Jogaku sekai* ("Women's learning world," 1901–1925) and *Fujin sekai* ("Lady's world," 1906–1933). Figure 4.3 is an advertisement for Pearl Paste Hair Oil in *Jogaku sekai* which appeared in 1912. The advertisement takes the form of a testimonial. Segment 4 contains the transcript. All bolded portions in the next three excerpts indicate Japanese sentence-final particles written in Romanized script.

Figure 4.3 Advertisement for Pāru Nerikōyu (Pearl Paste Perfumed Hair Oil), by Hirao Sanpei Shōten (Hirao Sanpei Company), *Jogaku sekai*, 1912, 12(15), unpaginated. © Hakubunkan Shinsha Publishers, Ltd.

Segment 4: Pearl Paste Hair Oil

I used to have very frizzy hair, and was really troubled-**desu-no**. I have tried all kinds of remedies and oils and did my best, but could not possibly do my hair in a chignon [*mage*]. So I wondered what to do. Then my husband *told* me that Pearl Paste Hair Oil has a reputation for being good for hair, and that I should try it. So I gave it a try. Good Heavens, before I knew it, I was able to do my hair chignon beautifully like this-**no**. Besides having a really nice fragrance, Pearl Paste Hair Oil makes your hair miraculously beautiful-**desu-noyo**.

This excerpt projects an interaction between a woman and the reader, with the woman talking to the reader about her hair. Deictics such as "I" and "this," as in the phrase "I was able to do my hair chignon beautifully like this," anchor the woman's speech in the imagined present conversation with the reader and tie it to the nearby image of the woman whose hair is arranged in a chignon. The text refers to two types of hair: "frizzy hair" and a "chignon." The woman has had both hair types. Indexicals characterize frizzy hair as undesirable ("troubled") and a chignon as desirable ("beautiful"). The woman's transition from undesirable frizzy hair to a desirable chignon involved failed attempts ("tried all kinds of remedies and oils," "did my best"), until her husband offers a solution. This solution—Pearl Paste Hair Oil—not only facilitates a "miraculously beautiful" chignon, but also has a good "reputation" and a "really nice fragrance." The text contains three linguistic elements that have been linked to "schoolgirl speech": *-desu-no, -no* and *-desu-noyo*. Ozaki, Takeuchi and Yanagihara construed "schoolgirl speech" as vulgar and low class. But here elements of "schoolgirl speech" are used by a woman who seems to be voiced more positively. She wants to fix her "frizzy hair," she is a good consumer who "gave it a try," and she appeals appropriately to authority ("my husband told me," "has a good reputation").

Figure 4.4 represents the narrating and narrated events in this excerpt. In the narrating event, a woman speaks and gives advice to the reader. In the narrated event, she tells a story about her frustrations with her hair, her attempts to fix it and the fulfillment of her desire through a product that was suggested by her husband. We represent the movement from desire to fulfillment with an arrow. Table 4.3 represents our brief discourse analysis of this one event. The narrated event is the woman's story about a desire being fulfilled. Several indexicals, like "troubled," "frizzy hair," "beautiful" and "chignon," voice the characters: the woman is a good wife and consumer struggling to improve herself, her husband is helpful and the product is beneficial. The "schoolgirl speech" forms (*-desu-no, -no, -desu-noyo*) associate the woman with the recognized way of speaking that has been called "schoolgirl speech" up until this historical moment. Given how Ozaki, Takeuchi, Yanagihara and others characterized this way of speaking, it seems puzzling why it would be associated with a diligent wife and consumer like the character in this advertisement. But we cannot draw any firm conclusions from this one event.

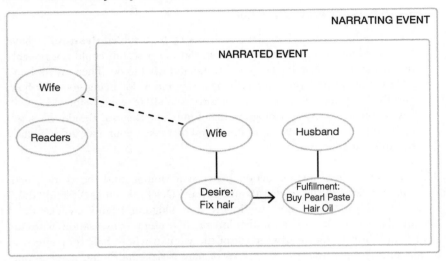

Figure 4.4 Advertisement

Table 4.3 Initial analysis of the 1912 advertisement

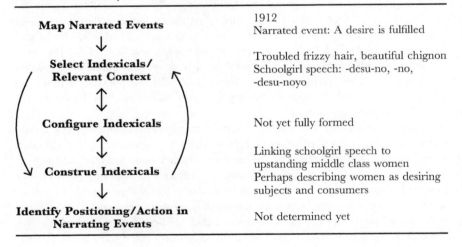

In order to interpret how this way of speaking positions women differently from 1910 onward, we need to examine more events in the trajectory. Figure 4.5 features a *moga* (modern girl) in the periodical *Fujin sekai* in 1931. She is presented as an avid consumer who expresses distinct desires and style in women's language. Segment 5 contains the transcript.

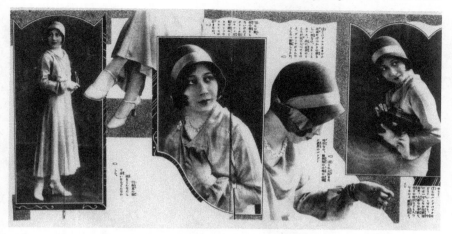

Figure 4.5 Untitled image of a *moga*, *Fujin sekai*, 1931, 26(5), unpaginated. © Jitsugyō no Nihon Sha, Ltd.

Segment 5: Items for a **moga** *(modern girl)*

This is a new-style dress that I just bought yesterday-**nano**. I really like the collar, cuffs, and I particularly like the right shoulder part-**noyo**. The brooch has moved up here-**wa**. This is my favorite watch-**nano**. It has a small, oval-shaped gold frame and a pitch-black band! These shoes are simple, but are made of cream-colored kid leather, and I like their light and smart style-**nano**. How wonderful it would be to walk in the early summer on the street in such a style-**kashira**.

Inoue argues that this advertisement forms part of a pathway with the one just described. Both advertisements involve a woman directly addressing the reader about fulfilling her desires through consumer goods. Both women use features of "schoolgirl speech" as they tell their stories, including *-nano, -noyo, -wa, -kashira*. Both project an interaction with the reader, creating immediacy with deictics like "I," "this" and "here." Instead of a married woman whose husband offers a solution that fulfills her desire, this advertisement features an unmarried woman, a *moga* (modern girl), who does not include anyone but herself in describing the fulfillment of her desires. Though she may not appeal to a male authority, she does appeal to the consumer good as a kind of authority that is able to fulfill her desire. The women in both advertisements are presented as experiencing fulfillment through consumption.

Consider one last example. Figure 4.6 is an advertisement for Victoria Menstrual Garment in *Fujin sekai* in 1925. It features a conversation between two sisters. Segment 6 contains the transcript.

Figure 4.6 Advertisement for Bikutoria Gekkeitai (Victoria Menstrual Garment), by Yamato Gomu Seisakusho (Yamato Rubber Manufacturing Company), *Fujin sekai*, 1925, 20(1): 333. © Jitsugyō no Nihon Sha, Ltd.

Segment 6: Victoria Menstrual Garment

Sonoko: Sister, you kindly *invited* me to the karuta game, but I . . . I can't make it tomorrow-**noyo**.

Older Sister: Oh, how come?

Sonoko: But . . . but, I have been in the moon disease all day-**nano**.

Older Sister: Period? . . . Sono-chan, don't you know about a menstrual garment called Victoria? If you wear it, you will not have to worry at all for hours-**wa**.

Sonoko: Ah, my friends are actually all *using* Victoria-desu-**wa**. Why
             didn't I think about that! Sister, I will go home right away
             and will definitely *visit* you tomorrow-**teyo**.
Older Sister: Oh my, you suddenly look all cheered up-**none**.

This example differs from the previous two in representing a conversation between two fictional characters, not projecting a conversation between the main character and the reader. The reader is instead recruited as an overhearer to this third conversation. The use of "all" in "my friends are actually all *using* Victoria" might invite the reader into the story, as a potential member of this group of Victoria users. As in the previous examples, the women in this advertisement use several emblems of "schoolgirl speech": *-noyo, -nano, -wa, -teyo, -none*. The women are also voiced as desiring subjects—wanting to go to the game, not wanting to worry about her period—and as consumers. As in the first advertisement, these desiring and consuming female subjects appeal to authority—not the explicit authority of men, like the husband in the first example, but of other young women ("sister" and "my friends") as well as the commodity itself.

Table 4.4 represents our analysis of these three events from 1912, 1925 and 1931. Various similarities provide evidence that the events are part of the same pathway. The narrated events from the three advertisements in women's magazines are parallel. Women fix their frizzy hair, feel "wonderful" while walking down the street and enjoy life while menstruating, thanks to consumer goods like Pearl

Table 4.4 Cross-event analysis of the three advertisements

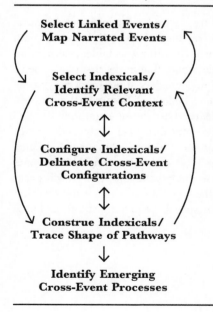

Select Linked Events/ Map Narrated Events	Linked Events: 1912, 1925, 1931 Narrated events: Desires are fulfilled through consumer goods
Select Indexicals/ Identify Relevant Cross-Event Context	Troubled frizzy hair, beautiful chignon, "I like," "want" to go to game I, my, me, you, this, here Schoolgirl speech: -desu-no, -no, -desu-noyo
Configure Indexicals/ Delineate Cross-Event Configurations	Tight linkage established between the linguistic forms associated with women's speech and the respectable, desiring, consuming subject
Construe Indexicals/ Trace Shape of Pathways	Mainstream, respectable women speak women's language Women who speak this way are desiring and consuming subjects
Identify Emerging Cross-Event Processes	Women's language helps constitute a new vision of women as desiring consumers

Paste Hair Oil, contemporary clothing and Victoria Menstrual Garment. All three events project conversations by "real" women, anchored in the here and now through deictics, either directly addressing the reader or inviting the reader to be an overhearer. Women in all three events also use linguistic forms that have been associated with "schoolgirl speech" (e.g., *-teyo, -none, -nano, -noyo, -wa, -kashira, -desu-no, -no, -desu-noyo*).

But the type of woman being associated with this way of speaking has changed from the one characterized by Ozaki, Takeuchi and Yanagihara. Women who speak this way in events from the 1910s, 1920s and 1930s are no longer respectable females who have been corrupted by speech that came from geisha. They are instead respectable middle-class women who appropriately have their desires fulfilled by consumer goods. Across the pathway of events, a configuration of indexicals emerges that associates these forms of speech with this new social type. Within any one event, we could not conclude that the earlier meaning of "schoolgirl speech" had changed. But across events the new presuppositions of these ways of speaking solidify, establishing a more rigid pathway across which a set of Japanese women came to be identified differently. The same set of linguistic forms became evaluated differently, as they presupposed the new social type of the respectable urban middle-class woman who both desires and consumes. By tracing these three (and other similar) speech events in this second phase of the pathway across which the meaning of "Japanese women's language" emerges, Inoue is able to identify a new social voice and show how advertisements recruit women into speaking and acting this way. Inoue argues that, in this second phase, the changing meaning of women's language helped constitute a gendered capitalist subject as allegedly "real" women defined their social positions through relationships with commodities.

By the second decade of the twentieth century, then, "schoolgirl speech" came to be understood as "women's language"—no longer a vulgar language with low-class origins, but a style of speaking associated with respectable, desiring and consuming middle-class urban women. Inoue argues that in the first phase men's denigration of "schoolgirl speech" expressed male anxiety about modernity in the late 1800s, while in the second phase "women's language" became an expression of the modern, consumer self who has learned to desire commodities. She supports these conclusions with careful cross-event discourse analyses that trace how the linguistic forms associated with "Japanese women's language" signaled certain social types and evaluations between 1880 and 1910, then different ones between 1910 and 1940. By doing discourse analysis beyond the speech event on her archival data, she is able to trace these pathways and substantiate her claims about the larger social processes that speech helped constitute in Japan a century ago.

Example 2: Irish English accent

Segment 7: A poor Irish haymaker

> When a poor Irish haymaker, who had but just learned a few phrases of the English language by rote . . . began his speech in a court of justice with these words: "My lord, I am a poor widow" it was sufficient to throw a grave judge and jury into convulsions of laughter.
>
> (Edgeworth, 2006 [1802], p. 22)

This excerpt appears in a book written in 1802 by Maria Edgeworth. The book is filled with reported speech from Irish speakers. In this excerpt, a type of Irish person ("poor Irish haymaker") is associated with a type of misspoken English often referred to as an "Irish bull"—an utterance that contains a humorous error and reveals the speaker's ignorance of English. Here the error occurs when a man reportedly refers to himself as a "widow" instead of a widower.

Figure 4.7 represents the narrating and narrated events in this excerpt. In the narrating event, Edgeworth writes for her readers. As described in the discussion of Inoue above, this kind of mass media both projects a speech event between Edgeworth and imagined readers and is taken up in various subsequent individual events of interpretation on the part of readers. The narrated event describes a "bull," an error in speaking English made by an Irishman, that Edgeworth has overheard. The main characters are "a poor Irish haymaker" and "a grave judge and jury." These characters represent two different social types, with corresponding styles of speech. The ignorant haymaker makes errors in his use of English, and the judge and jury recognize such errors and find them humorous.

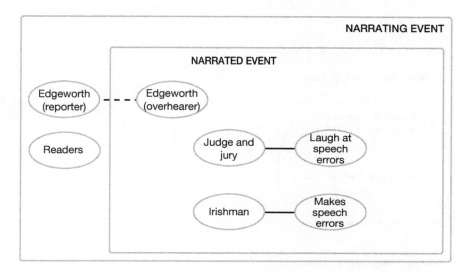

Figure 4.7 Haymaker

The judge and jury are represented above the Irishman because of their social superiority, as presupposed in the narrated event.

This social superiority is established through the author's voicing of the Irish and English characters (we presume that the judge and jury are English, as this characterizes many Irish bulls, although they could be more sophisticated Irish people). The author uses several evaluative indexicals to characterize the Irishman. He is a "haymaker," "poor" and has "just learned a few phrases of the English language by rote." Both the author and the English characters are unsympathetic to the poor Irish haymaker, regarding his manner of speaking as foolish. The author uses direct reported speech to present what the haymaker said—"My lord, I am a poor widow"—helping the reader experience the incongruity of the mistake in the gravity of the legal setting. The Englishmen in the narrated event are "judge and jury." They are "grave," serious men, who nonetheless cannot help but succumb to "convulsions of laughter" at the haymaker's error in English. The juxtaposition of their serious character with the convulsions of laughter creates drama in the situation.

Table 4.5 represents our analysis of this one brief excerpt. The narrated event contains an Irish plaintiff and the English judge and jury. Reported speech and several evaluative indexicals characterize the Irishman as poor and ignorant. Other evaluative indexicals and the metapragmatic expression "convulsions of laughter" characterize the judge and jury as serious people who cannot help but explode into hilarity at the ignorant Irishman's error. But we cannot draw broader conclusions from this one short excerpt. Which category of identity is most important here? Is it class (e.g., "poor"), profession (e.g., "haymaker"), education (e.g., "just learned . . . English") or something else? Is this just a brief joke at one Irishman's expense, or something more systematic? From just this one example, we cannot determine the implications of the brief social act.

Table 4.5 Initial analysis of the Irish bull

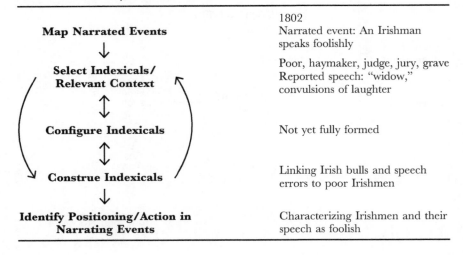

Map Narrated Events	1802 Narrated event: An Irishman speaks foolishly
Select Indexicals/Relevant Context	Poor, haymaker, judge, jury, grave Reported speech: "widow," convulsions of laughter
Configure Indexicals	Not yet fully formed
Construe Indexicals	Linking Irish bulls and speech errors to poor Irishmen
Identify Positioning/Action in Narrating Events	Characterizing Irishmen and their speech as foolish

Background

What does it mean to depict certain types of Irish people as poor speakers of English? Robert Moore (2007, 2011) answers this question by examining textual representations of Irish speech across three centuries. In this section we present data and analyses from Moore's work, as a second illustration of how discourse analysis beyond the speech event can be productively applied to archival data. Moore studies representations of "Irish English accent," exploring represented variation in phonology, morphology, syntax and discourse. He argues that contemporary portrayals of Irish English recycle elements of what he calls a long-standing Irish "accent culture" in which Irish people have been depicted in relatively stable ways—although the evaluations accomplished through these depictions change somewhat over time. Drawing on archival materials from the past several centuries, Moore shows how certain linguistic forms remain emblems of Irish identity and how a recurring type of speech event has often been used to portray "Irish accent."

In the following sections, we sketch Moore's account of Irish accent through excerpts from his analyses of three different texts that were compiled early in each of the past three centuries: *Essay on Irish Bulls* (1802), *English as We Speak It in Ireland* (1910) and *Overheard in Dublin* (2007). Moore shows how these texts create a consistent pattern in reporting Irish accent that relies on the figure of the "overhearer"—a narrated position for the author that is similar to what Inoue described. He focuses on reported speech, showing how authors use this device, along with evaluative indexicals, to characterize Irish voices in the narrated event and juxtapose these voices to the voice of the more sophisticated overhearer. He also shows how, in the narrating event, readers are positioned with respect to Irish people and with respect to the narrator.

In the sections that follow, we sample Moore's analyses of the three texts in chronological order. Unlike Inoue, who describes a historical shift from "school-girl speech" to "women's language," Moore describes how the figuration of Irish English emerged and then remains stable across three centuries. All data excerpts below are formatted following Moore's method of transcription. In order to contrast the framing speech of the reporter and the reported speech of the characters, Moore uses a technique that includes labels and indentations. Along the right-hand side of each example, he uses labels to identify various elements (e.g., "frame," "quote"). He presents framing speech at the left margin and reported speech indented. Spelling and punctuation remain as they appear in the original texts.

Essay on Irish Bulls *(1802)*

Bulls are brief spoken utterances that involve comic contradictions that the speaker does not seem to recognize. The excerpt that opened this section is a bull, with the Irishman describing himself as a "widow" instead of a widower. From the late seventeenth century through the twentieth century, bulls have consistently been associated with Irish speakers of English. Moore argues that Maria Edgeworth's *Essay on Irish Bulls* (2006 [1802]) is the most important contribution to establishing the genre of the Irish bull. The publication of this book was pivotal to the enregisterment of Irish "accent," to establishing the association between certain kinds of Irish people and errors in speaking English. Ironically, the book intended to criticize the stereotype that the Irish are prone to bulls. But, because it presents a collection of Irish bulls collected by Edgeworth, it served as a catalyst for associating this way of speaking with the Irish. Speaking as an overhearer, Edgeworth circulated bulls that established the stereotype she was trying to criticize. Like Japanese male intellectuals' accounts of "schoolgirl speech," Edgeworth's book both described a register and played a role in the creation of that register.

In the following example, a character does not quite understand what an echo is.

Segment 8: Paddy Blake

When Paddy heard an Englishman speaking of the fine echo at   FRAME
the lake of Killarney, which repeats the sound forty times, he
very promptly observed

'Faith that's nothing at all to the echo in my father's   QUOTE
garden, in the county of Galway: if you say to it
    "How do you do, Paddy Blake?"
it will answer,
    "Pretty well, I thank you, Sir"

(Edgeworth, 2006 [1802], p. 6)

In presenting this bull, Edgeworth clearly separates the framing speech and the reported speech. First she sets up the bull, then she quotes the speaker of the bull. This produces two distinct roles for Edgeworth, as an overhearer of the bull in the narrated event and as a reporter of the bull in the narrating event. This bull contains two characters in the narrated event: "Paddy Blake" and "an Englishman." Spatial cues link these characters to areas in Ireland: Paddy's garden is "in the county of Galway" and the Englishman mentions "the lake of Killarney." Upon hearing about a "fine echo" in Killarney from the Englishman, Paddy boasts about one in Galway. The joke is that Paddy apparently believes an "echo" does not repeat sounds ("How do you do"), but replies to them ("Pretty well"). The bull links spatially located characters to identifiable ways of speaking: Paddy from Galway makes speech errors, and an Englishman who visited Killarney does not.

Figure 4.8 represents the narrated and narrating events in this excerpt. In the narrating event Edgeworth projects an interaction with her readers, as someone reporting the speech of Irish people, and the mass distribution of her book made possible various narrating events in which readers interpreted her writing. The

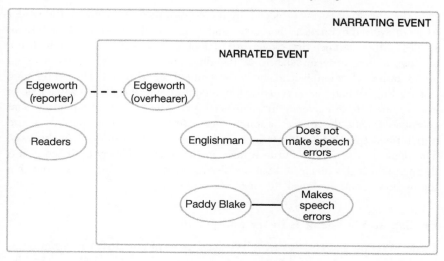

Figure 4.8 Paddy Blake

narrated event tacitly includes Edgeworth, presupposing that she is an overhearer of the bull such that she can report it to the reader, as well as the two characters Paddy Blake and the Englishman. Paddy and the Englishman speak in characteristic ways for people like them: Paddy makes speech errors, and the Englishman does not. We draw a dashed line between Edgeworth the overhearer in the narrated event and Edgeworth the reporter in the narrating event, because this connection establishes the credibility of her report in the narrating event.

We can compare this bull about the echo with the "haymaker's" bull presented above. Figures 4.7 and 4.8 show graphically that both excerpts use the same reporting structure, with two roles for Edgeworth, as an overhearer of bulls who becomes a reporter of bulls. Both excerpts voice two central characters in similar ways. In the first it is a "poor Irish haymaker" contrasted with "a grave judge and jury." In the second it is "Paddy Blake" from "Galway" contrasted with "an Englishman" discussing "Killarney." Each excerpt presents the speech of the Irish character as bad English: "a poor Irish haymaker" saying "widow" instead of widower, and "Paddy Blake" believing an echo gives an "answer" to a question instead of repeating what was said. Both excerpts describe the contrasting figures as serious people who do not make any errors. The first excerpt explicitly marks the humor of the Irishman's error by offering a coda in which the "judge and jury" who hear the bull are thrown "into convulsions of laughter." All these parallelisms begin to establish a cross-event configuration of indexicals. Moore shows how many Irish bulls from Edgeworth's book, and presumably in other circulating images of Irish people from the time, have a similar structure—one that positions Irish people as ignorant and makes fun of them.

In the narrating events projected by these bulls, the author invites the reader to align with the English characters and laugh at the ignorant Irish use of English. Moore argues that Edgeworth's book collected stories about Irish use of English that were circulating at the time and, by publishing them as an authoritative collection, helped codify the genre of the Irish bull. The lampooning of Irish English had been occurring for some time, but this recognizable type of event gained more currency through her book. The process of enregisterment culminated with the book, although there were many other published and unpublished speech events in which Irish people were positioned in this way. The book thus served as a crucial node in the broad pathway of linked events through which this image of Irish people was established. And it turns out that the pathway continued over the next two centuries.

English as We Speak It in Ireland *(1910)*

Patrick Weston Joyce's *English as We Speak It in Ireland* (1910) is regarded as "the beginning of modern scholarship on this variety" (Hickey, 2005, p. 18). Like Edgeworth's book on Irish bulls, Moore argues that Joyce's book was another pivotal moment in the establishment of stereotypes about Irish people's use of English. Moore describes the book as both a descriptive grammar of Irish English and a harsh critique of Irish English speakers. The author presents it as a scholarly, scientific text on Irish English, but in fact the book makes claims both about how the Irish do speak and about how they should speak. Like Edgeworth's book, Joyce collects many anecdotes of Irish English speech. Edgeworth and Joyce also use a similar reporting structure. Like Edgeworth, Joyce "overhears" Irish utterances and reports them to his readers.

Unlike Edgeworth's bulls, which focused on the misunderstanding of words and expressions, Joyce foregrounds pronunciation. In the following excerpts from Joyce's book, certain vowel sounds are presented as emblems of Irish accent. In this first excerpt, Joyce tells a story that centers on the pronunciation of the word "tea" as "tay."

Segment 9: A young gentleman

Many years ago I was traveling on the long car from Macroom   FRAME
to Killarney. On the other side—at my back—sat a young
gentleman—'a superior person', as anyone could gather from
his *dandified* speech. The car stopped where he was to get off:
a tall fine-looking old gentleman was waiting for him, and
nothing could exceed the dignity and kindness with which he
received him. Pointing to his car he said

    'Come now and they'll get you a nice refreshing   QUOTE
    cup of *tay*'.
    'Yes',

says the dandy,   FRAME

'I shall be very glad to have a cup of *tee*'   QUOTE

—laying a particular stress on *tee*.   FRAME

I confess I felt a shrinking of shame for our humanity.   CODA
Now which of these two was the vulgarian?

(Joyce, 1910, pp. 91–92; italics as in original)

Joyce uses a similar reporting structure as Edgeworth, with framing speech, reported speech and a coda. Also like Edgeworth, Joyce positions himself both as an overhearer of an instance of Irish English and as a reporter of it. He clearly locates himself as a participant in the narrated event, describing his own direct experience ("I was traveling," "at my back") and reactions ("I confess I felt"). The narrated event focuses on two characters, a "young gentleman" and an "old gentleman." The story takes place on a trip from Macroom to Killarney with the young gentleman exiting at an unspecified location, perhaps in a rural area between the two points. Several evaluative indexicals voice the young gentleman: "a superior person," "dandified speech" and "dandy." The old gentleman is characterized as "tall," "fine-looking" and exhibiting "dignity" and "kindness." Joyce emphasizes that the old gentleman says "tay," whereas the young gentleman stresses the pronunciation "tee." The story thus links spatially located characters to identifiable ways of speaking: the young gentleman, a traveler who has acquired dandified speech—like saying "tee" for tea—and an old gentleman, a dignified rural old-timer who says "tay" for tea.

Figure 4.9 represents the narrated and narrating events in this excerpt. In the narrated event are Joyce, the overhearer of the interaction, and the two main characters. Because Joyce presents himself as an overhearer in the narrated event,

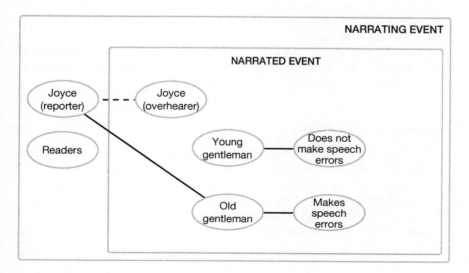

Figure 4.9 Young gentleman

he can be a reliable reporter in the narrating event. The young and old gentlemen are characterized through their speech in ways that run parallel to the voicing communicated in Edgeworth's Irish bulls described above: the old gentleman makes a speech error, using nonstandard pronunciation for "tea," while the young gentleman does not. By comparing the voicing represented in Figures 4.7 and 4.8, from Edgeworth, with the voicing represented in Figure 4.9, we can see the similarities that persisted across the intervening century. As we analyze further examples from Joyce below, we will see this pattern reinforced.

There is one significant difference, however. In the narrating events of her Irish bulls, Edgeworth aligned herself with the English who laughed at Irish speech errors. But Joyce aligns himself differently in this excerpt. Note how "a superior person" is presented in quotes, framing it as the words of various others who can recognize the social significance of the young gentleman's dandified speech. This might reinforce the voicing of the young gentleman as genuinely superior, by making the judgment broader than just Joyce's opinion. But it might also place the social category of "a superior person" into question, potentially undermining the value of the judgment. This latter possibility seems to take hold as the excerpt develops. Joyce emphasizes the old gentleman's "dignity" and "kindness," then he has the young gentleman rudely emphasize the appropriate pronunciation of "tee," obviously pointing out the old gentleman's speech error. And Joyce himself feels shame at the young gentleman's behavior, suggesting that the younger man may be more of a "vulgarian." He presents the young gentleman as an affected snob and seems to side with the old gentleman. Joyce does presuppose that nonstandard pronunciation is vulgar—the old gentleman's use of "tay" for "tea" is an error. But he directly addresses the reader, suggesting that elitist arrogance may be even more vulgar. We represent this partial alignment with the old gentleman by using a solid line from Joyce in the narrating event. The alignment is not complete, as Joyce himself would never say "tay," but he criticizes the young gentleman and shows some sympathy for the rural Irishman making the speech error.

In the next excerpt, Joyce tells a story about a schoolboy who imitates another's regional Irish accent and is punished for it. The emblem of the low-status accent is pronouncing the word "fine" as "foine."

Segment 10: Mick Hogan

In Tipperary the vowel *i* [ay] is generally sounded *oi*.   FRAME
Mick Hogan a Tipperary boy—he was a man indeed—was
a pupil in Mr. Condon's school in Mitchelstown, with the
full rich typical accent. One morning as he walked in, a fellow
pupil, Tom Burke—a big fellow too—with face down on desk
over a book, said, without lifting his head—to make fun of him—

'*foine* day, Mick'.   QUOTE
'Yes',

said Mick as he walked past, at the same time laying his hand   FRAME
on Tom's poll and punching his nose down hard against the desk.

Tom let Mick alone after that 'foine day'   CODA
(Joyce, 1910, p. 102; italics as in original)

In this excerpt Joyce uses the same structure as in earlier excerpts. He presents framing speech, reported speech and a coda, and he positions himself both as an overhearer of an event of nonstandard Irish speech and as a reporter of that event. Unlike the previous excerpt, Joyce himself did not overhear this interaction, but instead overheard a story about the interaction. This resembles the excerpts from Edgeworth, who also overheard the telling of bulls rather than the actual bulls themselves.

The excerpt begins more like a linguistic treatise, explicitly linking a phonological variant ("oi" for "ay") to a regional area (Tipperary). The story involves two characters: Mick Hogan and Tom Burke. These characters are explicitly linked to regions of Ireland, with Mick from Tipperary and Tom from Mitchelstown. Mick has "the full rich typical accent" of Tipperary, presumably including the phonological variation of substituting "oi" for "ay." This story has the same voicing contrast in the narrated event as the previous excerpts from both Edgeworth and Joyce. The story links spatially located characters to identifiable ways of speaking, with Mick from Tipperary using the nonstandard pronunciation "foine" and Tom from Mitchelstown presumably using the standard "fine." Tom greets Mick with "foine day" in an explicit attempt to "make fun of him." Mick responds to Tom with a "yes," but then responds to the insult by assaulting him physically.

As in the prior excerpt, Joyce positions himself differently in the narrating event than Edgeworth did. The final line, "Tom let Mick alone after that 'foine day'," distances Joyce from both characters. Unlike Edgeworth, he does not align himself with the character that speaks proper English. He presents Mick's violence against Tom as justified, given the insult. But Joyce also includes the nonstandard pronunciation in this final line, making clear that people like Mick do talk this way and presupposing that Joyce himself would never do so. So Joyce is not simply ridiculing Irish people like Mick who speak English in nonstandard ways. In fact, he opposes himself to those who ridicule such Irish people. But he is not aligning himself with Irish people who make speech errors either, as his examples foreground and even make fun of their speech.

Table 4.6 represents our cross-event analysis of these four events from Edgeworth and Joyce. In the narrated events, the authors portray two contrasting types. On one side there are Irish males who make errors when speaking English (haymaker, Paddy Blake, old gentleman, Mick). On the other side are those who do not make such errors (judge and jury, Englishman, young gentleman, Tom). Indexical cues seem to voice the error-prone Irish people as lower-class people tied to a backward region (e.g., "poor," "haymaker," "Galway," "on the long car from Macroom to Killarney," "Tipperary"). The parallelism across these characters and voices from the four events helps establish that they are part of

Table 4.6 Cross-event analysis of representations of Irish speech

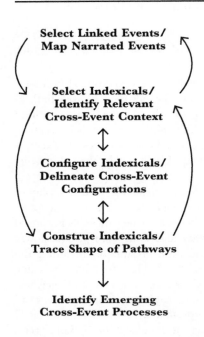

Select Linked Events/ Map Narrated Events	Four events from 1802 and 1910 Narrated events: Certain Irish speakers of English make speech errors and are criticized by Englishmen or other proper speakers
Select Indexicals/ Identify Relevant Cross-Event Context	Poor, haymaker, judge, jury, grave Englishman, gentleman, Tipperary Reported speech: "widow," laughter, "[echo] will answer," "tay," "foine"
Configure Indexicals/ Delineate Cross-Event Configurations	Systematic 2-part organization: Irish speakers make errors, contrasted with English who note errors
Construe Indexicals/ Trace Shape of Pathways	Low-class Irish speakers of English are ignorant, poor, rural, humorous 1802 reporter joins in laughing at Irish, but 1910 reporter criticizes the critics also
Identify Emerging Cross-Event Processes	Apparent shift from presenting Irish speakers of English as ignorant and laughable to presenting some Irish speakers as making funny mistakes but also sympathetic

a pathway. The events are also linked through a recurring stance for the writer, as both overhearer of an event and reporter of that event.

In all four cases the authors report instances of Irish speech errors. In doing so, they either explicitly or tacitly join the critics in making fun of the errors. Even Joyce, who shows some sympathy for the Irish who make mistakes, nonetheless displays instances of the errors and thus points out the mistakes. By displaying them, he inevitably invites a speaker of Standard English to laugh at the mistake. But despite the similarities across the events from 1802 and 1910, Joyce makes two important changes. First, in the narrated events he voices those who notice or point out Irish mistakes as bullies. They are vulgar and deserve retribution. Second, in the narrating event he positions himself against these bullies, evaluating their criticisms as inappropriate. We can see further transformation across this pathway of events by moving forward another century to contemporary reports of how certain Irish characters speak.

Overheard in Dublin *(2005 to the present)*

In summer 2007, the book *Overheard in Dublin* (Kelly and Kelly, 2007) reached first place on the Irish paperback nonfiction bestseller list. The books by Edgeworth and Joyce were also "nonfiction" and were also filled with overheard anecdotes about Irish speakers of English. But Kelly and Kelly's book used a different method for collecting stories—asking website visitors to report what they overheard. The website, established in 2005, is a collaborative blog with the same name as the book (www.overheardindublin.com). The website asks visitors: "Overhear anything funny, interesting, unusual in Dublin?? Tell us what you've heard!" Anyone can post a story by supplying a title, message, location and name. The 2007 book collects anecdotes that were posted on the website. As of this writing, the website is still active. A Twitter account linked to the website was established in 2011 (@OverheardDublin), and this appears to average about a dozen posts per day. We will explore the affordances of new media technologies like this in more detail in the next chapter.

Below we present two examples from *Overheard in Dublin* that Moore analyzes. The first one is from the website and the second one is from the book. In the first, "Anonymous" describes an interaction she or he overheard on the bus ride to "college":

Segment 11: A skanger youngwan

Awful sore it is!	TITLE
On the 78A to college the other morning a skanger youngwan gets on at James's with a crutch and bandaged knee. She sits beside me at the back and her mate sits up the front, turns around and says	FRAME
'jayziz jacintehhhh dat looks terrible sore!'	QUOTE
Jacintehhhh goes	FRAME
'yer i' is. . . . Like bleedin artrootis or sumtin'.	QUOTE
Awful affliction that artrootis. . . .	CODA
Overheard by Anonymous, 78A to ballyer Posted on Monday, 26th November 2007.	PROVENANCE

In this excerpt "Anonymous" reports "Irish accent" in a way that has many parallels with Edgeworth and Joyce. The report uses framing speech, reported speech and a coda. It includes the familiar double roles, with Anonymous first as an overhearer of the event and then as the reporter of that event. In compliance with the submission guidelines on the website, the report also includes an explicit title ("Awful sore it is!"), as well as a closing summary of the reporter's name, location and date posted.

In the narrated event, Anonymous describes a "skanger" (a derogatory term for lower-class Dubliners) "youngwan" (woman) and her "mate" and links them to a location, "James's" (an area of lower-class housing in the inner city). These evaluative indexicals voice the two characters as lower-class Dubliners. Anonymous positions him or herself as part of a different group, as a "college" student. One of the lower-class women sits in (perhaps) uncomfortable physical proximity to Anonymous ("She sits beside me"). Anonymous uses reported speech to convey the type of pronunciation overheard: "jayziz" for "Jesus," "jacintehhhh" for "Jacintha," "dat" for "that," "artrootis" for "arthritis." As in Joyce, the non-standard pronunciation of the vowel in "tea" as "tay" is also found here in the pronunciation of the vowel in "Jesus" as "jayziz." In addition, "th" becomes "t" or "d," and "ay" becomes "oo." These are all phonological variations that index lower-class Irish ways of pronouncing English.

As in the earlier excerpt Joyce reported about Tom and Mick, Anonymous also incorporates a quote from a character into his or her own utterances, in both the frame ("Jacintehhhh goes") and the coda ("Awful affliction that artrootis. . . ."). The speech that was just quoted and attributed to the characters ("Jacintehhhh" and "artrootis") is blended into the narrating voice. Anonymous clearly uses these quotations to ridicule the "skanger youngwan" and her "mate." The exaggerated pronunciation of "Jacintehhhh" is almost surely unsympathetic, and the sarcasm of "awful affliction" together with the exaggerated pronunciation of "artrootis" is clearly mocking the speaker. In the coda, the narrator directly addresses readers and invites them to align with her or him in laughing at the mistakes of the lower-class Irish speakers of English.

Figure 4.10 represents the narrating and narrated events. In the narrating event Anonymous writes for readers of the blog. The post both projects an interaction that involves alignment with the reader in laughing at the speech errors and makes possible subsequent acts of reading. The narrated event includes Anonymous, the overhearer of the interaction, and two characters, the "skanger

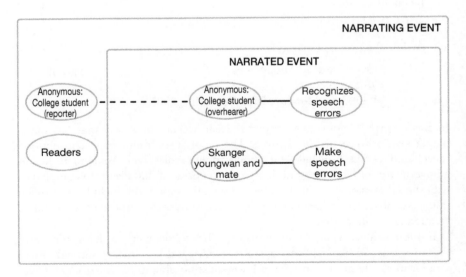

Figure 4.10 Skanger youngwan

youngwan" and her "mate." The "skanger youngwan" and "mate" are depicted as speaking very differently than Anonymous. Through reported speech that includes many nonstandard spellings to evoke the nonstandard pronunciation, Anonymous portrays their speech errors (along with their ignorance about medical conditions). Note the similarity between this discursive interaction and those described by Edgeworth (Figures 4.7 and 4.8) and Joyce (Figure 4.9). In all cases we have respectable speakers who notice speech errors by lower-class Irish people.

This case differs from the excerpts selected by Edgeworth and Joyce, however, in depicting only one type of narrated character other than the author. There is no "judge and jury" for a "haymaker," no "Englishman" for a "Paddy," no "young gentleman" for an "old gentleman," and no "Tom" for a "Mick." In this case the overhearer of this story becomes the contrastive figure. Anonymous, a "college" student, positions him or herself against the "skanger youngwan" and her "mate." As we have said, the narrating event in this case also returns to the simpler type of social action found in Edgeworth's examples: Anonymous simply laughs at the lower-class Irish speakers of English, without any sympathy for them or reservations about their critics.

Our last example is taken from the *Overheard in Dublin* (2007) book. Like Edgeworth, it reports a bull.

Segment 12: Two elderly ladies

Overheard two elderly ladies on the no. 2 bus discussing the   FRAME
drug problem in Dublin:

Mary:

'Jaysus, Josie, aren't them drugs terrible?'   QUOTE

Josie: FRAME

'Mary, if it wasn't for the Valium. I'd be on drugs meself'   QUOTE
(Kelly and Kelly, 2007, p. 22)

Here another anonymous reporter describes an interaction overheard on a Dublin bus. As with all the other excerpts, this report includes framing speech and reported speech, and it positions the author as both overhearer and reporter. Anonymous depicts "two elderly ladies," Mary and Josie. The instances of non-standard pronunciation ("Jaysus" and "meself") voice them as lower-class Irish speakers of a low-status variety of English. The pronunciation of the vowel in "Jesus" as "Jaysus" echoes not only the previous excerpt (which included "jayziz") but also Joyce's story in which "tea" was pronounced as "tay." This story also contains an Irish bull, because Josie does not recognize that Valium is a drug. This echoes events reported by Edgeworth in which lower-class Irish speakers make similar humorous mistakes. As in the previous excerpt about the skanger, the narrated event does not contain a separate character, beyond the overhearer,

Table 4.7 The final cross-event analysis of Irish accent

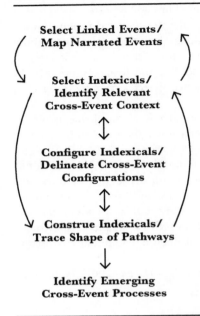

Select Linked Events/ Map Narrated Events	Six linked events from 1802, 1910, 2007 Narrated events: Certain Irish speakers of English speak incorrectly, and more respectable speakers notice these errors
Select Indexicals/ Identify Relevant Cross-Event Context	Haymaker, judge, Englishman, gentleman, Tipperary, skanger, elderly, anonymous Reported speech: "widow," laughter, "[echo] will answer," "tay," "foine," "Jaysis," "drug"
Configure Indexicals/ Delineate Cross-Event Configurations	Systematic 2-part organization: lower-class Irish speakers make errors, respectable speakers notice them Overhearer becomes reporter
Construe Indexicals/ Trace Shape of Pathways	Lower-class Irish accent is nonstandard, humorous, sometimes even repulsive Certain Irish speakers of English are ignorant, poor, uneducated, humorous
Identify Emerging Cross-Event Processes	Reporters display and laugh at Irish speakers Portrayals of "Irish accent" help identify internal others—initially Irish contrasted to English, then social class differences among Irish

who contrasts with the lower-class Irish characters. Anonymous fills the role of presumably respectable speaker, enlisting the reader to join him or her in laughing at the error-filled Irish speech.

Table 4.7 represents our cross-event analysis of "Irish accent" across the examples from the nineteenth, twentieth and twenty-first centuries. The narrated events all portray Irish people making errors while speaking English, contrasting those who speak with an "Irish accent" and those who recognize it. The contrasting figures are sometimes characters in the stories, as in the story of Paddy and the Englishman, and sometimes the overhearers themselves, as in the case of the skanger and the Anonymous reporter. The authors report these narrated events using a consistent structure, organized into framing speech and reported speech, with a narrator who reports an event she or he has overheard. These parallelisms provide strong evidence that the events participate in a common pathway despite their historical distance from one another.

Because many other events participate in this pathway and have similar structure, any given event need not be elaborated in order to be understood as a lampooning of lower-class Irish speech. These events and others like them provide cross-event context for each other, allowing hearers to recognize the structure and interpret the voicing, positioning and social action even in short instances that might themselves contain very limited information. All narrators recognize "Irish accent" when they hear it, and they construe it as nonstandard, ignorant, humorous and perhaps even repulsive. The authors invite readers to align with them in making fun of these speakers. Moore argues that the broad pathway of many such events, over the past three centuries, has established an Irish "accent culture." This way of portraying Irish speech encourages Irish people themselves to view their own language use in terms created by English colonialism, from an overhearer's perspective, creating distinctions among "accented" others within their own community.

Conclusion

The cases from Miyako Inoue and Robert Moore illustrate how our approach to discourse analysis beyond the speech event can be productively applied to projects that analyze archival data. In the first case on Japanese women's language from Inoue, we showed how our cross-event approach can illuminate the historical shift that Inoue describes—as depictions of women's language changed from vulgar "schoolgirl speech" in the late 1800s to consumerist "women's language" in the early 1900s. In the second case on Irish English accent from Moore, we showed how our cross-event approach could help document the emergence and solidification of a register across three texts from 1802, 1910 and 2007.

In some ways our approach to discourse analysis beyond the speech event has been the same in Chapters 3 and 4, applied to ethnographic and archival data. In both cases we start with the distinction between narrated and narrating events, then identify indexical cues that help establish relevant context and voice narrated characters both within and across events. In both cases we engage in an iterative interpretive process, locating potentially salient indexicals and the context they make relevant, then inferring the voicing, positioning and social action that these indexicals might be signaling, then considering other potentially salient indexicals given the new construal of social action, and so on—until a configuration of mutually presupposing indexical signs emerges and helps solidify one reading of an event or a pathway. In both cases we are then able to support inferences about the social action occurring and to trace the shape of relevant pathways.

Discourse analysis beyond the speech event done on ethnographic and archival data is also similar in relying on cross-event context. Events provide crucial context for other events, because the interpretation of one event would often not be possible without the larger configuration provided by the emerging pathway. Any one of the conversations about Maurice or nicknames, or about Japanese women's speech or Irish English, might in itself not be robust enough to sustain an interpretation about the social action and broader social processes occurring. Discourse analysis beyond the speech event allows an analyst to draw on emerging configurations from across a pathway of linked events, so that we can pick up patterns that would not be visible if we focused on discrete or typical events. Very often the phenomena we are interested in as social scientists only take shape across such pathways, and we need to do cross-event analysis in order to study them.

But discourse analyses of ethnographic and archival data also differ in some key ways. In ethnographic studies, the participants in one narrating event are often the same as those in subsequent events. In archival studies, because of the historical scale, participants more often change from one event to another. Archival studies are less local, identifying patterns with broader scope. Another way to say this is that ethnographic studies more often focus on pathways with individual events linked together, with relatively few linked events at any one point in the pathway. Archival studies, especially those focusing on mass media, involve streams or broad pathways with many concurrent and branching linked events. Often there are crucial nodes in such broad pathways, with links cascading outward from these, but archival studies generally cover a larger set of linked events. This means that archival studies require a sampling method more urgently than ethnographic ones. All discourse analysis beyond the speech event requires the analyst to identify those events that become part of relevant pathways, from a larger set of potentially relevant events. But those working with archival data have a larger set of potentially relevant events to choose from. The next chapter shows how the same challenge often arises in discourse analyses of new media data.

5 Discourse analysis of new media data

The last two chapters have shown the utility of discourse analysis beyond the speech event for ethnographic and archival research, and they have illustrated how to apply our methodological approach to different kinds of data. Ethnographic research typically collects and analyzes discourse data from living research participants over shorter timescales and more limited spatial scales. Archival research typically collects and analyzes discourse data from historical artifacts that cover broader temporal and spatial scales. Our approach allows discourse analysts to document pathways of linked events and the social actions accomplished across events for either kind of data, although some details of the approach differ in the two types of cases.

In this chapter we show how to apply our approach to a third and final kind of data, from "new media." New media technologies include various social media, from more traditional forms like email and blogs to newer forms like Facebook, Twitter and Instagram, with new platforms being developed constantly. These sites of communication have been made possible by the Internet and more recently transformed by the affordances of mobile devices. New media communication is usually densely networked, often with many recipients receiving messages and with linkages to other posts through forwarding and quoting. Websites or applications serve as hubs that connect virtual communities and networks. New media communication happens closer to real-time than traditional mediated communication, with responses expected more quickly and topics changing rapidly. People use new media to share information via text, image and video, and messages are often multimodal.

As with ethnographic and archival data, studies of "new media" represent an ideal type. Archival data is often incorporated into ethnographic research, and vice versa. Similarly, studies of new media often involve ethnographic and/or archival components. The logs of past communications that serve as the data source for new media studies are like archives in many ways, making new media studies an important type of archival work in the Internet era. New media studies can nonetheless also include archives of traditional media, together with data from Internet-mediated communication. And some studies include all three data types, if the research questions demand it and available data allow it. We have seen in the previous chapter how Robert Moore's work on Irish English accent combines analyses of archival data from nineteenth- and twentieth-century books with analyses of new media posts from a twenty-first-century website. With this hybrid data set Moore was able to show how the stereotyping of Irish speakers persists not only across historical time but also across types of media.

In this chapter we show how our approach to discourse analysis beyond the speech event can help document pathways across events of new media communication. We apply our model to studies of new media by Elaine Chun (2013) and Betsy Rymes (2014). We first consider Chun's study of a YouTube video and comments posted in response to it. She traces pathways of Internet commentary, showing how links across posts establish social action. Her work illustrates how the significance of communication is often not located in the original event itself (in this case, the video), but instead is shaped by how that event is taken up in subsequent linked events (in this case, the comments). Rymes traces the recontextualization of stock storyline elements in music videos, following them across events as others remix them. Even though the same formula is repeated across events of video storytelling, Rymes shows that the elements are recombined in ways that accomplish different kinds of positioning and social action.

Example 1: Internet commentary

Segment 1: "Act black" and two responses

"I subconsciously act black around black people and it's because I try really hard to fit in. Like for rizzles."—Kevin Wu

"How does one act black Kevin? What would you think if i said i try to act Chinese around Chinese people, whatever that means?"—MissAsaju

"I don't know if you were joking about tending to act black around black people, but I can't stop laughin cause that is so true for me."—lilfoot113

The first quote in the above segment comes from a YouTube video uploaded by Kevin Wu, a Chinese American. The second two quotes are two comments (among thousands) that were posted on the YouTube website in response to his video. In the first quote Wu describes a generic type of narrated event: he "subconsciously act[s] black around black people." This narrated event contains two types of characters: Kevin Wu and "black people." Wu describes his narrated self as unaware of his behavior in the actual moment of performance, and he offers a psychological explanation for this "subconscious" behavior ("try[ing] really hard to fit in").

By making this comment in the narrating event (the video itself), however, Wu positions himself as aware both of his tendency to act black and of the underlying reason for this behavior. This might create some tension between the narrated and narrating Kevin Wu. Is it the case that he used to be unaware of this tendency but now recognizes it? Or is he sometimes aware but at other times unaware? Neither of these explanations seems appropriate, given what he says next. "For rizzles" is a phrase often associated with African American rap artist Snoop Dogg and with a widely understood "black gangster style" that has been both widely emulated and parodied. Given that Wu is describing himself as someone who "acts black" sometimes, and that "for rizzles" is something stereotypically associated with "black people," Wu's use of the expression "for rizzles" seems to enact the same behavior he is describing. "For rizzles" seems to be reported speech that presupposes two distinct types of speakers: Wu reporting something that "black people" say, and Wu reporting the type of speech he himself performs when he is around "black people." Maybe Wu is being ironic, enacting what he is describing in order to make a joke. The video itself does not definitively establish the positioning and social action being performed, however. For that, we need to examine how the video was taken up in subsequent events.

The two comments by MissAsaju and lilfoot113 are clearly linked to Kevin's video—by virtue of where they are posted on the site, through repetition of the phrase "act black" and in MissAsaju's case by her use of Kevin's name. It turns out that Kevin's video and these comments set off a struggle about the appropriate way to discuss race in contemporary America. These three and other writers discuss how one should present racialized social categories and position oneself with respect to them. Wu, a Chinese American, presents "black people" as a bounded group and himself as someone whose desire to fit in leads him to "act black." MissAsaju questions the assumption that a racial or ethnic category like "black" or "Chinese" really involves some bounded set of characteristic behaviors. In doing so she distances herself from Wu and suggests that he perpetuates false ideas about race. Lilfoot113, on the other hand, seems to accept Wu's assumption and aligns herself with Wu as someone who also "acts black."

Background

Elaine Chun analyzes this and other new media communications in her study of how contemporary Americans use such media to produce, perform and contest the nature and boundaries of racialized groups like "black people" and "Chinese." In this section we draw on Chun's work to illustrate how discourse analysis beyond the speech event can be productively applied to new media data. Chun (2013) analyzes the YouTube video just introduced, which was posted by the popular Chinese American YouTube star Kevin Wu (YouTube username: KevJumba). In her analysis of the video, together with the YouTube comments posted in response to it, Chun focuses on verbal and nonverbal signs in Wu's performance that index "blackness" for those familiar with contemporary American popular culture. In her analysis of the comments, she traces how viewers collaborate with and contest each other as they interpret Wu's performance. Chun explores the broader racial ideologies indexed by Wu's performance, showing how they become resources as interpretations of the performance emerge through the linked commentaries made by Wu's transnational viewership.

The video is titled *I'm Not Cool*, which Wu opens by giving a rationale for making the video: it responds to people who are always telling him that he tries to act cool. He admits that he often tries to act cool, but says that he has decided to use the opposite approach and reveal his lack of coolness. The three-minute video presents "10 Reasons Why I'm Not Cool," shifting between shots where Wu is directly addressing the camera and scenes of him interacting with others. Wu uploaded the video to YouTube in August 2011. It received over five million views between August 2011 and March 2012. Chun's analysis is based on the 41,860 comments that were posted in response to Wu's video during that time period.

Chun argues that Wu self-consciously undermines his own performance of masculinity, producing what she calls "ironic masculine cool"—an ambivalent stance that simultaneously embodies and critiques hypermasculinity. "Ironic masculinity may sometimes destabilize a coherent sense of masculinity by giving voice to oppositional perspectives . . . whereas at other times maintain a hegemonic masculinity because of the potential for performers to safely voice heterosexist and sexist positions" (2013, p. 594). Chun shows how Wu's ironic masculinity marks his performance *as* a performance, rather than as an authentic presentation of self. This produces a tension between his apparently earnest desire for traditional, physical, dominant masculinity and his self-deprecating mockery of that desire. As one important part of her analysis, Chun explores how Wu's ironic masculine cool often draws on stereotypes of black masculinity, producing what she calls "ironic blackness."

Chun traces the interpretations and recontextualizations of Wu's performance as viewers wrote comments in the six months after he posted the video. Commenters pointed out and evaluated various features of the performance itself. Some subsequent commenters also commented on comments or presupposed aspects of previous comments as they commented on the video. Chun shows how Wu's performance invites others to voice Wu as a narrated character and to evaluate that voice. She traces links across a pathway of events, as comments coalesce into pathways that have stable voicing and evaluation of the types of people described and enacted in Wu's video.

In her analysis Chun identifies three types of evaluation that commenters offer: "direct quotations," "metalinguistic evaluation" and "love declarations." We will consider examples of the first two types. As part of her analysis of direct quotations, Chun explores how Wu's utterance "not in my house" is quoted by YouTube commenters, and how comments linked by this quotation presuppose stereotypes and evaluate Wu. As part of her analysis of metalinguistic evaluation, Chun considers how Wu's claim that he "acts black" is evaluated by YouTube commenters, and how evaluations of this claim across linked comments come to voice Wu and position commenters in the narrating events.

Direct quotations

At one point in the video Wu says "not in my house." Many YouTube commenters directly quoted this phrase. In the video segment in which this phrase appears, Wu is explaining that his "super competitive" nature is one of the reasons why he is "annoying" and "not cool." He then turns to Jeremy Lin, a Chinese American professional basketball player—who is physically there in the shot, interacting with Wu—and challenges him to throw a crumpled piece of paper into a wastebasket as if he were taking a shot in basketball. Lin "shoots" the paper, but Wu swats it away as if he is blocking or "rejecting" a basketball shot. Wu then stands up, aggressively approaches Lin, loudly states "I told you" and "not in my house," while lifting up his shirt and displaying his bare chest to Lin. He then jerks his head back to flip his hair off of his face. Below is a transcript of this segment. In the right column are Chun's notes on how a recurring vowel sound (the one in "my") is pronounced as the diphthong [ai] (sounds like "eye") or monophthong [a:] (sounds like "ah").

Segment 2: Super-competitive

1	*WU:*	My friends find me annoying? ((to Wu's audience))	Diphthong [ai] in *My*
2		cause I'm <u>super</u> competitive	Diphthong [ai] in *I'm*
3		<u>all</u> the time	Diphthong [ai] in *time*
4		even when it's unnecessary.	
5		Hey Jeremy Lin. ((to Lin, relaxing on Wu's bed and ironing))	
6		I bet you can't make this piece of <u>paper</u>	Diphthong [ai] in *I*
7		into this <u>trash</u> can right here.	
8	*LIN:*	<u>Al</u>right.	Diphthong [ai] in *alright*
9		((calmly tosses the paper ball from the bed))	
10	*WU:*	TOLD YOU. ((aggressively bats ball away with one hand))	
11		I TOLD YOU. ((stands up, thrusts hands in front of body))	Monophthong [a:] in *I*
12		NOT IN MY HOUSE BABY ((lifts shirt, fanning motion))	Monophthong [a:] in *my* Falsetto *house*
13		NO:T IN MY: HOU:SE. ((lifts shirt, fanning motion))	Monophthong [a:] in *my*
14		((flips bangs back, sits down))	
15		Anyways ((to Wu's audience))	
16		those are the ten reasons	
17		Why	
18		I'm <u>not</u> cool.	Diphthong [ai] in *I*

Figure 5.1 represents the narrated and narrating events in this segment. In the narrating event, Kevin Wu makes a presentation for his viewing audience. As with archival data, this communication does not allow for real-time interaction. Wu projects a type of interaction with the audience, imagining that they think

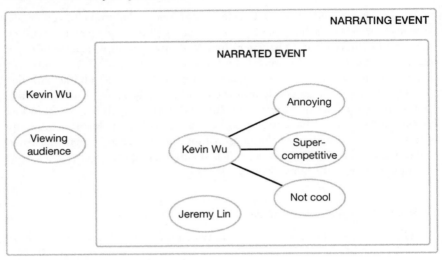

Figure 5.1 Super-competitive

he is trying to be cool, for example. As we will discuss below, the comments posted about the video create asynchronous narrating events across different pathways that unfold over the next several months. In the narrated event, Kevin Wu describes himself as "annoying," "super competitive" and "not cool." Jeremy Lin is in everyday life very cool, as a professional basketball player. But in this segment Wu acts superior to Lin, rejecting his shot. Lin is also ironing a piece of clothing, on a small ironing board placed on his lap, which is not commonly understood as a masculine activity. To mark this hierarchy, we place Wu above Lin in the narrated event.

Wu pronounces the vowel in "my," "I," "right" and "time" as the diphthong [ai] (sounding like the vowel in "eye") in lines 1–8 and 18. But in the segment from lines 10–14, where Wu is aggressively blocking Lin's shot, when he says "I told you" and "not in my house" he pronounces the vowel sound in "I" and "my" as "ah" (monophthong [a:]). Chun explains that diphthong [ai] is typically seen as mainstream American English pronunciation, while monophthong [a:] is associated with African American and Southern speech. Chun argues that other indexical cues in the speech event link the nonstandard pronunciation "ah" with African American speech. For example, the monophthongal vowels occur when boasting and playing basketball, two activities that are stereotypically associated with African American men and not with Southerners (Kochman, 1981). Wu's use of falsetto voice in "house" and the term "baby" are other cues that Chun cites in her argument that Wu is performing stereotypical "blackness" in the segment from lines 10–14.

Table 5.1 represents our within-event analysis of this event. Various indexicals link Wu with African American men, including the pronunciation "ah." Wu also

Table 5.1 Initial analysis of the "not in my house" event

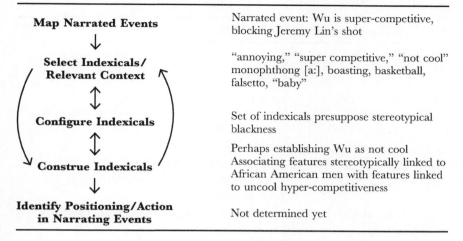

Map Narrated Events ↓	Narrated event: Wu is super-competitive, blocking Jeremy Lin's shot
Select Indexicals/ Relevant Context	"annoying," "super competitive," "not cool" monophthong [aː], boasting, basketball, falsetto, "baby"
Configure Indexicals	Set of indexicals presuppose stereotypical blackness
Construe Indexicals	Perhaps establishing Wu as not cool Associating features stereotypically linked to African American men with features linked to uncool hyper-competitiveness
Identify Positioning/Action in Narrating Events	Not determined yet

explicitly characterizes his narrated self as not cool, because he is "annoying" and "super competitive." He enacts these "not cool" qualities in the skit with Lin, inviting him to shoot, then swatting away his shot and gloating about his prowess. This might suggest that stereotypical African American men are super competitive and that his enactment of this stereotype is not cool, although we need more evidence to draw firm conclusions. Chun suggests that Wu is giving a performance of "ironic blackness," pretending to act like a stereotypical black male while assuming that everyone knows he is not. But this one event by itself does not make clear why Wu is doing this or what type of social action Wu is performing in the narrating event. We need to investigate how this segment is taken up in subsequent events as viewers post comments about it.

Chun systematically investigates how commenters take up various aspects of Wu's video. After offering a preliminary analysis of the segment with Jeremy Lin, she explores how commenters take up this part of the video and solidify certain interpretations of it across a pathway of events. To trace these pathways, Chun identified all of the comments in which viewers directly quoted "in my house." Table 5.2 displays the first 11 of the 319 total instances. Chun formats this table in three columns: the first column displays the comment number (e.g., "117" means the one hundred and seventeenth comment posted on YouTube in response to Wu's video); the second column gives the screen name of the commenter; and the third column presents the comment itself.

Each of these comments directly quotes Wu's utterance "not in my house" from the video, and this links them to one another as well as to the video segment in which the quote originally appeared. Several comments also include other instances of reported speech ("I told you," "baby") as well as reported action ("hair flip"). The repetition of these quotes links the comments and the

Table 5.2 First 11 comments that directly quote "not in my house" (adapted from Chun, 2013)

Item	Commenter	Comment
117	Fearlessthebestday	Told you! I told you! Not in my house baby not in my house! *Justin Bieber flip* Hahaha! xD
626	CourtneyPalma	not in my house baby not in my house <3 i love you kevin <3 i grew up watching your videos <3
862	duyzzigkeit789	not in my house!
1047	ilovmc	Not in my house baby!
1049	purplemandy817	NOT IN MAH HOUSE, BABY! *HAIR FLIP*
1176	littleninjaboi	lmfao. I TOLD YOU! I TOLD YOU! NOT IN MAH HOUSE!
1247	SaharHijazi	Mr. Simple ? .."not in my house" "you could've broken my neck" LMAO
1484	indiadude8	NOT IN MY HOUSE BABY, NOT IN MY HOUSE. *hair flip*
1557	shoyunkaku	TOLD YA, NOT IN MY HOUSE BABY, NAH!
1646	felisfeng	TOLD YOU! I TOLD YOU! NOT IN MY HOUSE BABY! NOT IN MY HOUSE! LMFAO
1791	ThePuppylovers1	not in my house baby! LOL

video together, creating a pathway of events that make this particular segment of the video seem worthy of metapragmatic commentary. In addition to the reported speech and action, most of the comments contain positive evaluations of Wu's action. Some include explicit statements such as "I love you kevin" (comment 626) and emoticons such as "<3" (a sideways heart in comment 626). Several comments also include laughter and abbreviations that indicate laughter: "Hahaha!" (comment 117); the acronym "LOL" ("laugh out loud" in comment 1791) and its variants (e.g., "LMAO," "LMFAO" ["laugh my (fucking) ass off" in comments 1176, 1247, 1646]); and the emoticon "XD" (a sideways laughing face in comment 117). These various indexical signs support a construal of Wu's video or at least the "in my house" segment as something that commenters find funny and perhaps endearing.

Table 5.3 represents our cross-event analysis of this pathway of events, from Wu's utterance of the phrase "not in my house" to the eleventh comment that directly quotes it. Across these comments the phrase "not in my house" becomes the central element in the narrated events, the object of metapragmatic commentary about Wu's video and his personality. The commenters react positively to Wu's utterance. Across the pathway of events, cross-event context emerges and helps establish the social action occurring. Indexicals across these 12 events

Table 5.3 Cross-event analysis of "not in my house"

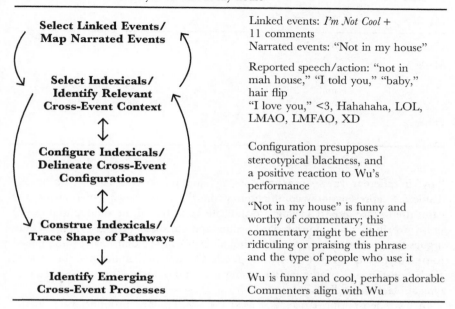

Select Linked Events/ Map Narrated Events	Linked events: *I'm Not Cool* + 11 comments Narrated events: "Not in my house"
Select Indexicals/ Identify Relevant Cross-Event Context	Reported speech/action: "not in mah house," "I told you," "baby," hair flip "I love you," <3, Hahahaha, LOL, LMAO, LMFAO, XD
Configure Indexicals/ Delineate Cross-Event Configurations	Configuration presupposes stereotypical blackness, and a positive reaction to Wu's performance
Construe Indexicals/ Trace Shape of Pathways	"Not in my house" is funny and worthy of commentary; this commentary might be either ridiculing or praising this phrase and the type of people who use it
Identify Emerging Cross-Event Processes	Wu is funny and cool, perhaps adorable Commenters align with Wu

begin to mutually presuppose one another, and the resulting configuration of indexicals establishes that Wu is funny and aligns the commenters with Wu.

Wu claims at the opening of his video that he is "not cool," but commenters' reactions to his performance in fact position him as cool and funny. This may be part of the ironic point—he claims to be not cool as a way of establishing himself as cool, and that's funny. In doing so, he draws on stereotypes of black masculinity. It is still not entirely clear how Wu and his commenters are positioning themselves with respect to this stereotypical identity. Chun describes Wu's stance as "ironic blackness." In some respects he acts according to the stereotype, inviting Jeremy Lin to shoot and then aggressively swatting it away, followed by a triumphant display. Wu acts not cool in this way, but commenters react to him as if he is acting cool while doing it. The humor comes from the irony, the fact that he is mocking and not genuinely inhabiting this aggressive, triumphant persona. But we do not yet have enough evidence to determine Wu and the commenters' evaluations of stereotypical black masculinity. Are they making fun of it? Are they enjoying enacting it? Are they simultaneously enacting and criticizing it? And how does the appearance of a Chinese American professional basketball player—an unexpected ethnic identity for this profession—who is ironing clothes, of all things, contribute to Wu's positioning and social action?

In exploring these questions, Chun argues that the nonstandard pronunciation "ah" is an important index of stereotypical blackness. She reviews all 319 comments that quoted "in my house" and analyzes how commenters spelled the word

Table 5.4 Comments with marked and unmarked orthographic representations of "my"

Orthography		Total
Unmarked	my	246
Marked	ma	38
	mah	32
	mah!	1
	mahh	1
Other	mi	1
		319

"my" in different ways—sometimes as "my" and other times as "ma" or "mah." Table 5.4 represents how commenters wrote the word. Seventy-two of the 319 cases used nonstandard spellings to indicate Wu's use of the monophthong [aː] in this word. By using nonstandard orthography to spell "my" as "ma(h)," Chun argues that commenters index the phonological variant that has become linked to stereotypically African American speech. Commenters notice and foreground Wu's nonstandard pronunciation, using it to index his performance of stereotypical black masculinity.

In his video performance, Wu used the nonstandard pronunciation "mah" when (ironically) enacting the stereotype of black masculinity in the brief scene where he blocks Jeremy Lin's shot. Many people who posted YouTube comments on the video indexed this pronunciation by using nonstandard spelling. The first person at the beginning of the pathway noted the contrast between standard and nonstandard pronunciation and used nonstandard spelling to mark it. Subsequent posts in the pathway may have been influenced by and certainly followed along with this phonological contrast. The distinction between stereotypical African American and standard English became salient, as more and more events in the pathway marked it with the nonstandard spelling. On a website like YouTube that is available worldwide, this sort of salient social distinction can spread across transnational space. Those who commented on Wu's "not in my house," for example, reported that they come from many nations. Table 5.5 shows the distribution of orthographic representation by country. Commenters who used "ma(h)" came from the United States, Canada, the United Kingdom, the Philippines, New Zealand, Israel, Netherlands, Norway, United Arab Emirates, Denmark, Ireland, Portugal, Bulgaria, Finland, Thailand, Bolivia, Spain, Turkey and Zimbabwe. The racialized contrast from Wu's performance became salient across a transnational pathway of events.

Metalinguistic evaluation

In order to analyze more extensively how Wu and his commenters position themselves with respect to stereotypical black masculinity, Chun turns to another part of the video in which Wu claims that he "acts black." She analyzes how

Table 5.5 Standard and nonstandard spelling by country

Country	my	ma	mah	mahh	mah!
United States	125	15	17	1	
N/A	22	6	5		1
Canada	15	2	2		
United Kingdom	11	3	1		
Philippines	7		1		
Australia, Germany	5				
New Zealand	3	2			
France, Hong Kong, Sweden	4				
Israel, Netherlands, Norway	3	1			
United Arab Emirates	2	2			
Denmark	2	1			
Ireland	2		1		
Portugal	1		2		
Brazil, Indonesia, Jamaica, Malaysian, Poland, Singapore	2				
Bulgaria	1		1		
Finland	1	1			
Thailand	1	1			
Austria, Bahrain, Belgium, Cambodia, Guam, Luxembourg, South Africa, Switzerland, Trinidad and Tobago, Vietnam	1				
Bolivia, Zimbabwe			1		
Spain, Turkey		1			
	246	**38**	**32**	**1**	**1**

commenters use explicit metalinguistic evaluations as they respond to this claim. In the video segment below, which we also presented earlier, Wu explains that his "acting black around black people" is another reason why he is not cool.

Segment 3: "Acting black"

1 Also
2 I: subconsciously?
3 act <u>black</u>.
4 around
5 black people.
6 and it's because I try
7 <u>real</u>ly hard to fit in.
8 Like
9 for (.)
10 rizzles.

Figure 5.2 represents the narrated and narrating events in this segment. In the narrating event, Kevin Wu projects an interaction with his viewing audience in which he acts "not cool" by performing stereotypical blackness in an attempt to be cool, and in which he simultaneously jokes about this in order to entertain

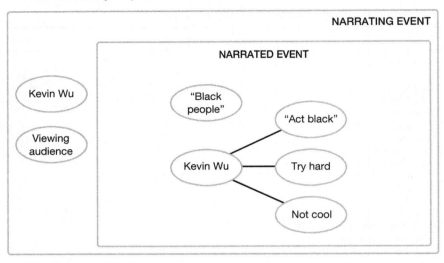

Figure 5.2 "Acting black"

the audience. The narrated event contains two characters, Kevin Wu and "black people." Wu describes his narrated self as "acting black" and "trying hard," which provide another reason why he is not cool.

Chun delineates a set of indexical cues that juxtapose Wu's apparently earnest desire and blatant incompetence to perform "blackness." His claims that "I subconsciously act black" and "I try really hard" explicitly describe Wu as "acting" and "trying" to "act black," presupposing that he does not do it well. Other cues, such as the pause after "for" at line 9 and the discourse marker "like" at line 8, suggest hesitation in using the "-izzles" morpheme, a sign widely associated in mainstream popular culture with a "black gangster style." Chun also describes how Wu's use of postvocalic /r/ in "for" (line 9) when coupled with "rizzles" (line 10) may underscore his incompetence at performing this utterance linked to "blackness." This configuration of indexical signs establishes a lack of alignment or amateur character in Wu's performance of "blackness."

Table 5.6 represents Chun's analysis of this event. The narrated event involves Wu "acting black." We have described the various indexicals Chun identifies that establish Wu as not cool. He describes himself as "acting black" and "trying hard," then enacts these qualities by saying "for rizzles" with hesitation and uncertainty. The juxtaposition of signs of insecurity and signs of "blackness" is "not cool," because Wu is a poor imitator, a wannabe cool person who is motivated by insecurities to try to "act black" and then does so awkwardly. So what is Wu implying about "acting black" itself? Is "acting black" cool, for people who are able to do it naturally? On the surface, this seems to be the implication. Wu is making fun of himself for failing to behave in a desirable way. In order to see whether this is in fact the case, we need to examine how this event is taken up by commenters.

Table 5.6 Initial analysis of the "acting black" event

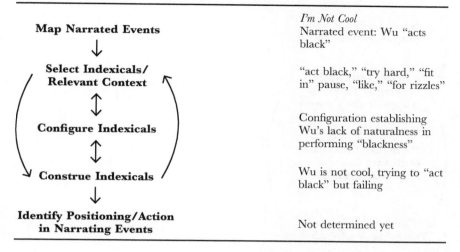

	I'm Not Cool
Map Narrated Events	Narrated event: Wu "acts black"
Select Indexicals/ Relevant Context	"act black," "try hard," "fit in" pause, "like," "for rizzles"
Configure Indexicals	Configuration establishing Wu's lack of naturalness in performing "blackness"
Construe Indexicals	Wu is not cool, trying to "act black" but failing
Identify Positioning/Action in Narrating Events	Not determined yet

Chun traces how commenters use metalinguistic evaluations as they respond to Wu's claim that he "acts black." These comments build a pathway across which Wu is positioned and evaluated. Chun identifies 163 metapragmatic evaluations that comment on Wu's claim that he "acts black." Five of these comments are represented in Table 5.7.

In the first three comments, the authors write "what is acting black" and "how does one act black," questioning Wu's assumption that "acting black" exists as a monolithic phenomenon. The last two comments dispute his assumption that "forizzle" is something that "black people" actually say. The comments treat Wu's performance of "acting black" as reflecting his own incorrect understanding of what it means to be "black." Black people, they suggest, do not all act the same, and he should not assume that they do. Apart from a single "lol," there are no indexical signs to suggest that these commenters evaluate Wu's notion of "acting black" as funny in the way that the comments reviewed above construed "not in my house" as funny. Instead, acronyms like "WTF" ("what the fuck")

Table 5.7 Five comments from the 15 that criticized Wu's racial essentialism (adapted from Chun, 2013)

Item	Commenter	Comment
14827	daniscrazy	What is acting black and how does one act black?
14852	MissAsaju	How does one act black Kevin? What would you think if i said i try to act Chinese around Chinese people, whatever that means?
27782	mindsight1	WTF is acting black? GTFO
28819	09wedabest	Kev I'm black . . . and I don't say forizzle lol
36800	kesha12523	HEY FIRST OF ALL BLACK PEOPLE DONT SAY FRIZZLES WTF DOES THAT MEAN ANYWAY!

Table 5.8 Analysis of the initial pathway of events about "acting black"

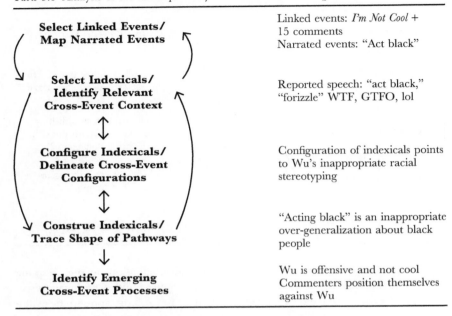

Select Linked Events/ Map Narrated Events	Linked events: *I'm Not Cool* + 15 comments Narrated events: "Act black"
Select Indexicals/ Identify Relevant Cross-Event Context	Reported speech: "act black," "forizzle" WTF, GTFO, lol
Configure Indexicals/ Delineate Cross-Event Configurations	Configuration of indexicals points to Wu's inappropriate racial stereotyping
Construe Indexicals/ Trace Shape of Pathways	"Acting black" is an inappropriate over-generalization about black people
Identify Emerging Cross-Event Processes	Wu is offensive and not cool Commenters position themselves against Wu

and "GTFO" ("get the fuck out") suggest that the commenters are offended. These comments criticize Wu's racial and linguistic essentialism. The commenters characterize Wu as someone who perpetuates false stereotypes about language and race, and they position themselves against him.

Table 5.8 summarizes our analysis of the cross-event trajectory that emerges across these initial comments about "acting black." The phrase "act black" becomes the focal point of the narrated events themselves, repeated across the linked events. We have mentioned several indexical cues that establish relevant context for inferring how the idea of "acting black" is understood by the commenters. These signs and the relevant context they index support an inference that Wu's statements are problematic in at least two ways: he mistakenly assumes that "acting black" exists as a coherent way that black people behave and that "forizzle" is something that black people say. Across the pathway of events Wu himself seems to be positioned as more than "not cool." He could be considered offensive and could be seen as perpetuating problematic racial stereotypes. Certain people, such as these commenters, may position themselves against him.

Not all comments on Wu's "acting black" segment were negative, however. Table 5.9 represents selected comments that position Wu differently and align commenters with him.

All of these commenters align themselves with Wu, claiming that they too "act black around black people." They write: "Yup, I done that shit before," "that is so true for me," "I talk black . . . too," "I do the exact same thing" and "I totally do the black thing to[o]." Using first person participant deictics, these commenters

Table 5.9 Selected comments from the 60 that aligned with Wu's experience of "acting black" (adapted from Chun, 2013)

Item	Commenter	Comment
18485	San45501	I subconsciously act black around black people because I try really hard to fit in. Yup, I done that shit before:)
21683	lilfoot113	I don't know if you were joking about tending to act black around black people, but I can't stop laughin cause that is so true for me.
21931	renesmecullen212	i accidently talk black around black people too . . . XD
31985	DancinDaisyDoodleBu9	OMIGOD i do the exact same thing around black people!!!!!!!! :D :D :D o god im so not cool . . .
32925	thatcrazyass	OMG lmfao i totally do the black thing to, i said for shizzle to this black girl once and she just started laughing her ass off

identify with Wu's experience of "acting black." The comments contain other indexical cues that indicate the authors' alignment with Wu: statements like "I can't stop laughin," acronyms like "lmfao," and emoticons representing smiling and laughing faces, such as ":)" and ":D" and "XD." These comments help create a pathway that starts with the segment about "acting black" in Wu's video and extends across many linked comments in which the authors identify with Wu's experience and align with him. Unlike the previous set of commenters, these authors do not question Wu's presupposition that "acting black" exists.

Table 5.10 contains similar comments aligning with Wu, posted by authors who explicitly identify as "black."

Table 5.10 Four of the seven comments by black authors who align with Wu (adapted from Chun, 2013)

Item	Commenter	Comment
7752	Neonlights715	omg i act black around black ppl too so i can fit in and well im black..
9911	aisoleil	I'm Black . . . and I find myself acting "black" around other Black people to fit in. It never goes over well. :-\
10849	XDpeaceout	I too try to act black in front of black people so that I can fit in :[
		Only its a little diferent because Im also black, but either way I can never quite pull it off . . . dawg
28219	marikachica	i subconsciously act black around black people lol everyone does that, even me . . . and im black !!!!! XD

As in the comments just reviewed, these black authors align with Wu's experience of "acting black": "I act black . . . too," "I find myself acting 'black'," "I too try to act black," "everyone does that, even me." The laughing face emoticon "XD" appears again in this set, but there are other emoticons that express ambivalence (":-\") or sadness (":["). These ambivalent emoticons co-occur with the statements "It never goes well" and "I can never quite pull it off." Like Wu, these black authors claim that they cannot quite manage to "act black" authentically, despite the fact that they are black. One comment ends with "dawg," which may echo Wu's "for rizzles," as another attempt to perform "blackness" by using a term that indexes this social type. The pathway of comments that align with Wu and his struggles with "acting black," then, is both expanded and complicated by these somewhat ambivalent additions from black authors.

Table 5.11 represents Chun's cross-event analysis of these last two sets of comments about "acting black." As in the set of comments represented in Table 5.8, the phrase "act black" itself becomes the main topic in the narrated events represented in Table 5.11, across the pathway of linked events. Indexicals across the last two sets of comments come to presuppose one another and contextualize Wu's segment on "acting black" differently than the comments analyzed in Table 5.8. In this case Wu's representation of trying to "act black" but failing is evaluated not as problematic but as true, and as an experience these commenters have also had. Commenters say "I too" and "talk black," and they evaluate "acting black" as an amusing social reality (through indexicals such as smiling emoticons, "lol" and "lmfao") or as a sad truth (through indexicals such as ambivalent emoticons and comments like "never goes well"). Across this pathway

Table 5.11 The cross-event analysis of "acting black"

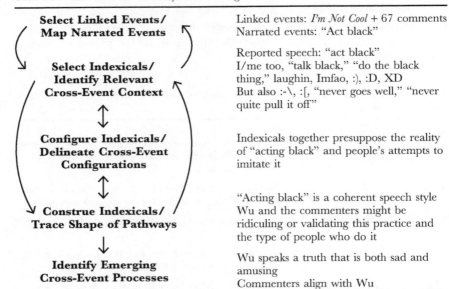

Select Linked Events/ Map Narrated Events	Linked events: *I'm Not Cool* + 67 comments Narrated events: "Act black"
Select Indexicals/ Identify Relevant Cross-Event Context	Reported speech: "act black" I/me too, "talk black," "do the black thing," laughin, lmfao, :), :D, XD But also :-\, :[, "never goes well," "never quite pull it off"
Configure Indexicals/ Delineate Cross-Event Configurations	Indexicals together presuppose the reality of "acting black" and people's attempts to imitate it
Construe Indexicals/ Trace Shape of Pathways	"Acting black" is a coherent speech style Wu and the commenters might be ridiculing or validating this practice and the type of people who do it
Identify Emerging Cross-Event Processes	Wu speaks a truth that is both sad and amusing Commenters align with Wu

of events, commenters align with Wu and act as if he is pointing out a funny but sad truth about racial categories in America—that "blackness" is a set of recognizable behaviors and that "acting black" is a practice they (sometimes ambivalently) find themselves engaging in.

Chun offers a sophisticated analysis of Wu's complexly layered performance of "ironic blackness" and the emergent construals produced by his transnational viewership. In the segments analyzed above, and in the rest of her analysis, she shows how Wu claims to aspire to stereotypical black masculinity, makes fun of this aspiration and his inability to enact it fully (in significant part because of his identity as an Asian American male) and also makes fun of the stereotype and Americans' love of and aversion to this stereotyped male behavior. These potential accounts of Wu's performance emerge across pathways that start with the video and solidify across mutually presupposing comments posted to YouTube. She shows how Wu's ironic stance foregrounds an ambivalence toward stereotypical black masculinity, even though his humorous stance never deeply challenges stereotypes of black hypermasculinity. In sections of her argument not summarized here, she also shows how reactions to Wu's videos may help reshape common images of Asian masculinity. Wu and his commenters do not generally challenge typical stereotypes of race, gender and authenticity, but they do raise a disparate set of interpretations that, taken together, challenge unitary readings of race in America. Her cross-event analyses usefully illustrate how our approach to discourse analysis beyond the speech event can facilitate research on new media data.

Example 2: Video storytelling

Those familiar with viral videos might recognize the screen shots in Figure 5.3. A video becomes "viral" when it is watched by large numbers of people in a short period of time and broadly shared on social media sites. The image on the left in Figure 5.3 comes from *Lazy Sunday*, one of the first videos to go viral on YouTube. Produced in 2005 as an "SNL Digital Short" by the late-night comedy show *Saturday Night Live*, *Lazy Sunday* mimics the genre of a hip hop music video with SNL actors Andy Samberg and Chris Parnell rapping. It received over five million views in a two-month period on then-fledgling YouTube. The image on

Figure 5.3 Lazy Sunday and Friday!

the right is from *Friday!*, which is a music video from 2011 featuring then-unknown teenager Rebecca Black singing a song in a video paid for by her parents. It received over 167 million views on YouTube in a three-month period. Both videos tell stories and use similar genre elements to do so. But Betsy Rymes (2014) argues that they achieve very different effects because of the distinct ways in which they deploy these elements.

In this section we apply our model of discourse analysis beyond the speech event to Rymes' research on video storytelling, further illustrating how our approach can enrich analysis of new media data. This case also shows how the model can be used with nonverbal data as well. In her study Rymes traces how videomakers use a set of stock storyline elements across several music videos. The music video genre predates the current era of new media, but the videos Rymes analyzes were produced for a new media ecosystem that facilitates instantaneous viewing, sharing and commenting—and this rapid communication can catapult such videos into enduring or fleeting eminence, notoriety or oblivion. Although each video incorporates similar stock elements, Rymes traces these elements across pathways of usage, illustrating how use of the same element often does not produce the same result. Elements are recontextualized in ways that accomplish different kinds of social action.

This case differs substantially from the others we have analyzed, because images and genre elements play a more central role than speech. In the age of new media, communication is becoming more multimodal and less centered around written and spoken language. This section illustrates how our approach to discourse analysis beyond the speech event can be applied to multimodal and nonverbal sign use. The events Rymes describes also participate in a broader pathway of events, including Wu's video reviewed above, that index stereotypes about black masculinity and produce what Chun calls "ironic blackness."

Background

In *Communicating beyond Language*, Betsy Rymes (2014) uses the concept of "communicative repertoire" to analyze how people draw on a range of semiotic resources as they position themselves both interactionally and across time. Instead of identifying people as members of bounded, homogeneous groups who share a stable set of capacities and beliefs, she describes the heterogeneous repertoires that characterize both individuals and groups. Demographically similar individuals often have very different repertoires, and groups overlap in complicated ways. Furthermore, both culture itself and communicative capacities expand and shift as individuals and groups create and master new signs, models and genres. Rymes shows why we must do discourse analysis beyond the speech event in order to trace the emerging intersections and divergences of identities and capacities as individuals expand their repertoires and as group repertoires shift.

In this section we briefly sketch two analyses from one of Rymes' chapters— entitled "Storytelling Repertoires"—in order to illustrate how our model of discourse analysis beyond the speech event can be applied to the multimedia, new media genre of "video storytelling." Like Chun, Rymes uses YouTube videos as data. Instead of following pathways of YouTube comments, however, Rymes follows storytelling elements as they move across several music videos posted to YouTube. She examines how these videos incorporate stock storyline elements with varying degrees of self-reflexivity, and how the same elements can produce various results as they are recontextualized differently.

Rymes argues that storytelling involves a central tension in which most narrators want to tell a unique story but rely on routine storylines to do so. In order to explore this tension, she samples viral YouTube music videos and analyzes a subset. In her focal YouTube video storytelling genre, Rymes identifies six stock storyline elements that appear across the music videos.

1. Wake up in a youthy bedroom
2. Get together with friend(s)
3. Visit a convenience store and/or get food
4. Drive in a car
5. Walk down a street
6. Dissolve into fun/reverie/vague destination

These six elements function as a preformed scaffold for video storytellers in the genre Rymes examines, and together they form a recognizable story trajectory. But Rymes finds that these elements are deployed in different ways, sometimes as unimaginative replications but at other times as creative recontextualizations. According to Rymes, replication merely reproduces these stock elements without reflexive awareness and without telling a unique story. Recontextualization, in contrast, juxtaposes the stock elements with other forms to produce ironic awareness and to say something clever.

In the following sections we sketch Rymes' analyses of how these storyline elements are combined differently in replication and recontextualization. Within each video story, Rymes shows how the six elements form a narrative with movement from beginning to end. The video storytelling events also participate in cross-event pathways, as they juxtapose elements that are drawn from prior events. Rymes traces the elements across videos, analyzing how the storytellers embellish and recombine each element with others as it is recontextualized. Her analyses show how each storytelling event participates in a narrower pathway with similar video stories, as well as broader pathways across which widely circulating social stereotypes emerge.

Storylines recurring across events

This section describes how the six stock storyline elements are used in *Lazy Sunday* and *Friday!* Figure 5.4 displays screenshots from the two music videos, for each of the story elements. In *Lazy Sunday*, which features *Saturday Night Live* actors Andy Samberg and Chris Parnell, Samberg wakes up in what Rymes calls a "youthy" bedroom (one with indexical signs of youthfulness) and arranges to meet his friend Parnell. They go to a bakery and a convenience store to get food. They ride in a taxi and then walk down the street. They arrive at their

VIDEO ELEMENT	LAZY SUNDAY (2005)	FRIDAY! (2011)
1. Wake up in a youthy bedroom		
2. Get together with friend(s)		
3. Visit a convenience store and/or get food		"Gotta get my bowl, gotta have cereal."
4. Drive in a car		
5. Walk down a street		
6. Dissolve into fun/reverie/vague destination		

Figure 5.4 Storylines in *Lazy Sunday* and *Friday!*

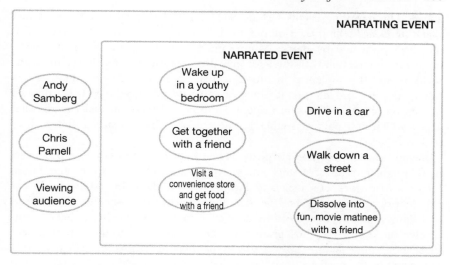

Figure 5.5 Lazy Sunday storyline

destination, a matinee screening of the film *The Chronicles of Narnia*. In *Friday!* at-that-time unknown teenager Rebecca Black wakes up in a youthy bedroom and talks about getting food (saying, "gotta get my bowl, gotta have cereal"). She gets together with friends and rides in their cars. Finally, she walks toward a party at some unspecified location.

Figures 5.5 and 5.6 represent the narrated and narrating events in *Lazy Sunday* and *Friday!* The narrated events contain the six storyline elements described

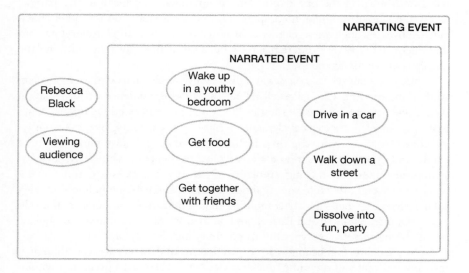

Figure 5.6 Friday! storyline

above. The narrating events include Samberg and Parnell in *Lazy Sunday* and Black in *Friday!* telling their stories to the viewing audiences. As discussed in the cases presented by Inoue, Moore and Chun above, the narrating events project an interaction with the audience, presupposing certain things about the speakers and the audience. In subsequent narrating events, individual viewers watch the video and interpret it. Some viewers have produced recycled or mashed up versions of these videos in response, and posted these on social media sites across which new pathways emerge, but we do not have space to follow these pathways here.

Beyond the six storyline elements, Rymes also describes how the producers used several recognizable story enhancements in both *Lazy Sunday* and *Friday!* Figure 5.7 provides screen shots to illustrate each of these. In addition to the car ride that occurs as a storyline element, both videos use strobe-like video effects and flash words on the screen in distinctive fonts. Two further enhancements involve the use of "hip hop grammar" and "tough guy attitude." Both videos make use of these features associated with hip hop and African American speech. For example, the speakers use copula deletion in *Lazy Sunday* (e.g., "tru dat") and *Friday!* (e.g., "we so excited"). "Tough guy attitude" is displayed nonverbally throughout *Lazy Sunday*, as Samberg and Parnell sneer and swagger in ways associated with urban thuggishness. A similar attitude is displayed briefly in *Friday!* when one of the producers of the song, Patrice Wilson, drives a car and raps about fast and furious driving (e.g., "fast lanes, switching lanes, with a car up on my side").

Lazy Sunday and *Friday!* draw on a remarkably similar set of stock elements and story enhancements, even though they were created six years apart by people from very different social locations—established actors and a nationally recognized television show, on the one hand, and an unknown teenager and her parents who paid a small production company to produce a video, on the other. Each video moves through these elements in order to create a similar storyline. But the videos achieve very different effects because of the way they combine the elements and enhancements.

Table 5.12 analyzes *Lazy Sunday* as a discrete event. The narrated event involves Andy Samberg and Chris Parnell telling the viewing audience about a day in their lives. Several indexicals, such as "tru dat," profanity and "gangster" hand gestures, suggest stereotypical elements of hip hop masculinity. But several other indexicals, such as discussing map technology, seeing a fantasy film and eating candy and cupcakes, presuppose stereotypical elements of white nerd identity. Juxtaposing these contrasting emblems of identity produces an ironic meta-commentary on both white youthy thoughtlessness and urban toughness, making each seem somewhat silly. By combining these contrasting stereotypes in a self-aware manner, Samberg and Parnell position themselves not as simply reproducing or inhabiting these stereotypes but as commenting cleverly on them.

Friday!, in contrast, becomes a very different kind of event even though it incorporates many of the same indexical elements. Table 5.13 presents a within-event analysis of this video. The narrated event here is nearly identical to that

VIDEO ELEMENT	LAZY SUNDAY (2005)	FRIDAY! (2011)
Obligatory car ride		
Strobe like video effects		
Distinctive fonts flashing on screen		
"Hip Hop Grammar" (e.g. copula deletion; word choice)	"Tru dat" "movie trivia's the illest"	We so excited!
"Tough Guy attitude"		

Figure 5.7 Story enhancements in *Lazy Sunday* and *Friday!*

in *Lazy Sunday*: Rebecca Black tells a story about her day—in this case Friday, not Sunday. Indexicals, like waking up in a youthy bedroom, meeting friends and riding in cars, suggest youthful behaviors. Other indexicals, such as "we so excited" and a black man rapping in a car, presuppose hip hop culture. However, unlike in *Lazy Sunday*, these two potentially contrasting models of identity are not juxtaposed. Instead, they simply appear as stock elements and enhancements from the music video genre that Rymes describes. *Friday!* merely replicates these elements, instead of cleverly recontextualizing them like *Lazy Sunday* does. *Friday!*

Table 5.12 Within-event analysis of *Lazy Sunday*

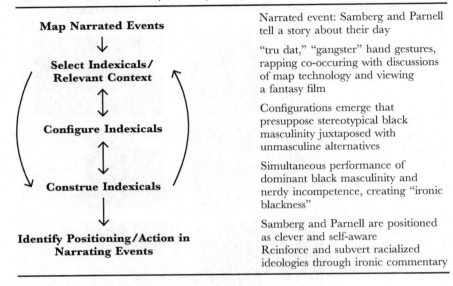

Map Narrated Events	Narrated event: Samberg and Parnell tell a story about their day
Select Indexicals/ Relevant Context	"tru dat," "gangster" hand gestures, rapping co-occuring with discussions of map technology and viewing a fantasy film
Configure Indexicals	Configurations emerge that presuppose stereotypical black masculinity juxtaposed with unmasculine alternatives
Construe Indexicals	Simultaneous performance of dominant black masculinity and nerdy incompetence, creating "ironic blackness"
Identify Positioning/Action in Narrating Events	Samberg and Parnell are positioned as clever and self-aware Reinforce and subvert racialized ideologies through ironic commentary

Table 5.13 Analysis of *Friday!* as juxtaposed with *Lazy Sunday*

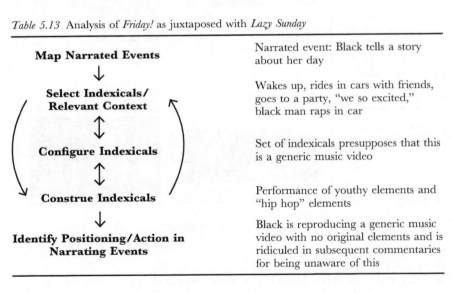

Map Narrated Events	Narrated event: Black tells a story about her day
Select Indexicals/ Relevant Context	Wakes up, rides in cars with friends, goes to a party, "we so excited," black man raps in car
Configure Indexicals	Set of indexicals presupposes that this is a generic music video
Construe Indexicals	Performance of youthy elements and "hip hop" elements
Identify Positioning/Action in Narrating Events	Black is reproducing a generic music video with no original elements and is ridiculed in subsequent commentaries for being unaware of this

does not combine storyline elements playfully, nor does it juxtapose styles in order to create ironic effect. The narrative simply follows the now familiar storyline, without telling a unique story or positioning Rebecca Black in an ironic or otherwise complex way. She is simply a girl wanting to have fun on Friday.

Although Rymes does not analyze them in the same detail as Chun, many commentaries about each of these videos have been posted both on and off the

YouTube website. Both *Lazy Sunday* and *Friday!* were posted to YouTube and received millions of views in only a few months. YouTube comment threads are available for *Friday!*, which was reposted to YouTube in September 2011 and as of June 2014 has over 670,000 comments. Although YouTube comment threads are not available for *Lazy Sunday*, which has since moved to the Hulu website where no comments can be posted, there are numerous commentaries elsewhere—in blog posts, news media, critical reviews, and so on. These commentaries form pathways extending forward in time from the videos themselves. In general, commenters and critics have ridiculed *Friday!* for replicating stock elements earnestly, with no ironic distance and no apparent awareness of the irony in the original video being copied. *Lazy Sunday* has more often been praised for recontextualizing stock elements with irony and self-awareness. As with the irony we saw in Wu's video, the positioning and social action in *Lazy Sunday* echoes with more possible voices and stances, juxtaposing social types and creating a more complex and ambiguous type of social action. Despite these differences, the two music videos participate in a common pathway, one marked by the shared storyline elements and embellishments. Across these and other events, Rymes shows how a music video genre emerges and becomes recognizable.

"Ironic blackness" across events

In addition to participating in this pathway of storytelling music videos that share several features, *Lazy Sunday* and *Friday!* also fall within a broader pathway of events that presuppose and comment on stereotypes of black masculinity. Rymes describes various hip hop elements from the two music videos. Like Kevin Wu's *I'm Not Cool* YouTube video, *Lazy Sunday* and *Friday!* deploy both verbal and nonverbal indexicals that presuppose stereotypes of blackness that are linked to urban, "tough guy attitude." In *I'm Not Cool*, Wu draws on a range of linguistic and nonlinguistic behaviors linked to black masculinity—such as "for rizzles," monophthong [a:], boasting and aggressive basketball moves—to "act black." The creators of *Lazy Sunday* and *Friday!* draw on stereotypical behavior of hip hop artists, having characters rap and use "gangster" hand gestures and body postures associated with this stereotype. Because of this similarity, all three videos participate in a broad pathway across which stereotypes of black masculinity have emerged and been evaluated.

I'm Not Cool and *Lazy Sunday* also participate in a narrower pathway of events that perform what Chun calls "ironic blackness." Like *Lazy Sunday*'s use of "hip hop grammar" and "tough guy attitude" discussed above, Wu also performs linguistic and behavioral displays that are stereotypically linked to black masculinity. When he used the phrase "for rizzles" and the monophthong vowel [a:] in "not in my house," he presupposes "hip hop grammar," a set of nonverbal behaviors, linguistic expressions and grammatical patterns that index stereotyped black male speakers. Wu also enacts a "tough guy attitude" when he boasts and postures after blocking Jeremy Lin's shot in the basketball scene. Like Wu, Samberg and Parnell perform an ironic masculine cool that relies heavily on ideologies of blackness. The respective authors use similar strategies in the two videos, recontextualizing hip hop emblems by juxtaposing them with contrasting signs. In *Lazy Sunday*, hip hop elements are juxtaposed with signs of white nerdy privilege. In *I'm Not Cool*, hip hop elements are juxtaposed with signs of self-deprecating incompetence. The juxtaposition creates distance between the performer and the stereotype he is partly enacting, such that the performer is seen as ironically commenting on an absurd stereotype rather than unwittingly perpetuating it. Chun explores whether this type of performance actually challenges or reproduces stereotypes of blackness, and she concludes that the challenge is limited. But these two ironic performances do complicate ideologies of blackness by establishing what Chun calls "ironic blackness." *Friday!*, in contrast, simply replicates stereotypical hip hop elements without any self-reflexive distance or commentary. Thus *Friday!* seems substantively empty and painfully earnest, while *Lazy Sunday* and *I'm Not Cool* seem ironic, aware and clever.

Table 5.14 represents our analysis of *I'm Not Cool* and *Lazy Sunday*, two events that participate in the pathway of events in which people perform "ironic blackness." The narrated events in both videos tell stories about the narrators, reasons why Wu is not cool and a day in the life of Samberg and Parnell. Both videos use many indexical signs that presuppose stereotypical blackness—like "forizzles," monophthong [a:], "tru dat" and "gangster" hand gestures. But these indexicals co-occur with others that presuppose contrasting social identities, like Wu's "try hard" and hesitation, and Samberg and Parnell's discussing map

Table 5.14 Analysis of "ironic blackness" across events

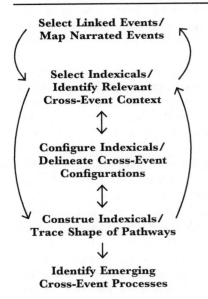

Select Linked Events/ Map Narrated Events	Linked events: *Lazy Sunday* and *I'm Not Cool* Narrated events: Telling stories about their personalities and experiences
Select Indexicals/ Identify Relevant Cross-Event Context	"forizzles," monophthong [a:], "tru dat," "gangster" hand gestures, rapping co-occuring with: "try hard," hesitation, discussing map technology, seeing fantasy film
Configure Indexicals/ Delineate Cross-Event Configurations	Configurations emerge that simultaneously presuppose stereotypical black masculinity and contrasting unmasculine alternatives
Construe Indexicals/ Trace Shape of Pathways	Simultaneous performance of dominant black masculinity and nerdy incompetence, creating "ironic blackness"
Identify Emerging Cross-Event Processes	Samberg, Parnell, and Wu positioned as clever and self-aware Both reinforces and subverts racialized ideologies through ironic commentary

technology and seeing a fantasy film. The emerging configuration of indexicals within both cases, and across the pathway of similar events, juxtaposes these contrasting stereotypes. The contrast leads viewers to infer a self-reflexive distance between the central characters and their enactment of stereotypes of black masculinity. They are not literally hoping to be seen as cool or masculine, but are instead performing Chun's "ironic blackness." Samberg, Parnell and Wu thus position themselves as clever and self-aware. They also point out the complexity of contemporary American attitudes toward stereotypical "blackness," while both reinforcing and subverting these stereotypes.

By presenting selected analyses from Rymes' account of video storytelling, we have illustrated how our approach to discourse analysis beyond the speech event can reveal patterns in new media data, including data with substantial nonverbal elements. Rymes shows how configurations of indexicals across events can establish pathways that cohere because of a shared storyline. The music videos *Lazy Sunday* and *Friday!* rely on the same set of stock elements to organize their stories, and thus they participate in a pathway of music videos that are organized in this way. But *Lazy Sunday* and *Friday!* differ in the degree to which the story elements are replicated or recontextualized. *Friday!* simply reproduces the stock storyline without creating any self-reflexive distance, while *Lazy Sunday* juxtaposes stock and contrasting elements to produce ironic commentary. Even though *Friday!* comes later in the pathway, it fails to reproduce the ironic distance in the videos it imitates, and commenters ridicule it for this. *Lazy Sunday* and Kevin Wu's *I'm Not Cool* participate in a different pathway of events, one in which speakers perform "ironic blackness" and position themselves as clever and self-aware. Discourse analysis beyond the speech event can document the types of broader, multiuser pathways that are created in new media environments.

Conclusion

Like all other kinds of discourse analysis beyond the speech event, analyses of new media data allow us to uncover social actions that only take shape across events. Wu's video *I'm Not Cool* has various possible meanings when taken by itself. But by examining how it is taken up in YouTube comments, Chun shows how it comes to accomplish clearer social actions when we consider it part of a pathway of events. In some cases discrete events have obvious implications, but more often we must trace a subsequent pathway of events in order to uncover the positioning and social action being accomplished through discourse.

Compared to ethnographic and archival studies, cross-event patterns accomplished through new media tend to occur at more extended (virtual) spatial scales but at intermediate timescales. Discourse analysis of new media data is thus in some ways similar to archival and in other ways similar to ethnographic research. Like archival research, studies of new media data typically analyze contributors who are separated from each other in space and time. Sometimes interlocutors know each other, but often people who never meet communicate and accomplish joint social action in new media environments. Also like archival data, analyses of new media data often reveal broader, larger-scale pathways. Ethnographic data often traces a chain of interactions that is a single link wide and extends only across a small number of events. Archival and new media data more often reveal pathways that are amplified by mass or social media, with one-to-many links from various nodes to a broad range of addressees.

The timescale of social actions accomplished through new media data is more similar to ethnographic work, however, with patterns emerging and shifting over hours, days and months instead of years and decades. Participants in new media interactions expect rapid responses, and topics shift quickly—more often like an extended interaction instead of a sociohistorical process. The resulting patterns can be widely distributed but evanescent. Analyses of new media data sometimes focus on very short contributions that add up to larger patterns, like the brief comments analyzed by Chun. This means that analyses of new media data often do not take the canonical form of analyzing an extended event, as in the classic format for discourse analysis, but instead piece together patterns from across individual events that do not themselves have extensive structure. Similar patterns have been found in "small stories" research, which shifts the focus from detailed analyses of extended narrative performances to many smaller-scale analyses of brief narrative events that collectively form a larger pattern (Georgakopoulou, 2007). Methodologically, in order to do discourse analysis beyond the speech event on new media data the analyst must identify many smaller segments that might contribute to a pathway and show how they add up to a larger whole. This requires exploring a broad set of potentially relevant events and selecting those that contribute to a relevant pathway.

6 Conclusions

Recent work in linguistic anthropology and related disciplines has shown that we must move beyond the speech event in order to analyze the role language plays in constituting social life. We now have a solid theoretical account of this new approach to language and society and a robust collection of empirical work illustrating its productivity. But researchers who study discourse need methodological guidance about how to implement the approach in their empirical work. In this book we provide such guidance, and in this final chapter we summarize our four primary contributions. First, we build on existing linguistic anthropological approaches to develop a systematic method for doing discourse analysis of discrete speech events. Second, we show how many central human processes require analysts to move beyond a focus on discrete and recurring types of events to study emergent cross-event patterns. Third, we present a method for doing discourse analysis on the pathways of linked events across which many central human processes occur. Fourth, we illustrate the heterogeneous ways in which events are linked into pathways and accomplish various social actions. In addition to being methodologically useful, our approach also has implications for how discourse analysts conceptualize social life.

Discourse analysis of discrete events

Linguistic anthropologists in the semiotic tradition from Sapir (1921) and Peirce (1932) to Whorf (1956), Jakobson (1960) and Silverstein (1976, 1992, 1993) have articulated the concepts required to support a systematic methodological approach to analyzing language use as social action in cultural context. Many linguistic anthropologists have productively applied this approach to discourse data from around the world (e.g., Haviland, 1996; Irvine, 1992; Koven, 2013; Lempert, 2005; Reyes and Lo, 2009). Some have developed methodological approaches based on this work (e.g., Briggs, 1986; Wortham, 2001), but in this book we develop a more concise package of discourse analytic tools and techniques that are inspired by the linguistic anthropological tradition.

Silverstein (1992, 1993) describes how relevant context emerges such that a speech event and its constituent utterances come to accomplish denotation and other social actions. He explains how key utterances in an interaction come to have functions, and how the overall event comes to be identifiable as some recognizable type, as indexical signs point to relevant aspects of context that support construals of voicing, evaluation, positioning and social action. Silverstein describes how a configuration of co-textual indexical signs establishes certain aspects of context as relevant, while other potentially relevant signs and the contexts they might have indexed become irrelevant as subsequent signs do not presuppose them. Thus he describes an iterative inferential process that moves between an emerging conception of what is happening in the event as a whole and construals of particular signs and the context they make relevant. This is what he calls the dialectic of contextualization and entextualization, through which participants and analysts build accounts of relevant context and social action that come to buttress each other as a plausible construal solidifies over interactional time.

In Chapters 1 and 2 we showed how this theoretical account undergirds a methodological approach to discourse analysis of discrete speech events. The approach involves five components, organized into three phases. In the first phase, the discourse analyst asks what characters, objects and events are referred to and characterized as the narrated contents of the discursive interaction. Narrated events provide resources that participants use to position themselves and others in the narrating event, so the first step in discourse analysis involves mapping the central characters and happenings in the narrated events. We have used a standard diagram for representing this mapping visually, as in Figures 1.1, 1.2, 2.1, 2.2, etc.

In the second phase the discourse analyst engages iteratively in three component tasks, mimicking the dialectic of contextualization and entextualization. First, attending particularly to types of signs that often signal social actions accomplished through discourse, the analyst asks which indexical signs become salient and signal context that may be relevant to interpreting the social action occurring in the narrating event. We recommend that analysts attend initially to three types of signs that often index context important for interpreting social action: deictics, reported speech and evaluative indexicals. Each of these three types contributes to the denotational message about narrated events while also presupposing information about participants' positions and actions in the narrating event. In almost all discursive interactions some indexical signs beyond these three types will communicate information important to the analysis, and occasionally none of these three types of signs will be salient, but in most cases analysts will uncover some relevant context by doing a first pass through the data focusing on deictics, reported speech and evaluative indexicals.

In the second component of the second phase, analysts ask which accounts of voicing, evaluation, positioning and social action participants use, explicitly or tacitly, to construe salient indexical signs and interpret narrated and narrating events. Having made one pass through the data and identified potentially salient indexical signs and the context they make relevant, the analyst infers the types of social action that might be compatible with this context. Analysts make inferences about social presuppositions communicated through the narrating event, including the voices participants assign to central characters. They draw conclusions about how speakers are evaluating those voices. And they infer the types of positioning and social action participants enact in the narrating event.

As represented by the circular arrows in the tables we use to represent discourse analysis of discrete speech events—like Tables 1.1, 1.4, 2.2, 3.1, etc.—analysts iteratively engage in the two components of selecting indexicals and construing indexicals. A provisional account of salient indexicals and relevant context limits plausible construals of social action, but presupposed construals also shape participants' and analysts' judgments about which indexicals and contexts are salient. In theory, this circle has no end. In practice, inferences about salient indexicals and plausible construals normally converge such that some account of social action emerges as the most plausible. Silverstein (1992, 1993) shows how this convergence is facilitated by and results in a configuration of mutually presupposing indexicals. Such configurations provisionally end the dialectic of contextualization and entextualization and the analyst's iterative process of selecting and construing indexicals. In the third component of the second phase, then, a discourse analyst explores how salient indexical signs coalesce into stable configurations within events, such that relevant context and recognizable types of social action are established.

In the third phase, the discourse analyst makes inferences based on the salient indexicals and relevant context, configurations of indexicals and construals of those salient indexicals. The analyst selects an account that best explains the positioning and social action occurring in the narrating event, looking for evidence that participants themselves explicitly or tacitly adopted a similar account. As discussed in Chapter 2, not all approaches to discourse analysis will take interactional positioning and social action as their central foci. For other types of research questions, other approaches will be more appropriate. But our approach to discourse analysis aims to produce empirically warranted assertions about the social action being accomplished through discourse in cultural context.

Cross-event processes

For decades, linguistic anthropology and related fields focused on the speech event as the focal unit of analysis (Hymes, 1964). Some studied typical speech events, describing how certain events recur among and characterize a group of speakers or social locations (Heath, 1983; Philips, 1983; Wortham, 1994). Others focused on the emergence of social action over interactional time, as interlocutors enact contingent patterns (Duranti and Goodwin, 1992; Erickson and Shultz, 1982; Ochs, Schegloff and Thompson, 1996). This work has been enormously productive conceptually, empirically and methodologically. It has allowed us to conceptualize and observe the central role of language in constituting social life and the central role of sociocultural context in making linguistic communication possible. It has provided vivid empirical accounts of how language facilitates action in context. And it has yielded a powerful methodological approach to the discourse analysis of discrete speech events.

More recently, linguistic anthropologists have begun to look beyond the speech event, studying the cross-event chains or pathways involved in social identification, cultural change and ontogenesis (Agha, 2007; Agha & Wortham, 2005). Many discursively mediated social processes take shape across and not merely within events—as an individual comes to be identified ontogenetically, as a way of speaking gets established and characterized sociohistorically, etc. These processes take place at a different scale than event-level processes, temporally and often spatially. It is crucial to distinguish this claim about cross-event pathways from the important but distinct fact that analysis of any speech event requires inferences from patterns that extend beyond the speech event itself. Discourse analysis of a discrete speech event requires that participants and analysts know about signs, models and regularities from the broader sociocultural context (Goffman, 1981). But this is different than our claim about moving beyond analyses of discrete events to pathways across events. It is true both that any event of speaking can only be understood by presupposing information, models and evaluations from beyond that event and that many discursively mediated actions can only be understood in terms of cross-event pathways.

Building on prior work, we argue that discourse analysis across pathways of linked events is essential to studying language and social life—because many processes in the human world only occur through such pathways. If we study only discrete events or recurring types of events, we will not be able to analyze central processes like learning, socialization, the emergence of social groups and associated ways of speaking, etc. This book provides several illustrations of such cross-event processes. For example, Tyisha and Maurice traveled pathways of social identification that shifted in unpredictable ways across the year. If we had studied only discrete events or types of events, we would not have been able to trace their complex, shifting social identities across time. Inoue shows how Japanese women's language came to have different meanings across a century, as similar linguistic forms were taken to index different models of female personhood. If she had studied only discrete events, she would not have been able to document the historical emergence and transformation of the register. Some types of processes in the human world can be studied by focusing on discrete but pivotal events or on recurring types of events. But many cannot, and in these cases we need to do discourse analysis beyond the speech event.

Discourse analysis across pathways of linked events

The central goal of this book has been to develop and illustrate a method for doing systematic discourse analysis across pathways of linked events. We have argued that discourse analysis across events requires analysis of individual events in a pathway, using the method described above, but that it also requires three additional components. The discourse analyst must identify the events that make up a pathway, tracing how events become relevant to each other as they are linked through reported speech, parallelism across narrated events and other devices. The analyst must delineate cross-event configurations of indexical signs, studying how these signs come to presuppose each other across events and create relevant context that establishes more rigid pathways. And the analyst must trace the shape of pathways, showing how they become stable and establish more complex and durable processes like socialization and learning.

Adding these three new tasks to our approach, we have developed a revised three-phase/five-component strategy for doing discourse analysis across speech events. In the first phase, the discourse analyst selects linked events and maps narrated events. Once the analyst identifies a pathway of linked events, s/he maps the narrated events within each of them. Narrated and narrating events have been established in prior discursive interactions, and these are often presupposed and become resources in subsequent events. Analysts must identify linked events that might make up a pathway by looking for potential links—reported speech that occurred in an earlier event, reference to the same topic or individual, parallelism of various sorts, the use of similar registers or types of linguistic form, etc. Any event could potentially participate in a pathway with an indeterminately large number of other events, so the process of selecting linked events requires inference. The analyst identifies events in a pathway based in part on the research questions and in part on patterns that emerge in the ongoing analysis. A given construal of the voicing or positioning in an event, for example, might make a particular prior event important to the pathway because that construal includes a position that was also established in the earlier event. As the analysis of potentially relevant events proceeds analysts engage in an iterative inferential process, with emerging construals of social action supporting the inclusion of certain other events and the analysis of certain other events shaping the analysis. This iterative process stops when a configuration of cross-event indexicals solidifies, supporting certain construals and the events that those construals make relevant.

Because any event participates in many potentially relevant pathways, it can be challenging to gather data when doing discourse analysis beyond the speech event. No empirical study can collect or analyze all possibly relevant events. Analysts solve this problem in part through research design. The research questions asked will constrain the types of pathways that might be relevant, and analysts can focus on collecting data from predetermined kinds of events. But in almost every case there might be relevant pathways that include events the analyst did not anticipate, pathways that will only be visible in retrospect. The only solution to this problem is to look actively during the research process for other possibly relevant events and pathways that might require collection of additional data, and to collect as much data as possible.

In the first component of the second phase, the analyst selects indexicals and identifies relevant context across events. One central part of relevant context is the other events in the pathway. Indexical signs within each event point to past and future events along the pathway, tying events together through indexical links like reported speech, shared narrated events and recurring evaluations. These events form what we have called "cross-event context." When analyzing a pathway of events analysts must attend to indexicals both within and across events, identifying the aspects of context that become relevant to interpreting cross-event processes. Relevant context will always include both cross-event context and other context indexed by indexicals across events. Focal indexical signs from across linked events point to salient voices, cultural models and other aspects of context that become relevant to understanding social actions accomplished across the pathway. Analysts start by looking for potentially salient deictics, reported speech and evaluative indexicals in events across the pathway, but in subsequent iterations they will also look for other salient indexicals that index context relevant to interpreting social action in the particular pathway.

In the second component of the second phase, analysts construe indexicals and trace the shape of pathways. As indexicals in linked events collectively come to presuppose overlapping relevant context, like relevant cultural models, a pathway becomes more rigid and particular interpretations of social action become more plausible. Participants and analysts construe the social actions occurring and the implications of the broader social pathway, by inferring from salient indexicals and relevant context. Instead of entextualization, this involves the broader process of enregisterment, with a pathway of events collectively accomplishing social actions and broader processes like socialization and learning. This is a dialectic process, with newly relevant context providing opportunities for reinterpreting actions and processes that take shape across the pathway, while a firmer account of the pathway constrains the events, indexical signs and context that might be relevant. When cross-event configurations of signs become stable, analysts can make inferences about the shape of pathways, about the form that actions and broader social processes are taking.

In the third and last component of the second phase discourse analysts delineate cross-event configurations of indexicals. Relevant context and plausible construals of social action are established as indexicals across events become configured, as signs from several events come to presuppose each other. As this cross-event configuration of signs solidifies, it provisionally ends the iterative selection and construal of indexicals and relevant context, and it establishes the social actions that are being accomplished across events. Metaphorically, this establishes a more "rigid" pathway, one that has the "shape" of one process or another. In the case of Maurice, for example, the pathway went from events in which he was easily able to act both like a high-status male and a diligent student to events in which the girls made it increasingly hard for him to sustain both aspects of his social identity. Toward the end of the pathway, Maurice was forced to choose one or the other, and he ended up being shut out of classroom conversation. The emergence and transformation of his identity across speech events that occurred from October through May established the shape of this pathway.

In the third phase, analysts interpret emerging cross-event actions and processes. Participants and analysts attend to relevant context across events and make tacit or explicit inferences about positioning and social action both within and across events. Pathways across events can accomplish more complex, durable social actions and processes like socialization, learning and social identification. Over time pathways across events become rigid and presuppose certain outcomes, although these can change as pathways are extended and signs are recontextualized. It is important to see that this phase does not represent a purely cognitive process. Terms like "inference" and "construal" might suggest that participants are consciously assessing information and drawing conclusions. This happens sometimes, but more often participants orient to relevant contexts in a more embodied and performative manner. The analyst makes an argument about what has been happening, but participants often orient to emerging semiotic patterns without conscious reflection. They "infer" in the sense that they respond systematically to patterns in language and other material signs, but we should not imagine this as a purely cognitive process.

Heterogeneous pathways

Pathways of linked events take various forms, along more than one dimension. Pathways vary in the type of element that links events together, they vary in temporal and spatial scale and they vary in the type of media through which they propagate. We have examined some of this heterogeneity, and we have shown how our approach to discourse analysis should be applied somewhat differently for different types.

Agha (2007) provides a comprehensive account of the various factors that can link events together into pathways or speech chains. Events can be linked together because they describe or include some individual(s), because they include certain signs, grammatical categories or emblems, because they contain parallel discursive patterns in narrated or narrating events, because they describe the same topic or presuppose the same cultural models, and in various other ways. Our six case studies illustrate some of these linkages. In the case of Tyisha and Maurice, events in the pathways were linked because of the individuals who were described as characters in the narrated events and who themselves participated in the narrating events. In the case of nicknames in the supplementary school classroom, events in the pathway were linked by the recurrence of nicknames for two students. In the cases of Japanese women's language and Irish English "accent," events in the pathways were linked by recurring linguistic forms—instances of forms understood to index women's speech and instances of Irish characters using English in non-standard ways—as well as emerging evaluations of these ways of speaking. In the case of Kevin Wu's YouTube video, events were linked in part by the structure of the website, as comments about the same video, as well as through mention and similar evaluations of certain moments from the video. In the case of video storytelling, the events were linked by recurrence of stock genre elements. These six cases do not illustrate all ways in which events in a pathway can be linked, but they do show that pathways can be held together by various kinds of linkages.

We have also illustrated heterogeneity in the temporal and spatial scale of pathways and in the channels through which pathways develop. Some pathways, like the series of events across which Maurice was identified in one classroom over an academic year, are just one event "wide"—with each discrete event happening in a limited spatiotemporal envelope and building serially on the prior chain of events about that topic. Other pathways, like the series of events across which Japanese women's language was established, evaluated and transformed, are many events "wide." In this type of case, concurrent events occur across a broad spatiotemporal envelope, with discrete events linked directly to some other events in the pathway but not to most others, even though the accumulation of events collectively establishes the register that links forms, types of people and evaluations of them. Events in some pathways are linked only through direct experience, with participants in one event also participating in subsequent events. Events in other pathways propagate through media like YouTube that allow one-to-many communication and the rapid dissemination of signs and messages from central nodes to many receivers. Some media or institutional nodes provide legitimation as well as wide dissemination.

We have clustered these types of variability into three types, in order to give guidance to discourse analysts who should adopt somewhat different approaches to the different kinds of data. Ethnographic data cover more limited temporal and spatial scales and narrower pathways in which the same participants appear across events. Discourse analysis of ethnographic data must collect data from enough times and places to capture events that may turn out to participate in crucial pathways. Archival data generally involve broader spatial and temporal scales, as well as broader pathways and many participants who do not interact directly with each other. Analyses of new media data often capture widely distributed but shorter timescale, evanescent patterns. Discourse analyses of archival and new media data must identify relevant sources and then sample them appropriately, so as to demonstrate the existence of relevant pathways.

As we have argued, these three are ideal types. Ethnographic data can involve extended temporal scales—like the decades-long circulation of gossip described by Haviland (2005) and the shifting stances toward Catalan across the lifespan described by Woolard (2013). Archival and new media data can focus on limited temporal and spatial scales, and on tracing individual speakers or pathways that are one event "wide"—such as Faudree's (2013) analysis of one sixteenth-century text used to formalize Spanish conquests in the Americas. As we argue above, discourse analytic studies often need to analyze more than one type of data because heterogeneous processes are interconnected in the world. In such cases, discourse analysts will have to combine tools and approaches described under our three ideal types. In general, analysts must attend closely to the details of any given case and explore the particular configuration of devices for connecting events, relevant scales and channels of propagation.

We offer three ideal types partly because these seem to be the most useful clusters of cross-event pathways for contemporary discourse analytic studies. But we also deliberately offer more than two types in order to undermine a common dichotomy between "macro" analyses of repeated patterns across wide spatial and temporal scales and "micro" analyses of local, contingent patterns across narrow spatial and temporal scales. This distinction leads discourse analysts and others to misperceive the heterogeneous nature of the social world. Pathways do vary in scope, but we have shown that they vary along several dimensions such that the variation cannot be captured in a simple dichotomy.

Beyond "micro" and "macro" to contingent, heterogeneous networks

Discourse analysis is typically seen as "microanalytic," focused on small pieces of social life. This type of work is often contrasted with "macroanalytic" approaches that focus on more spatially and temporally extensive processes and institutions. Most forms of discourse analysis presuppose a "macro–micro dialectic," in which purportedly homogeneous "macro" processes constrain events and actions but are also simultaneously constituted by "micro" events and actions. Once we move beyond the speech event to study pathways across events, however, it becomes clear that a "macro–micro" account does not suffice. Under scrutiny, neither "macro" nor "micro" represents a coherent level of explanation, and combining them does not solve the problem (Wortham, 2012). Instead of imagining two allegedly homogeneous scales, we must ask which of many potentially relevant processes and resources—from interactional through local and global, from instantaneous through those emergent over months, years or centuries—facilitate and constrain focal actions and how these heterogeneous processes interrelate in a given case.

By criticizing a "macro–micro" account, we do not mean to dismiss the insights contained in such an approach. Those who study "macro" processes have shown that constraint plays an important role in meaningful human experience. As we have argued above, following many others (e.g., Bourdieu, 1972/1977; Silverstein, 1992), any analysis of signs within a discrete event presupposes standards of value and cultural models from beyond the "micro" speech event. Participants in discursive interaction themselves presuppose more widely circulating models as they construe discursive social action, and discourse analysts must do the same. An analysis limited to the "micro" cannot even make sense of "micro"-level events. Individual actions, interactional patterns and the social processes accomplished across pathways of events are all constrained by processes at wider temporal and spatial scales.

Despite their important point, however, analysts interested in the "macro" too often explain this core insight about constraint with reference to allegedly homogeneous "structure." As the term is typically used, structure in fact includes very heterogeneous processes: practices of capitalist exchange that have emerged over millennia, practices of European colonization that occurred over several centuries in the past millennium, the global movement of people and ideas that has accelerated over recent decades, the emergence of new styles that emerge and disappear in a few years and the adoption of a new approach over months or years in an organization or a family hoping to change. Each of these constrains, but these heterogeneous practices and models are not one kind of "macro" thing that constrains in the same way. Any process that takes place at a wider scale can constrain processes at narrower scales (Lemke, 2000). A novel presupposition established over a few seconds of interactional time can constrain the action of subsequent speakers even though transient interactional accomplishments do not normally qualify as "structure." Constraints can also emerge from local, more evanescent patterns that mediate and sometimes undermine more enduring regularities.

"Macro" and "structure," then, are often misleading terms. Constraint is crucial to explaining discursive and other human processes, but it is not a homogeneous entity grounded in one "macro" level of explanation. Many types of material objects, ideas and practices constrain, in various ways. Constraints can support or undermine each other, and various constraints always operate in any given case. Sometimes a constraint is institutionalized in enduring practices, but sometimes institutions play no important role in effective constraint. Sometimes constraints are established within a small group and remain irrelevant to others, but they can nonetheless powerfully limit action within the group. Sometimes constraints are ephemeral, salient for a while but then disappearing quickly. Instead of assuming that an analyst's favorite type of "structure" plays a crucial role in constraining thought and action, we must investigate the heterogeneous constraints actually influencing our object of study in specific cases.

"Micro" has similar strengths and weaknesses as an analytic category. Discourse analysts' emphasis on contingency, on the unexpected patterns and actions that can emerge despite sociocultural expectations, captures a crucial aspect of social life. Habits change and new ways of understanding emerge, sometimes in far-reaching ways. To explain change we must account for the emergence of unexpected practices, models and behaviors. As long as this insight about contingency and emergence does not imply that more enduring patterns do not constrain, it is crucial. But if we construe emergence as necessarily arising from the "agency" of individual actors or from "micro" interactional improvisation, we make a mistake. Contingent patterns emerge at various scales, sometimes at scales more extensive than individual actions or discrete events.

The concept of "agency" carries misleading assumptions about autonomous rational minds and about the individual as the relevant level of analysis for meaningful phenomena. Using this sort of "agency" to explain unexpected, emergent patterns is incomplete and often unproductive. Individuals do sometimes develop novel plans and execute unexpected actions, and these sometimes influence larger social patterns, although this is always mediated through collective artifacts. Contingent emergence, however, is more often accomplished by groups. Sometimes this happens interactionally, when participants create an unexpected pattern through improvisation (Sawyer, 2003; Schegloff, 2007). It can also happen over longer scales, as when a group engages in what Shotter (1993) calls "joint action" that cannot be reduced to the contributions of discrete individuals. A couple can create a new way of relating, across months or years, and its emergence is not typically reducible either to the actions of an individual or to a pivotal event. A system that includes both humans and tools can develop new practices, such that we must describe the whole system of individual dispositions and actions, along with nonhuman contributions, in order to explain change (Latour, 2005; Michel and Wortham, 2009).

Most emergent patterns cannot be reduced to individual actions in discrete events. Sometimes seminal actions of individuals do occur, but most change does not happen this way. More often change emerges across events, through co-constructed and sometimes unintended contributions. In explaining contingent emergence in a given case, we must determine the levels of analysis relevant to the focal phenomenon. If we assume that either individual agency or interactional creativity is the only way to explain emergence, we will misinterpret cases that centrally involve resources and processes from other scales.

Discourse analyses that rely solely on "macro" or "micro," "structure" or "agency" will thus be inadequate. A simple combination of the two will not suffice either. Many have proposed a "macro–micro dialectic," moving back and forth between the constraining force of the "macro" and the creative potential of the "micro." On such an account enduring practices and models constrain events while action in particular events reproduces or helps to transform those sociohistorical patterns. Giddens (1976) articulated an early version of this argument, calling it "structuration," but many others adopt a similar position. We agree that both constraint and emergence are crucial, but we disagree that "macro" and "micro" are the right categories for analyzing them. Constraint and emergence occur at various scales. "Macro–micro" accounts misconstrue heterogeneous resources from various scales, forcing them into two artificial scales instead of exploring how diverse resources become relevant in any given case. Instead of one monolithic type of structure, various types of constraining processes occur at various scales. And innovation occurs not only through individual intentions actualized in discrete events, but also from collective processes at various scales (Wortham, 2012).

Latour (2005) provides a useful theory of how people mobilize resources from various scales. He argues that the social world is constructed out of heterogeneous "assemblages." For any focal phenomenon a "network" has been constructed, and this network is heterogeneous in both scale and type. Ideas, objects and dispositions from different scales come together to do the relevant work (Lemke, 2000). In Maurice's case, for example, the process of social identification depended on resources from various scales: the decades-long change in Americans' expectations that girls will be more successful in school; the local intensification of this gender stereotype in Mrs. Bailey's classroom; the centuries-long exclusion of African American males from mainstream American institutions; whatever ontogenetic trajectory led Maurice to desire both academic success and high status as a male; and so on. A network is also heterogeneous in type. Material objects matter, like the spatial organization of the classroom with certain students sitting nearer the teachers in more central positions. Ideas matter, like the models of personhood circulated in the media that represent African American males in certain ways. And embodied dispositions matter, like the tension between Maurice and Mr. Smith that was palpable in the classroom.

Latour helps us see how analyses of typical events or simple "macro"-level regularities obscure the heterogeneous cross-event processes that actually constitute social life. Instead of relying on sociological essentializations, we must study the complex emergence of identities, groups, registers, habits and models across events at various scales. Different research questions and different focal phenomena will require attention to different configurations of resources. In order to explain complex processes like learning, social identification and enregisterment, analysts must attend to a configuration of heterogeneous, interconnected resources across several scales, instead of attending to one or two scales selected a priori. Participants' sense of the unproblematic, "natural" establishment of social facts in any given case depends on a contingent configuration of resources from various scales.

Discourse analysis beyond the speech event is a method that helps analysts overcome the tendency to collapse analyses into "macro" and "micro." Our approach helps analysts look beyond one or two scales and uncover intermediate-scale regularities that take shape across pathways of linked events. In this book we have shown how discourse analysis beyond the speech event allows us to capture the heterogeneity of relevant resources and study the contingent emergence of social actions that draw on resources from various scales. In practice, participants mobilize heterogeneous resources and establish links across events in ways that accomplish complex social processes. Our approach to discourse analysis beyond the speech event provides one important methodological window into these processes.

Appendix A

Transcription conventions

'-'	abrupt breaks or stops (if several, stammering)
'?'	rising intonation
'.'	falling intonation
'_'	(underline) stress
(1.0)	silences, timed to the nearest second
'['	indicates simultaneous talk by two speakers, with one utterance represented on top of the other and the moment of overlap marked by left brackets
'='	interruption or next utterance following immediately, or continuous talk represented on separate lines because of need to represent overlapping comment on intervening line
'((...))'	transcriber comment
':'	elongated vowel
'º...º'	segment quieter than surrounding talk
ALL CAPS	segment louder than surrounding talk
','	pause or breath without marked intonation
'(hh)'	laughter breaking into words while speaking
'(...)'	doubtful transcription or conjecture

Appendix B

Abbreviations of names in Wortham transcripts

Teachers

Mrs. Bailey	T/B
Mr. Smith	T/S

Students

Brenna	BRE
Candace	CAN
Jasmine	JAS
Linda	LIN
Maurice	MRC
Tyisha	TYI

Unidentified Students

Female Student	FST
Female Students	FSTS
Male Student	MST
Student	ST
Students	STS

References

Agha, Asif (2005) Voicing, footing, enregisterment. *Journal of Linguistic Anthropology* 15(1): 38–59.

Agha, Asif (2007) *Language and social relations*. New York: Cambridge University Press.

Agha, Asif and Wortham, Stanton (eds.) (2005) *Discourse across speech events: Intertextuality and interdiscursivity in social life*. A special issue of *Journal of Linguistics Anthropology* 15(1).

Bakhtin, Mikhail (1935/1981) Discourse in the novel. (C. Emerson and M. Holquist, translators). In Mikhail Bakhtin (ed.) *The dialogic imagination*. Austin: University of Texas Press.

Bauman, Richard and Briggs, Charles L. (1990) Poetics and performance as critical perspectives on language and social life. *Annual Review of Anthropology* 19:59–88.

Blommaert, Jan (2007) Sociolinguistic scales. *Intercultural Pragmatics* 4(1):1–19.

Bonilla-Silva, Eduardo and Forman, Tyrone A. (2000) "I am not a racist, but . . .": Mapping white college students' racial ideology in the USA. *Discourse and Society* 11(1): 50–85.

Bourdieu, Pierre (1972/1977) *Outline of a theory of practice*. (R. Nice, translator). New York: Cambridge University Press.

Briggs, Charles (1986) *Learning how to ask: A sociolinguistic appraisal of the role of interview in social science research*. Cambridge: Cambridge University Press.

Bucholtz, Mary and Lopez, Qiana (2011) Performing blackness, forming whiteness: Linguistic minstrelsy in Hollywood film. *Journal of Sociolinguistics* 15(5):680–706.

Chun, Elaine (2013) Ironic blackness as masculine cool: Asian American language and authenticity on YouTube. *Applied Linguistics* 34(5):592–612.

Duranti, Alessandro (1997) *Linguistic anthropology*. New York: Cambridge University Press.

Duranti, Alessandro and Goodwin, Charles (1992) *Rethinking context: Language as an interactive phenomenon*. Cambridge, MA: Cambridge University Press.

Eckert, Penelope (1989) *Jocks and burnouts: Social categories and identity in the high school*. New York: Teachers College Press.

Edgeworth, Maria (1802/2006) *Essay on Irish Bulls*. London: J. Johnson Publishers.

Erickson, Frederick and Shultz, Jeffrey (1982) *Counselor as gatekeeper: Social interaction in interviews*. New York: Academic Press.

Faudree, Paja (2013) How to say things with wars: Performativity and discursive rupture in the *Requerimiento* of the Spanish Conquest. *Journal of Linguistic Anthropology* 22(3): 182–200.

Fludernik, Monika (1993) *The fictions of language and the languages of fiction*. New York: Routledge.

Garfinkel, Harold (1967) *Studies in ethnomethodology*. New York: Prentice Hall.

Georgakopoulou, Alexandra (2007) *Small stories, interaction and identities*. London: John Benjamins.

Giddens, Anthony (1976) *New rules of sociological method*. New York: Basic Books.

Goffman, Erving (1981) *Forms of talk*. Philadelphia: University of Pennsylvania Press.

Gumperz, John Joseph (1982) *Discourse strategies*. Cambridge: Cambridge University Press.

Halliday, Michael A.K. (1978) *Language as social semiotic*. London: Edward Arnold.

Hammersley, Martyn and Atkinson, Paul (1995) *Ethnography: Principles and practice*. New York: Routledge.

Haviland, John (1996) Text from talk in Tzotzil. In Michael Silverstein and Greg Urban (eds.) *Natural histories of discourse*, pp. 45–78. Chicago: University of Chicago Press.

Haviland, John (2005) "Whorish old man" and "one (animal) gentleman": The intertextual construction of enemies and selves. *Journal of Linguistic Anthropology* 15(1):81–94.

Heath, Shirley B. (1983) *Ways with words: Language, life, and work in communities and classrooms*. New York: Cambridge University Press.

Heidegger, M. (1927/1962) *Being and time*. (J. Macquarrie and E. Robinson, translators). New York: Harper and Row.

Hickey, Raymond (2005) Irish English in the context of previous research. In Anne Barron and Klaus Schneider (eds.) *The pragmatics of Irish English*, pp. 17–44. Berlin: Mouton de Gruyter.

Hill, Jane H. (2008) *The everyday language of white racism*. Malden, MA: Wiley-Blackwell.

Hymes, Dell H. (1964) Introduction: Toward ethnographies of communication. *American Anthropologist* 66(6):1–34.

Hymes, Dell H. (1974) *Foundations in sociolinguistics: An ethnographic approach*. Philadelphia: University of Pennsylvania Press.

Inoue, Miyako (2006) *Vicarious language: Gender and linguistic modernity in Japan*. Berkeley: University of California Press.

Irvine, Judith (1992) *Insult and responsibility: Verbal abuse in a Wolof village*. In Jane H. Hill and Judith T. Irvine (eds.) *Responsibility and evidence in oral discourse*, pp. 105–134. New York: Cambridge University Press.

Jakobson, Roman (1957/1971) Shifters, verbal categories and the Russian verb. In Roman Jakobson, *Selected writings*, vol. 2, pp. 130–147. The Hague: Mouton.

Jakobson, Roman (1960) Closing statement: Linguistics and poetics. In Thomas A. Sebeok (ed.) *Style in language*, pp. 350–377. Cambridge, MA: MIT Press.

Jefferson, Gail (1978) Sequential aspects of storytelling in conversation. In Jim Schenkein (ed.) *Studies in the organization of conversational interaction*, pp. 219–248. New York: Academic.

Jespersen, Otto (1924) *The philosophy of grammar*. London: Allen and Unwin.

Joyce, Patrick Weston (1910) *English as we speak it in Ireland*. London: Longmans, Green and Co. and Dublin: M.H. Gill and Son, Ltd.

Kelly, Gerard and Kelly, Sinead (2007) *Overheard in Dublin*. Dublin: Gill and Macmillan, Ltd.

Kiesling, Scott F. (2004) Dude. *American Speech* 79(3):281–305.

Kochman, Thomas (1981) *Black and white styles in conflict*. Chicago: The University of Chicago Press.

Koven, Michèle (2013) Speaking French in Portugal: An analysis of contested models of migrant personhood in narratives about return migration and language use. *Journal of Sociolinguistics* 17(3):324–354.

Latour, Bruno (2005) *Reassembling the social: An introduction to actor-network theory*. New York: Oxford University Press.

Lee, Stacey J. (1996) *Unraveling the model minority stereotype*. New York: Teachers College Press.

Lemke, Jay (2000) Across the scales of time. *Mind, Culture, and Activity* 7:273–290.

Lempert, Michael (2005) Denotational textuality and demeanor indexicality in Tibetan Buddhist debate. *Journal of Linguistic Anthropology* 15(2):171–193.

Mehan, Hugh (1996) The construction of an LD student: A case study in the politics of representation. In Michael Silverstein and Greg Urban (eds.) *Natural histories of discourse*, pp. 253–276. Chicago: University of Chicago Press.

Michel, Alexandra and Wortham, Stanton (2009) *Bullish on uncertainty: How organizational cultures transform participants.* New York: Cambridge University Press.

Moore, Robert (2007) Images of Irish English in the formation of Irish publics, 1600–present. *Irish Journal of Anthropology* 10(1):18–29.

Moore, Robert (2011) Overhearing Ireland: Mediatized personae in Irish accent culture. *Language and Communication* 31:229–242.

Ochs, Elinor, Schegloff, Emanuel, and Thompson, Sandra (eds.) (1996) *Interaction and grammar.* Cambridge: Cambridge University Press.

Ozaki, Koyo (1994 [1888]) Hayari kotoba [Vogue speech]. *Kijo no tomo* [*The lady's friend*]. In Ooka Makoto et al. (eds.) *Koyo zenshuu*, vol. 10, pp. 4–5. Tokyo: Iwanami Shoten.

Peirce, Charles (1932) *Collected papers of Charles Sanders Peirce*, vol. 2. Cambridge, MA: Harvard University Press.

Philips, Susan U. (1983) *The invisible culture: Communication in classroom and community on the Warm Springs Indian Reservation.* Prospect Heights, IL: Waveland Press.

Putnam, Hilary (1975) *Mind, language and reality*, vol. 2. London: Cambridge University Press.

Reyes, Angela (2007) *Language, identity, and stereotype among Southeast Asian American youth.* Mahwah, NJ: Lawrence Erlbaum.

Reyes, Angela (2011) "Racist!": Metapragmatic regimentation of racist discourse by Asian American youth. *Discourse and Society* 22(4):458–473.

Reyes, Angela (2013) Corporations are people: Emblematic scales of brand personification among Asian American youth. *Language in Society* 42(2):163–185.

Reyes, Angela and Lo, Adrienne (eds.) (2009) *Beyond Yellow English: Toward a linguistic anthropology of Asian Pacific America.* New York: Oxford University Press.

Rymes, Betsy (2014) *Communicating beyond language: Everyday encounters with diversity.* New York: Routledge.

Sacks, Harvey, Schegloff, Emanuel, and Jefferson, Gail (1974) A simplest systematics for the organization of turn-taking in conversation. *Language* 50:696–735.

Sapir, Edward (1921) *Language: An introduction to the study of speech.* New York: Harcourt, Brace and Company.

Sawyer, R. Keith (2003) *Improvised dialogues: Emergence and creativity in conversation.* Westport, CT: Greenwood.

Schegloff, Emanuel A. (2007) *Sequence organization in interaction: A primer in conversation analysis*, vol. 1. New York: Cambridge University Press.

Shotter, John (1993) *Conversational realities.* London: Sage.

Silverstein, Michael (1976) Shifters, linguistic categories, and cultural description. In Keith Basso and Henry Selby (eds.) *Meaning in anthropology*, pp. 11–55. Albuquerque, NM: University of New Mexico Press.

Silverstein, Michael (1992) The indeterminacy of contextualization: When is enough enough? In Peter Auer and Aldo Di Luzio (eds.) *The contextualization of language*, pp. 55–75. Amsterdam: John Benjamins.

Silverstein, Michael (1993) Metapragmatic discourse and metapragmatic function. In John Lucy (ed.) *Reflexive language.* New York: Cambridge University Press.

Silverstein, Michael (2003) Indexical order and the dialectics of sociolinguistic life. *Language and Communication* 23:193–229.

Silverstein, Michael and Urban, Greg (eds.) (1996) *Natural histories of discourse*. Chicago: University of Chicago Press.

Takeuchi, Kyuichi (1907) Tokyo fujin no tsuuyoogo [The common language among women in Tokyo]. *Shumi* 2(II):24–26.

Whorf, Benjamin Lee (1956) *Language, thought, and reality: Selected writings of Benjamin Lee Whorf.* Cambridge, MA: MIT Press.

Woolard, Kathryn A. (2013) Is the personal political? Chronotopes and changing stances toward Catalan language and identity. *International Journal of Bilingual Education and Bilingualism* 16(2):210–224.

Wortham, Stanton E.F. (1994) *Acting out participant examples in the classroom*. Philadelphia: John Benjamins.

Wortham, Stanton E.F. (2001) *Narratives in action: A strategy for research and analysis*. New York: Teachers College Press.

Wortham, Stanton (2005) Socialization beyond the speech event. *Journal of Linguistic Anthropology* 15:95–112.

Wortham, Stanton (2006) *Learning identity: The joint emergence of social identity and academic learning*. New York: Cambridge University Press.

Wortham, Stanton (ed.) (2012) *Beyond macro and micro in the linguistic anthropology of education.* A special issue of *Anthropology and Education Quarterly* 43(2).

Wortham, Stanton, Mortimer, Katherine and Allard, Elaine (2009) Mexicans as model minorities in the new Latino Diaspora. *Anthropology and Education Quarterly* 40:388–404.

Wortham, Stanton and Rhodes, Catherine (2013) Life as a chord: Heterogeneous resources in the social identification of one migrant girl. *Applied Linguistics* 34(5):536–553.

Wortham, Stanton and Rhodes, Catherine (in press) Narratives across speech events. In Anna De Fina and Alexandra Georgakopoulou (eds.) *Handbook of narrative analysis.* Malden, MA: Wiley-Blackwell.

Yanagihara, Yoshimitsu (1908) Teyodawa kotoba no kairyo: mazu hyojungo o tsukure [The reform of teyo-dawa speech: First, establish the standard Japanese language]. *Jokan* 18(1):13–15.

Zhou, Min (2009) *Contemporary Chinese America*. Philadelphia: Temple University Press.

Index

Page references in **bold** refer to tables, references in *italics* refer to figures.

acting black: comments debating 155–8, **156–7**; discourse analysis of **155**; Wu's concept of 144–5, 153–5

advertisements 110, 120–6, *120*, **122**, *123–4*

African Americans: aligning with Wu **157**, 158; and masculinity *see* black masculinity, stereotypes of; pronunciations used by 148, 151–2, **152**; *see also* blackness

agency 180–1

archival data: discourse analysis of 110–11, 114, 120, 141–2; in new media studies 143; scales of 178

archival studies 38–9, 72, 112, 142, 169

Asian American supplementary schools 96–7, 99

assemblages 181

audience, interaction with 147–8, 153–4, 163–4

Black, Rebecca 160, 163, 164, 165

black masculinity, stereotypes of 146, 149, 151–2, 159–60, 164, 166–9

blackness: complexity of attitudes to 169; incompetent performance of 154, 158, 168; signs indexing 39, 145, 148; stereotypes of 149, 151, 153, 167–8 (*see also* stereotypes); *see also* ironic blackness

black people 144–5, 153–7; *see also* African Americans

Chinese Americans 39, 144–5, 147, 151

communicative repertoire 160

configurations of indexicals: in archival data 113; in characterization 28, 31–2, 88, 90; cohering 24–5, 41–3, 173; and context 21, 65–6, 71, 172; and contrasting stereotypes 169; and entextualization 60–1; in poetic structure 62; and relevance of models 76; *see also* cross-event configurations of indexicals

consequentialism 61

constraints 179–81

construing indexicals 79

contextualization: dialectic with entextualization 14–15, 38, 41, 60, 172–3; and indexicals 53–4; signs performing 13–14; use of term 12

contingency 180

conversation, projected by advertisements 121, 123, 125–6

copula deletion 164

corporate names 95, 99, 101, 108

co-text 16

cross-event configurations of indexicals: and humor 150–1; and nicknaming 104; social categorization of speech types as 117–19, 126, 131; studying 174–6

cross-event context 90, 108, 140–1, 175–6

cross-event discourse analysis: ironic blackness **168**; Maurice **83**, **93**; representations of Irish speech **136**, **140**; Samsung **107**; schoolgirl speech **125**; Tyisha **24**, **37**; YouTube video and comments **151**, **158**

crying "racist" 43, 59, 63–4, 67–71, 110

cultural models: as context 15, 73; creating pathways 176–7

deictics: across pathways 176; first person
    participant 156; as indexical signs 12,
    46–7, 172; information inferred from
    48–9; in narrated events 45; and reported
    speech 50, 94–5; and social action
    5–7; types of 47–8; and voicing 57
denotational text 45
difficult children 76
discourse analysis: context in 11;
    ethnographic 39, 72; goals of 13;
    linguistic anthropological approach to
    1, 10; phases and components of 41–3,
    42, **67**; unit of 16–17, 20; within and
    across events **22–3**; within-event **14**,
    30, **63**, **77**, **149**, **166**; *see also* cross-
    event discourse analysis
discourse deictics 48
discrete speech events, discourse analysis
    of 10, **14**, 17, 37–8, 41, 64, 172
discursive interaction: circle of
    interpretation 60–1; elements of 3;
    identifying patterns in 15–16; narrated
    contents of 45; segmentation of 13;
    social action in 11–13
discursive patterns, parallel 177
domain, use of term 18

Edgeworth, Maria 127, 130–2
emblems: and linked events 64; types of
    52–3; use of term 52
emergence 179–81
emergent emblems 52
emoticons 150, 157–8
enregistered emblems 52, 119
enregisterment: interdiscursive 20; process
    of 32; shaping pathways 35, 37, 65,
    176; use of term 19–20, 64–5
entextualization: and configuration of
    indexicals 60–1; dialectic with
    contextualization 14–15, 38, 41, 60;
    and enregisterment 64; intradiscursive
    20; provisional accounts 55; use of term
    13, 61
essentialism 155–6
ethnographic data: chains of interaction
    in 170; discourse analysis of 73, 142;
    scales of 178; sources of 72–3
ethnographic studies 38–9, 43, 72, 110, 142
evaluation: habitual 64; and positioning 59
evaluative indexicals: in accounts of Irish
    English 128, 133, 137–8; across
    pathways 176; interpretation of 53; and
    social action 113, 116; types of 52; use
    of term 46, 51–2, 172; and voicing 58

event of speaking 3
exclusion, and speech events 7, 10–11

focal signs, reinterpreting 19
framing speech 129–30, 133, 135, 137,
    139–40
Friday! *159*, 160; comments on 167; lack
    of irony in 168–9; storyline of *162–3*,
    163–6

gender: in classroom model 80–7, 91;
    and speech types 114, 126
Goth persona 69
grammar: of deictics 47; and indexical
    signs 53; in narrated events 45
grammatical categories 53, 61, 177

hermeneutic circle 60
hip hop grammar 164, 167
hip hop masculinity, *see* black masculinity,
    stereotypes of

ideational function 40
identity: discursive formation of 18, 20,
    25, 32, 75; formed along pathways
    36–7, 65; *see also* social identity
indexical signs: accumulation establishing
    context 12–13, 28, 38, 40;
    configurations of *see* configurations of
    indexicals; of contrasting identities
    168–9; identifying 14–15, 172; iterative
    selection of 41–2, 53–4, 60, 173;
    metapragmatic construals of 54–7, 69;
    pointing across pathways 175–6;
    referents of 73; types of 46–7; *see also*
    salient indexicals
interactional positioning: identifying
    14–15, 173; interpreting 42–3;
    use of term 59
Internet commentary 144
interpersonal function 41
interpretation: convergent 62;
    cycle of 15
Irish bulls 127–32, **128**, 134, 139
Irish English: archival and new media
    sources of 143–4; enregisterment of
    130; pronunciation of 132–3, 138–9;
    recurring forms of 177; social
    categorization of 110, 127–9, 136,
    140–1
ironic blackness: discourse analysis of
    168; in music videos 160, 167; in Wu's
    video 146, 149, 151, 159
iterative inferential process 172, 175

Japanese women's language *see* schoolgirl speech
joking: and nicknaming 107; signals of 76, 150
Joyce, Patrick Weston 132–9

language, and social life 171
Lazy Sunday 159; comments on 167; discourse analysis of **166**; ironic blackness in 167–9; narrated and narrating events in *163*; storyline of 161–5, *162–3*
learning, and pathways 1, 17, 174, 176
legitimation 178
Lin, Jeremy 147–9, 151, 167
linguistic anthropology 1, 18, 171, 173
linkages, tracing 18
love declarations 146

macro-micro dialectic 178–82
masculinity, performance of 146; *see also* black masculinity
metafunctions 40–1
metalinguistic evaluation 146, 152–3, 155
metapragmatic commentary 56, 71, 128, 150
metapragmatic discourse 55–6, 60
metapragmatic models: choosing 54–5, 57, 59–60; emergence through pathways 65–6; and indexical signs 61
metapragmatic verbs 50–1
metasemantics 54
mobile devices 143

narrated and narrating events 3–4, *4*; in accounts of Irish English *131, 133, 138*; in advertisements 121, *122*; in commentaries on speech styles *116, 127*; connections between 5–6, 8–9, *9*; constructing identity between 85, 87–93, *88*, 111–12, *112*; courageous liar example *26*; deictics linking 48–9; in music videos 163–4; in nicknaming *100, 102*; parallelism between 8, 28–9, *29*, 45–6, *46, 92*; and voicing 58; in YouTube video *148, 154*
narrated characters: characterization of 4, 11; conversation between 125; distinct from participants 77–9, **79**; indexicals voicing 58; social identification of 57; and verbs of speaking 50
narrated events: creating pathways 21; descriptions of 24–6, 48; and indexical signs 172; mapping 41, 44–5; parallelism between 174; and

positioning 28, 33–6, *35, 68*, 75–6, *75*,148; as resources for social action 41, 50, 54; in YouTube videos 144
narrated self: characterization of 6–7, 26, 28; and narrating self 144–5
narrating events: in archival data 111–12; asynchronous 148; deictics organizing 94–5, 99; and indexical signs 172–3; inferences about 60; interactional positioning in 8, 63, 75, 164; as interpretations 130; signs carrying information about 5
networks, heterogeneous 179, 181
new media: cross-event patterns in 169–70; multimodal communication in 160
new media data, scales of 178
new media studies 38–9, 43, 72, 143–4
nicknames: establishing 103–4, **105**, 107; experimenting with potential 97–102, **103**; recurrence of 177; resisting 95–6, 108; as targeting 107–8
nonverbal data 160, 167
not cool, acting 147–8, 151, 153–4, 156

ontogenetic development 64
out-groups 5
Overheard in Dublin 136–9
overhearers: in accounts of Irish English 129–33, 137, 139–40; alignment of 134–5, 138–9; commenters on speech styles as 112, 117, 119; in nicknaming 94–5; as participants 10; readers of advertisements as 125–6

paradigmatic sets 51
parallelism: and configuration of indexicals 62–3; creating pathways 21, 28–9, 32–3, 38, 66, 174
Parnell, Chris 159, 161, 163–4, 166–9
participants: links to narrated characters 6; orientation to signs 15–16; social identification of 57; understandings of 73
pathways of linked events: advertisements as 123; commentary on speech styles as 118; comments on videos as 146, 150, **156**, 167; different types of 71; discourse analysis across 1, 10, 16–18, 171, 174–5; in ethnography 73; heterogeneous 177–9; identity formation along **86, 89**, 94; in new media 170; nicknaming as 96, 100, 106–7, 109; parallelisms in 140;

positioning in *34*; scope of 142; and
social processes 64–5, 169, 174; tracing
shape of 21, 24–5, 38, 66–7, 176
person deictics 48
pivotal events 17, 174, 180
poetic structure 62–3
positioning: of absent participants 33;
along pathways 175; and evaluation 59;
and models 35; of participants 10–11,
13; self- 28, 30; signs inferring 172–3

quotation 66; direct 146–7, 149–50, **150**
quoted and quoting speech 115

race: in American classrooms 97;
contemporary discussion of 145
racism, accusations of 58–9, 71; *see also*
crying "racist"
Received Pronunciation 64–5
recontextualization: and replication 161,
165, 167; study of 18; in YouTube
comments 146
reference and predication 51, 57
register: describing and creating 130;
elements of 18; emergence and
transformation of 19–20; use of similar
175
relevant context: emergence of 171–2;
establishing 11–13, 21, 176–7;
inferences from 60; possible extent of
16; selecting 57
replication 161, 165
reported speech: in accounts of Irish
English 130, 133, 135, 137–9; and
characterizations 112–13, 128; creating
pathways 21, 38, 49, 64, 174, 176; as
indexical sign 46, 49, 172; and
positioning 9, 33, 95, 105; in print
media 115; and social action 6, 9, 110;
types of 49–50; use of term 6; in
YouTube comments 150
resources, configurations of 181–2

salient indexicals: interpreting 54–5, 172;
in nicknaming 101; selecting 41–2, 60,
76, 173; and voicing 58
Samberg, Andy 159, 161, 163–4, 166–9
sampling methods 142
schoolgirl speech: early categorization as
disreputable 115–19; origins of
113–14; recurring forms of 177;
re-evaluation of 174; scale of pathway
178; use in advertisements 119–21, 126
semiotic tradition 171

signs: in discourse analysis 4–5, 9–10;
emergence of configurations of 15,
20–1; inferred social function of 19, 40;
linguistic 5–6, 52, 54, 65; nonlinguistic
52–3; performing contextualization
13–14; and register 18
sign–stereotype links 19–21
small stories research 170
social action: and entextualization 61;
indexical signs signaling 19, 54, 57,
172–3; metapragmatic models
describing 55–7; nicknaming as 96,
101, 104; plausible construals of 173,
176; in speech events 3–5, 13–15,
40–1; timescales of 170; unintended 11
social categories: and African-American
pronunciation 152; in American high
schools 57; and Irish accent 130, 134;
and Japanese women's speech 112,
115–19, 122; racialized 159
social domain 19, 32, 57
social identification: and metapragmatic
construal 57; process of 25, 32,
40, 176
social identity: emergence of 65–6;
shifting 174; and speech events 65
socialization, and pathways 1, 16–17, 64,
174, 176
social position, recognizable 6, 57
social processes, as pathways 1, 174
social types: emergence of 18–19, 64,
174; indexicals presupposing 19, 52;
stable 17–19
solidification 20, 61, 65, 141
spatial deictics 47
spatial scales: narrower 109; of types of
data 38, 72, 143, 178; wider 111, 169
speaker alignments 58–9
speech chains 19, 177
speech events: boundaries of 13; context
beyond 16–17, 173–4; describing 2–3;
metafunctions of 40–1; parallelism
between *32*; recontextualization of 18;
social functions of 10; *see also* discrete
speech events
speech types, recruiting to 126
spelling, nonstandard 139, 152, **153**
stereotypes: as context 15, 76; ironic
distance from 164, 168–9; opposition
to 156; persistence of 19–20; and
storytelling 161
storylines: enhancements to 164, *165*;
recurring 161–3, 169
structure, heterogeneous 179–80

temporal deictics 47
temporal scales 37, 39, 178
textual function 41
teyo-dawa speech *see* schoolgirl speech
tough guy attitude 164, 167
transcription methods 129, 183
trying hard 154–5, 168
typifications 17–21

uptake 12, 61

verbs of speaking 28, 30, 50
video storytelling 144, 159–61, 169, 177
viral videos 159
voicing: along pathways 175; and context
   15; indexical signs inferring 28, 40–1,
   58, 172–3; of narrated characters 79;
   resources for 38; and social action 7–8,
   10, 14; and speaker alignments 58–9;
   use of term 6, 55, 57

white nerd identity 164, 168
women's magazines 114–16,
   120, 125
women's speech, *see* schoolgirl speech
Wu, Kevin: as acting black 144–5,
   151, 154–9; commenters'
   construal of 149–51; *I'm Not Cool*
   video 145–8, 152–4, 177; and ironic
   blackness 167–9; narrated self of
   148–9

YouTube comments: direct quotation in
   146, 148–52, **150**; identification
   across 39; metalinguistic evaluation
   in 152–6, **155**, **157**; on music videos
   166–7
YouTube videos: ironic blackness in
   144–6, 148–55, 159; pathways through
   178; storytelling in 39, 144, 160–1,
   167, 169

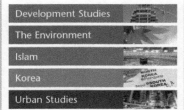